The Red Blazer

Volume 1

Dr. Carl D. Wilson Jr.

HAVANA BOOK GROUP LLC
HAVANABOOKGROUP.COM

In Dedication To

Marjorie Wilson
Matriarch of the Wilson Family

My mother is the source of my inspiration for this anthology dedicated to honoring women from all walks of life. She has always been there to support the family — the glue that has held us together regardless of any adversity. She helped my father put five children through college, Carla Wilson, Michelle Wilson, Marjorie Wilson, Jermaine Wilson and me.

As a result of my mother's undying devotion to her family, all of her children are successful. My mother has been the pillar of our family and the guiding force behind all of her children's success. She is loved unconditionally.

My mother has always been a provider, a wonderful example for her daughters and a devoted wife who stood by my father, Pastor Carl Dean Wilson Sr., during 47 years of their marriage. Unfortunately, my father passed away in May 30, 2011. She celebrated my father's passing and although she misses him, she has always stayed strong for her children. Today, she's still going to church, serving God, and standing strong by her legacy.

She's the source of my inspiration to honor and celebrate women around the world for their business success and contributions to society as humanitarians, philanthropists and community leaders. My mother, Marjorie Wilson rocks!

The Red Blazer Book: Volume 1

Dr. Carl D Wilson
Author/Creator

The Red Blazer Book is an Anthology of Phenomenal Women Co-authors. These Women take the time to prepare and write their chapters to Inspire and Encourage others Women to be Great and Achieve their Goals. The chapters are about their Bios, Lifestyles, Goals, Family, Travels and things that make them Women who Support Women Empowerment and Entrepreneurs. The goal of the 1st volume of The Red Blazer Anthology is to Inspire, Uplift, and Encourage other Women to write a Book or Anthology to Impact other Women. The Red Blazer Book is Dedicated to Dr. Carl D. Wilson, Jr.'s Mom who Supported, Encouraged, and Guided her to Success. The Ultimate Goal is to become a Best Selling Author with the phenomenal Co-authors of this great book. It will be a Phenomenal Accomplishment for all Women involved in The Red Blazer Vol. 1 Anthology. I want to say Thank you in advance to the Editor, Publisher, Co-Authors, Charitable Foundation, and Readers. The Launch will be 28 October 2021.

Dr. Carl D Wilson Jr

Founder/CEO

+9512415343

www.cdwilsonevents.com

carldean619@gmail.com

All rights reserved. No part of this publication may be reproduced, stored in a retrieval system, or transmitted in any form or by any means – electronic, mechanical, photocopying, recording or otherwise – without the written permission of the publisher.

HAVANA BOOK GROUP LLC
43537 RIDGE PARK DRIVE
TEMECULA, CA. 92590

COPYRIGHT 2021 All rights reserved.
ISBN: 978-1-73531-175-3

Foreword

From that first night over a year ago when I met Dr. Carl D. Wilson, Jr. online in a Facebook messenger chat, I knew we were going to be close friends. His genuine passion to honor, highlight, and empower exceptional women around the world became even more evident as I followed him on this remarkable journey. Dr. Wilson unselfishly has gifted hundreds of women so far with his prestigious and beautiful red blazer without any cost to the women. These women are now part of a unique group of ladies known as the "Red Blazers".

The Red Blazer book became the genius idea of Dr. Wilson as a perfect opportunity for these Red Blazer ladies to share their voices---their inspirational stories with other women, in particular. Many discuss their childhoods, their families, and their failures and problems along the way as they dreamed bigger and achieved their ultimate successes. The readers will appreciate the sincere openness of the women in these heart-warming stories. As the readers peruse these stories and become involved in the lives of these amazingly brilliant women, beneficial business and life skill advice will be acquired. The readers will definitely connect with many women in this book. These international women come from many diverse backgrounds economically, socially, culturally, etc. However, the one thing they all have in common is the desire to achieve their personal dreams and at the same time unselfishly guide others to find the success they desire. They are true humanitarians in many ways.

Why am I so positive the readers will thoroughly enjoy this book and learn essential business and life skills? Why am I convinced the readers will be so incredibly inspired they will not be able to put the book away until the last story is thoroughly read? Why do readers need to add this book to their personal business libraries? I am one of the proud authors and the Editor-in-Chief of this wonderful anthology. I have read each story several times, have personally interacted with many of the ladies featured in this book, and have learned new skills as well. These ladies and their stories have deeply impacted my heart as they will other readers. They have overcome many obstacles and have risen to the top of their fields of expertise.

This book should become a professional guidebook for today's young and/or new female entrepreneurs. Future entrepreneurs still unsure of their new career paths or businesses will definitely find the diversity of careers represented appealing and advantageous in their search. The Do's and Don't's discussed by these Red Blazer ladies will help to prevent novice entrepreneurs from making some of the mistakes they have made along their journeys. The ladies in this engaging and informational book humbly but also proudly share their wisdom and their vastly acquired knowledge so others can learn from them. These ladies were carefully selected by Dr. Carl Wilson to ensure the highest quality of stories in this first volume of the Red Blazer book.

Enjoy these extraordinary stories and learn from the BEST.

Dr. Randi D. Ward, Educator, Best-selling author, Visionary Book Writing Coach, Master Editor, International Speaker, Humanitarian.

Endorsements

I, Robbie Motter, CEO/Founder of GSFE, endorse the Red Blazer book by Carl Wilson featuring all his dynamic co-authors from across the world with their heartfelt stories that will touch many lives globally and make a difference in so many lives.

I, Dr. Randi D. Ward, Educator, Author, Visionary Coach, and Master Editor, highly endorse this Red Blazer book by the prestigious Dr. Carl D. Wilson, Jr., and the incredible award-winning female entrepreneurs whose powerful stories will not only deeply touch the readers' hearts but will inspire women of all ages to "dream bigger" and achieve success as they have done.

I, Desziree Richardson, Vibratory Voiced Healer, Visionary, Global Leader, International Best-Selling Author, Humanitarian, Executive Producer and Face Model, distinctly endorse the Red Blazer book by the sensational Dr. Carl D. Wilson, Jr. and the remarkable award-winning global women concurrently powering compelling stories that will shift the mindset of readers to believe in the possibility of existing through belief and determination by making the right decisions to elevate their success.

I, Dr. Barbara J. Hopkinson, endorse the Red Blazer book because it contains a wealth of women's success stories which are inspirational to young women on their journeys.

I, Dr. Shamila Ramjawan (Dr, Ph.C.), Entrepreneur, UNISA Business Management Lecturer, Founder: Red Corner Show and PrincessD Menstrual Cup endorse the Red Blazer by Dr. Carl D. Wilson, Jr. who shares his remarkable life story and irrepressible spirit of empowerment in this phenomenal book along with the inspirational stories of exemplary female entrepreneurs through their journeys of growth and success.

I, Maria Renee Davila, MBA, Educator, Author, CEO of the Global Trade Chamber, Co-Founder and Author of the 100 Successful Women in Business Network, endorse the Red Blazer book by Dr. Carl D. Wilson, Jr. because the amazing stories from female entrepreneurs will inspire women of all ages to achieve great things and succeed in all areas of their lives.

I, Jo Wiehler, the owner of La Belle Sabbioneta and the Incredible International Powerball Team, endorse this fantastic and powerful book specifically dedicated to those fearless women "blazing" the trail for all of us!

Chapter Overview

1. Alma Dang.. 14
2. Corazon Yellen Armenta 22
3. Dr. Randi D. Ward 34
4. Robbie Motter.. 44
5. Sue Phillips.. 48
6. Sarifa Alonto-Younes... 60
7. Caprice Crebar 70
8. Clarisa Romero 78
9. Robbie Moss Manning.. 86
10. Traci Jeske.. 96
11. Dr. Angelica Benavides 106
12. Godella Mary Petty 116
13. Ava Fang... 122
14. Isabelle Stephenson 132
15. Sharon Martin.. 142
16. Jo Wiehler.. 150
17. Dr. Shamila Ramjawan 160
18. Dr. Nephetina Serrano 170
19. Rene Huffman... 180
20. Ilona Parunakova.. 186
21. Madeleine Wober.. 196
22. Amelia Johnson 206
23. Dr. Rosalind Willis.. 214
24. Anna Smulowitz-Schutz.. 224
25. Michelle Delizio-Podlesni 228
26. Desziree Richardson 234
27. Michele Lee Malo... 244
28. Donna Sparaco Meador 254
29. Shawn Saxton 262
30. Carolyn McGee... 270
31. Dr. Imelda Yap-Ugalde 278
32. Caroline Velasco 288
33. Rebecca Garcia 298

34. Elma Kamari Bidkorpeh 308
35. Yolanda Core Pastrana 320
36. Dr. Janet Smith Warfield 326
37. Songwriting Shane's 338
38. Sharon Tanyag 350
39. Nancy Smith 354
40. Sonia D. Bermejo 364
41. Latasha Fennell 372
42. Di Carter 382
43. Dolly Cortes 394
44. Marie Lee Jenkins 402
45. Cheryl Broughton 412
46. Any P. Oliva 422
47. Diane Curley 430
48. Dr. Miyoshi Umeki Gordon 438
49. Dr. Barbara J. Hopkinson 448
50. Patti Rae Miliotis 458
51. Dr. Tania Simmons 468
52. Lynda Bergh Herring 476

Aknowledgements 487

Alma Dang

Queen Alma Dang
By Alma Dang

I am a preschool teacher, queen, model, actress, dancer, volunteer, and founder CEO of the organization Alma's Angle Care, which protect vulnerable kids. I strongly believe that education is one of the things that cannot be taken away from you because ignorance doesn't let you be free!

I was born in Mexico City, Nahauat Mexico, Spanish ciudad de Mexico or in full Ciudad de Mexico, D.F., City, and capital of Mexico, synonymous with Federal District (Distriro Federal; D.F.). The term Mexico City can also apply to the capital's metropolitan area, which includes the Federal District but extends beyond it to the west, north, and east, where the state (estado) of Mexico surrounds it on three sides. In contrast, the southern part of the Federal District sustains a limited population on its mountain slopes.

Spanish conquistadors founded Mexico City in 1521 atop the razed island-capital of Tenochtitlan, the cultural and political center of the Aztec (Mexica) empire. It is one of the oldest continuously inhabited urban settlements in the West Hemisphere, and it is rank as one of the world's most populous metropolitan areas.

The city's rich heritage is palpable on the streets and in its parks, colonial churches, and museums. The valley of Mexico constitutes a broad area of convergence for species of the tropical and temperate realms--a land of beautiful beaches and rich culture that includes traditional cuisine, handicraft artwork, and ancient architecture.

I grow up as a happy child, daughter of teachers, and then I met my husband Charlie Dang. We married and moved to San Diego, CA, thirty-nine years ago. San Diego is a city on the Pacific Coast of California known for its beaches, parks, and warm climate with the immense Balboa Park, the renowned San Diego Zoo as well as numerous art galleries, artist studios, museums. and gardens. A deep harbor is home to a large active naval fleet with the USS Midway and aircraft carrier turned museum open to the public.

I have one daughter and one son. My daughter is a high school teacher in the World Art of History, and my son graduated from the University in Art and technology.

I am a retired happy wife house.

My passion is helping others, praying, playing piano, playing tennis, modeling, dancing, playing golf, and doing cross fit.

I really enjoy being a volunteer at St. Vincent de Paul Medical Clinic for homeless and in the organization Alma Angel Care. I am founder, president, and CEO of this organization, www.almasangelcare.com

As a Christian, I strongly believe in giving back to others including my community because my mission in this world is to bring love, hope, and faith and to raise my voice to provide the necessary help that is need fully support the loss fortunate kids to continue their education successfully. Mentally, spiritual, physical, and this organization also guides and protect children who are vulnerable and who are in danger to be forgotten. This organization utilizes its resources to help children grow strong.

Vision: No more children working at the border.

Purpose: Ending ignorance and exploration of children

Benefits: Personal satisfaction
Club Alma's Angel Care (reading books free)
Acknowledgment

Special thanks to my wonderful husband Charlie Dang for always supporting the organization with love, time, and dedication.

To my son Kevin Bryant Dang who makes the Logo Alma Angel Care, love you always.

To Jesse Moore, Chairman Board Director, who always comes with a smile, love, and great ideas to helping more the organization in order to benefits the kids.

To the very talented Legend of the Music Sheldon Reynolds (Earth, Wind and Fire), (Music consultant) for making the Honor to donate to the organization the wonderful song "THE ANSWER"; it is a great contribution. I am feeling very blessed and grateful.

To Rein Hanston for supporting the organization with donations for buying food, books, and all those needs of the kids.

To Rosalyn Kahn (Speaking coach) for your support to the organization. You are always enthusiastic and very positive, giving clothes to all kids, including their families. She includes me as one of the leaders 2021. Thank you, Rosalyn Kalm.

To Mary Avina (Vice president in Mexico) for all your contributions with the organization. The King Garden "Real Madrid" works with a library in order to the kids can read books every day without paying for it.

To Penelope Decire (Vice president in Orange County) for your support.

To Beatriz Sanchez (Vice president in USA) for your wonderful guidance and contribution to the organization. Priceless.

To Amelia Johnson (Calendar Designer) for your marvelous participation---always smiling and guiding me with your lovely way of doing everything.

To all people who send donations to the organization making dreams come true and creating big smiles for all these sweet and lovely kids.

All my gratitude and admiration, God blessing all of you in every way.

With love,
Alma's Angel Care Organization.

Because education is important not only on an individual level but as productive member of society. It is a bridge for us to communicate effectively with people from all walks of life and to be able to help others in their future.

I am writing this biography to give my advice to you: Keep up the good work. Pray each morning and night to have faith and strength. Always help others and look out for others, treat others with respect, and love each other. There are always ways to help others such as looking out for them and treating them with respect, your parent, teachers, friends, and pets. I want you pass that love on to someone else and affect your community in a positive way.

As a preschool teacher, realtor, investor and professional dancer, my life suddenly changed 360° when they started inviting me to participate in Pageant events:

- Mrs. Maeya in 2018. Lynn Tang in representing her event "Universe Multicultural Film Festival" for two consecutive years in San Diego, California.

- Mrs. Asia USA Virgelia Productions. I was crowned in 2018-2019 as Mrs. Latina Global California 2019. In this amazing Beauty Pageant full of diversity, I met very beautiful queens and sisters around the world. Virgelia Villagas brings us to part of the winning prize to Thailand, which is one of my most wonderful experience in my life. This is the first time I started acting and filming the video for a TV commercial for "The Cancer Hope Village" in Chiang Main. I keep taking my acting classes with the teacher Chamo Gabriel Fernandez with the very prestigious group H2O from Venezuela and Colombia. We started making the movie "La u Hima Cena". India Rosa foundation teatral www.indiarosateatro.com from Jose Ferrer under the direction of director and producer Gabriel Fernandez a great and very talented teacher.

- Mrs. Tourism Mexico/USA 2019 Mina Tahayeri and Riza Asa in Portland Oregon USA. Also winning the award of "Beauty for Cause" for the best National Costume 2019 designed by the International High Couture Fashion. Designer Tommy Lee who is great honor for me because I am representing my country Mexico.

- Sra. México y sus Contrastes. 2020 Blanca Madrigal Rosarito Baja California (MEXICO) TV Channel 73 to representing Mexico and all states for traveling. During the Covid-19 Pandemic the project was stopped to prevent people from getting sick, but this also helped me to go to the Zoom world which is an amazing tool to keep in touch with others, family, and friends and allow me to keep working on all my projects and study more and more every day in order to prepare me better.

- Mrs. All Woman Rock Global Elite 2021-2022. Dr. Carl Wilson, this amazing man, gave me the great opportunity to be part of the Red Blazer group, which is Global group who empowers women each day. He is always sending beautiful gifts to us to make us feel loved, special, and appreciated which is very importance for every woman. He also made me part of this great book as a co-author. Thank you, Carl. It is an honor, and I really appreciated.

- 2021 Outstanding Model of the year (Paris) Paulette Mouquest. As the model, this title is very important for me. It also gave me the opportunity to be a part as an actress on the TV Reality Show "Hollywood Star in Paris" which is a very fun, interesting TV show in Paris. Thank you, Paulette Mouquest, for this great opportunity. This will be the First Annual Celebrity Awards in Paris. She also awarded me as a 2021 Outstanding Model of the year. This event will be in Paris on May 8th, 2022, and I will be modeling and receiving my award.

- Mrs. Eliunn Universe Humanitarian 2020-2021. Penelope Ladron de Guevara. This wonderful woman gave me two very important and prestigious awards for my dedication to the community and for helping others as a "Humanitarian Queen" and the Presidential Humanitarian Award 2021. Lifetime Achievement. Thank you, Penelope Ladron de Guevara, for your friendship and trust in me.

- Mrs. Cyberspace Universe 2021, Rein Hanston and Mrs. Outstanding Humanitarian Queen of Mexico 2021, Rein Hanston. In addition, she gave me the Award of the Cyber Excellence 2021. Thank you, beautiful Rein Hanston.

As a multiple Award-winning Mexico beauty Queen and Model, my responsibility with serving others keeps me going. I also have the recognition from Amit Singla International Global Peace & Icon as Best Social Activist Award 2021.

My participation as a model keeps going. I will be participating in the fourth Hollywood International Talent Show, Galina Capanni.

I also have too many interviews in very prestigious programs like VIP Latinos in Hollywood with Fernando Sanchez and Angeles Jacuinde Viveros TV Channel KDHK (Hispanic World Television in San Diego with Mrs. Kahn and Rosalina Alvarado. TV Channel 73 in Rosarito Mexico with Blanca Madrigal.

I had a dancing presentation and interview with "Javier Bautista y sus Estrellas" in San Diego, California.

I am a judge for the beauty pageant in 2018 for Mrs. Asia USA, Miss Philippines 2019, Miss perfect Lady 2021, which I will be crowned as a queen with Groupo Versage N G in Santa Anna 2021.

I modeled in various Fashion Shows in San Diego, Las Angeles, Hollywood, and Mexico. I am one of the models of Victoria Guadron Cosmetic line in USA and now am modeling for my own line Alma's Queens Care Accessories.

I appear in many magazines like "Gene Bonita" San Diego, and Tijuana 2018 LMA Awards 2021 "High Fashion", International Magazine June 15th, 2021 "Luxury Ready Lady" International Magazine (London, Paris, Los Angeles, New York, Singapore, Dubai, Japan, Manila, Taiwan. "Celerity World Paris" International Magazine 2021. "World Elite" Magazine 2020-2021 International Magazine. "Hollywood People" Perfect Lady 2021. The Prestigious Book of Queens from Virgelia Productions. International Beauty Pageants for two years consecutive.

The books are always one of your best friends like the Bible.

In my spare time, I enjoy meditating in God. You are born to follow the right path to dream, to have faith, and to always prepare to be a better human being. This will bring you peace, enjoyment, and happiness. The pandemic offers the opportunity for people to change mentally, physically, emotionally and the most important SPIRITUALLY. I expanded my vision to helping more kids around the world.

Always enjoy your present!

With love,
Alma Dang

Corazon Yellen Armenta

Beauty Queen with a Great Cause
By Corazon Yellen Armenta

I am proud to be a Filipina-Eurasian-American. I love my roots, the Philippines, Europe, and USA. My paternal grandfather was from Spain, and my heritage is a mixture of Filipino, Polynesian, Asian, Spanish, and Middle Eastern. I lived in California for many years and maintained a dual citizenship with both the Philippines and USA. I truly believe as they say that "America is the land of freedom and opportunity". USA and the Philippines are both beautiful countries, some of the best places in the world to live and enjoy life!

I cherish the memory of my childhood and life in the Philippines. I can still recall the friendly and hospitable people, the bustling, modern city, and some of the most beautiful tropical island paradise surroundings with magnificent beaches. I was born in Quezon City, Metro Manila. Being Catholic, I was raised strictly and conservatively with love and respect. My father, Aurelio Ugalde Sr., was a Brigadier General in the Philippine Air Force, Superintendent of Philippine Military Academy, and Vice President at Feati University. My mother Corazon Lucero Ugalde was a loving housewife and mother. They are both in Heaven now. We are six children in the family. The oldest is Cynthia followed by Christine, Aurelio, Jr., Eloisa, Corazon (me) and Reynaldo. Being the youngest girl among six children, I was pampered and spoiled and treated like the baby. My parents and grandmother's love and support played an important role in my upbringing. I was raised knowing deep inside I was loved. It taught me to be confident and independent. My family has always been close-knit. I was the favorite grandchild (among 30 grandchildren) of my maternal grandmother Brigida Lucero. She was my role model. My memories of her will live on. With her and my parents, I was always sheltered with their traditional values and love. We always had maids and housekeepers to do chores and do things for us. I was never a problem child. I was obedient and courteous, pleased everyone, and did what they expected me to do. But through the years, I have learned to be my own person, saying no if I must and saying exactly what I feel, instead of what others want.

I had my crush when I was ten with a boy named Benito, who sent me love notes in school. I started experimenting with make-up and different hairstyles when I was only eleven and have since followed fashion fads, dances, and trends. I will always have some child in me. I have read several books about life, and I am still interested in beauty, fashion, love, and life but with more meaning and greater depth. I am glad that I still have retained that sense of adventure and fun.

I was always chosen to be Princess or Queen at school - Miss Primary, Miss Grade School, Miss Grade 5, Miss Freshman, Miss Sophomore, and Miss College of Education. I started modeling at the young age of thirteen. I did print advertising for Pepsi Cola, followed by several modeling jobs for Frigidaire, Joanne Drew Salon, Firestone Calendar, and Fil Hispano Tiles. It was exciting for me to do TV Commercials for Pepsi Cola, Breeze detergent, and Caltex Oil. My first ramp fashion show was held at The Hilton Hotel for renowned Fashion Designer Emil Valdez and then a trip to Cebu for a fashion show for Designer Goulee Gorozpe sponsored by Seven Up.

I studied at Siena College (a Catholic private school) for grade school and high school) and the University of Santo Thomas for an Associate's degree. I was offered to appear in movies and to join the Miss Philippines. I declined the offers. These matters did not interest me since I was involved with my boyfriend Harry. My love life was more important for me. I enjoyed modeling, but fame and glory were not top priority in life; instead, my interest then was to have a family of my own and to live happily ever after. My parents were against young marriages; therefore, I became rebellious, eloped, and got married right after my 18th birthday party, changed my last name to Ikdal, and moved to Oslo, Norway (my husband's father was Norwegian), changing abruptly my sheltered life. I rebelled and did what I wanted to do, but it was a huge mistake! Norway and the Philippines are two different worlds. I had to adjust to the cold winter and learn the language. I did not have my family or maids to rely on. I worked for a shipping company and modeled part time. Unfortunately, this marriage did not work out. After four years in Norway, I moved to New York City to settle and separated from my husband. I was depressed; all my fairy tale dreams were destroyed. I learned that I could turn my life around if I explore the goodness of life and trust in God. I had family in New York, my older sisters Cynthia, Eloisa, and brother Junior, who supported me with their love and understanding. I met new friends, worked part time jobs, and started working as a model. I did numerous print ads and promotional modeling for Macy's, Simon Shirts, Conair Showerheads, and Florsheim Shoes and did several Fashion Shows for Alfred Angelo Bridals, Macy's, and Maloof Lingerie. I worked as a model for major trade shows and Conventions and appeared in several TV commercials for Macy's, Omron Calculators, and Arrow Shirts. It was especially thrilling for me when I was chosen to be one of the models for print work and fashion shows with all expenses paid to travel to Puerto Rico, the Caribbean. We stayed at the iconic El San Juan Hotel and had a grand time! I went to Herbert Berghof Acting School, and I had a part in a New York University Film. Then I auditioned and got a part for the TV movie Law and Order by Paramount Pictures and became a member of the Screen Actors Guild. I also did Brenner for The People, an ABC TV Movie. Everything was going great for me in the field of modeling and acting. I met distinguished and interesting people and different experts in the field of entertainment. I socialized and attended several parties and celebrations. I learned to be more independent and focused more on my career for almost 2 years in Manhattan which was interrupted when I finally got my divorce and remarried for the second time with my boyfriend Stephen Jaffee. This marriage brought me to live in San Francisco Bay Area for ten months. I modeled in the Bay area doing print work and fashion shows for Clinique Cosmetics, Bullocks, and Saks Fifth Avenue.

After ten months of residency in San Francisco, Stephen got a promotion as sales manager and a transfer location to Los Angeles, California. Four weeks after we moved to Los Angeles, I met Robert Yellen, a building contractor, and Real Estate Developer with a whirlwind romance. After three weeks of meeting and dating him, we lived together at his Beverly Hills home. We remarried after both of our divorces were granted, eight months after we had met. It was his second and my third marriage. With a wonderful husband, a great marriage, and the births of my daughter Bridgette and my son Sean Yellen, I was totally complete and fulfilled. My life in Beverly Hills was like a Fairy Tale at times. To have a family filled with true love and happiness is intensely fulfilling and beautiful. I had my share of sorrow and my share of blissful happiness. I have experienced life from all angles. To really know life itself, you must get involved in your existence. I felt I have lived my life to the fullest. I stopped my modeling and acting career when my children were born. I started my career again when they started school. Bridgette and Sean both attended the private school The Center for Early Education and Westwood Elementary School, and both graduated at Beverly Hills High School. Bridgette graduated at the University of Southern California with a Bachelor's degree in Communications. She is a school teacher at the L.A.U.S.D and is happily married with Matthew Rosenberg, an architect. Sean graduated with a Bachelor's Degree at Cal State University

Northridge. He is an executive for an App Company and is happily married to Sheila, a nurse. They have a five-year-old son Charles and a one-year-old daughter Sophie. I am very proud of them and love them so much. Being a mother and grandmother is the most rewarding experience! They are my greatest achievements and treasures in life! We have so many unforgettable memories that I will cherish forever from our travels all over the world to their childhood memories. When Sean was 3 to 11 years old, his best friend was Christopher Rogers, son of the late well known singer Kenny Rogers and Marianne Rogers. Sean had sleepovers several times at their Beverly Hills home, and Christopher had sleepovers at our house. I remember Kenny visiting our home to pick up Sean to join them in Palm Springs with their private jet. They also took Sean with them to Hawaii and Beaver Dam Farms in Georgia for vacations. When Bridgette was 5 to 7 years old, one of her close friends from school was Adam Levine of the famed Maroon Five. They both had several friends from famous family when they both attended Beverly Hills High School. I was very involved in PTA meetings, helping with their homework, field trips, and carpooling. I resumed my career as model and actress. I had fun in Phoenix, Arizona, for the filming of a Documentary for the US Air Force. I was booked for several Fashion Layouts and advertisements for California Mart in Los Angeles; I filmed a national TV Commercial for Taco Bell, The World's Fair in New Orleans World Expo, and Public Service against Alcoholism.

I was a guest at *Wally George Talk Show* and appeared in a Music Video for Alicia Bridges. I attended Professional Artists Group for acting classes and got a part in the TV Series *Days of our Lives* on NBC Channel 4. I played the role of former Philippines First Lady Imelda Marcos (even though she is older than me at least 30 years) for a humorous satirical play *I Weakness News* for the Gridiron Fundraisers and won Best Actress by The Filipino American Press Club. I also hosted several Celebrity Night

Fundraisers. While interviewing for the "Filipino Specials" and *Entra Pinoy TV Show*, which I co-hosted, I have met numerous, interesting personalities including Dan Inosanto, A Filipino American Martial Artist and training partner of the legendary Bruce Lee, Ed Sotiangco, CEO of Sotiangco Companies, and other successful entrepreneurs. I modeled for print advertising for Kings Hawaiian Sweet Bread for The Los Angeles Times and posters for supermarkets all over California. I modeled for advertisements for Western Airlines and San Miguel Beer!

My career as a columnist for *Limelight* for Asian American News is rewarding. I enjoyed tremendously writing about socials, charity events, fashion, and community news. I became very active with my social life, the community, and fundraisers. In between my schedule, Robert, Bridgette, Sean, and I traveled all over the USA, Canada, Asia, and Europe. My lifestyle became more hectic, demanding, and exciting when I wrote my book Total Beauty and Life and had my own business - Corazon Ugalde Yellen Cosmetics. This meant double responsibility and work but also fun. It changed my lifestyle. My family was still my number one priority, but I devoted myself to this book and the cosmetics business. My distributor was Jeffrey Light, CEO of Jason Natural Products. My products were Corazon Fragrances, Emotion Perfume, and Corazon Shampoos. My book was endorsed by Gloria Diaz, former Miss Universe and Marianne Rogers, wife of the legendary Kenny Rogers. It was launched at The Philippine Consulate in Los Angeles and at The National Bookstore in Makati, Philippines. It had a great turnout and was a huge success. I was a guest at several TV shows to promote my book, fragrances, and Beauty Queen title, Mrs. Travel of the World. I was featured in several publications both in the Philippines and USA.

Robert was a building contractor and real estate developer for many celebrities and film producers in Hollywood. He remodeled Sylvester Stallone's office and art studio in Santa Monica. He remodeled the home of Lawrence Gordon, film producer. We were invited to attend Movie Premiers - *Waterworld, Roadhouse,* and *Rocketeer* among others and through the years met several well-known movie stars - Julia Roberts, Arnold Schwarzenegger, Kevin Costner, and Patrick Swayze! It was an awesome experience to attend movie premieres with lavish reception!

One of my hobbies is collecting dolls. I started when Bridgette was born. I collected all kinds of dolls with over 2000 dolls in my collection. Some of my favorites are the Barbie dolls. I was the Founder and President of the Beverly Hills Barbie Club and had members all over the world. We had regular meetings about our common interests as a Barbie collector and discussed new collections and events. During the holidays, Christmas time, we donated dolls and toys for different Charity Groups. I was co-chairperson for the Mini Barbie Convention held in Southern California. I organized a Barbie Fashion Show at the famed Queen Mary Ballroom in Long Beach. For many years, I modeled Life size Barbie outfits during the Fashion Show of several Barbie Conventions in Maryland, Niagara Falls, New York, Nebraska, Florida, California, and Koblenz, Germany. I was featured in several Barbie Bazaar magazine and Japanese and German Magazines! I was one of the Barbie collectors' guests on the *Phil Donahue TV Show, Mo Gaffney,* and *Roseanne Barr TV Show.* I was interviewed by the late Dick Clark during his TV Game Show-It Takes Two. It was an amazing experience! It was thrilling to be the first Filipina to model for a major mannequin manufacturer Greneker Co. They sculpted my face and made a face mask to be immortalized as an Asian Mannequin for several Department Stores worldwide. To stay healthy and fit, I took yoga, aerobics, dance lessons, and Martial Arts. I met Dennis Alexio, the World Kickboxing Champion in the late 1980's. Dennis and I became good friends, and he trained me in kickboxing. He was my best instructor in self- defense.

I played the role of Cora Fischman, Nicole Simpson's friend, for "O.J. Simpson Trial Reenactment" for *E! Entertainment TV Show*, a role in the film *Dangerous Man*, Julia Styles, as Serafina in the movie *Fortune Teller*, TV Movies *Black Sheep, Behind the Dark, Botyok sa America* with Vandolph and "*Corazon*" TV series with Lloyd *Samartino*. I was filmed for the Fashion Video by Beverly Sassoon, former wife of Vidal Sassoon and starred in numerous stage and musical plays-*Balikbayan, New Yorker in Tondo, Regina of Greenwich, Ramona, Blind Curves* and *The World Is an Apple*. I won Best Actress by Virgo Awards for my role as Luisa, a poor prostitute in the dramatic play, *There Was a Soldier*, by Cebu Performing Arts. It is evident that I am passionate about Theatre Arts, so I founded my own business, CorYellen Theatre Company. I acquired sponsors, wrote, directed, produced, and starred as Queen Puso in the musical play *The Legend of Queen Puso*. I produced, directed, wrote, and starred in two more theatrical plays-*Deep in the Heart of Paradise* and *A Collectors Heart and Soul*. We had rehearsals, trained, and directed the actors and actresses. It was very challenging.

But at this point, my personal life was in chaos. After 18 years of marriage to Robert, sadly, we separated. We had marital problems and saw marriage therapists, but it was too late to make it work. It was devastating for both of us, especially for Bridgette and Sean who were teenagers. We had a live-in housekeeper since my children were very young, and I had to let her go. We had to sell our beautiful Beverly Hills home, and we both spent so much money for our attorneys. Finally, our divorce was granted, and we moved on. I received my generous settlement, and I invested it in Real Estate. I got my Real Estate license in 2000. My business in Real Estate was very successful. I was an independent contractor with Coldwell Banker in Beverly Hills. I represented both buyers and sellers and met many Hollywood celebrities. Most importantly, with my business, I was able to invest several properties in California and Nevada successfully. As investments, I purchased and sold a four-bedroom house in Sacramento, a three-bedroom house in North Hills, a triplex rental property in Koreatown and a three-bedroom beach house in Redondo Beach, all with great profits. I kept two properties for myself in a living trust for Bridgette and Sean. One property I own is a vacation house in Las Vegas. The other property which I purchased in 2001 is a fabulous Double Duplex in Wilshire Vista, close to LACMA. The value has tripled, and it is a great rental property with high rent. I named my 4 plex Casa Corazon.

I moved to Las Vegas in 2007 and met Frank Armenta, Jr., a network engineer. We dated and fell in love and after 8 months got married. Our Bridesmaids were my daughter Bridgette, Frank's daughter Heather, and groom's men were my son Sean, Frank's son Shane. It was my fourth marriage. After 8 years, we moved back to Los Angeles. I joined the beauty pageant by Virgelia Productions from Virgelia Villegas's invitation. It was a wonderful experience! It was joyous to be crowned Mrs. Asia Glamour among 40 international candidates on November 18, 2018, in Redondo Beach. Through the years, I have acquired 15 Beauty Queen Titles - Americas Ms. Charisma, Mrs. Travel of the World, Ms. Gandang Pilipina, Ms. Travel and Trade Love of Country Ambassador, Mrs. Philippines, Ms. InterContinental Universe, Mrs. Asia USA California, Mrs. Asia Glamour, Ms. Amerasia International, Most Beautiful Filipina, Ms. Global America World, Ms. Gawad Amerika Universe, World Class Beauty Queens USA Ambassador, Ms. Paris International, and Ms. All Women Rock Global Elite by Dr. Carl Wilson, CD Wilson Events.

I have many wonderful memories walking the ramp for amazing Fashion Shows, modeling for distinguished International Fashion Designers-Kenneth Barlis, Katrina Ponce Enrile, Diem Nguyen, Letty Alvarado, Ximena Valerio, Juhi Jagiasi, Marvin Bendana, Jane

Okida, and ShailK. During luncheons at The Excelsior on Rodeo Drive in Beverly Hills, I modeled couture ensembles for Yves St Laurent, Celine, and Fendi. As an internationally published Cover Girl, I have graced the covers of 32 international magazines. I am the Brand Ambassador of Luxury ReadyLady Lingerie by Designer Paulette Mouquet, also the Producer of Hollywood Star in Paris Reality TV Show, and I am thrilled to be one of the Stars!

To fulfill my bucket list, I visited Antarctica via M/V Ortelius. It was glorious to land on the coldest and windiest place on earth and observe the different types of wildlife. It was an adventure of a lifetime! I traveled extensively to the seven continents seeing the seven Wonders of the World and exploring 100 countries worldwide.

In Los Angeles, I started my business, Corazon Productions. I founded my company because of my love, passion, and support for the Arts and culture so I can further my cause and advocacy to showcase and promote talents who excel in their fields. I will be producing my second book launching events and Fashion Show in 2021. In Manila, I founded my business Queen Corazon Scents Trading Co. offering Queen Corazon Scents, sanitizers, and Queen Corazon Dolls. Part of Proceeds goes to Gasa Charities and Lighthouse Organization. I am one of the Ambassadors of this organization for helping victims of domestic violence. I believe in giving back to the community and charity work. I was filmed for a TV commercial in Thailand for Cancer Hope Village to promote Cancer awareness. I have volunteered to feed the homeless, donate goods, visited sick US Veterans in the Military hospital, and donated my contributions to charity events for a great cause. I was given an award for my charitable contribution and support to the community as a Humanitarian of the Year by the World Elite Organization.

The legacy I want to leave behind is my advocacy and women empowerment. Women can be anything they want - an entrepreneur, beauty queen, or homemaker. Everyone has the strength and power to conquer anything, to make a difference in society, and to inspire everyone that they can be the best of themselves.

My name "Corazon" means "Heart" in Spanish, and heart is the Symbol of Love. I believe in giving and receiving Love. I love life and I live life to the fullest. I love my family, my friends, my business, my lifestyle, and my blessings from God. I am having an amazing journey in life, and I thank God for everything.

I can be reached at corayellen@aol.com,
Instagram @beautyqueencorayellenarmenta
Facebook - Queen Corazon Yellen Armenta
You Tube channel - Beauty Queen Corazon Ugalde Armenta

Dr. Randi D. Ward

Believe, Dream Bigger, and Reach for the Stars
By Randi D. Ward

Life has so many twists and turns and detours and winding roads with bumps and cracks that often try to change the directions in life we desire to take or are meant to take. Learning how to deal with these obstacles and roadblocks takes perseverance, courage, and a never-ending belief you can accomplish everything your heart desires. My life philosophy is the following: "Believe. Don't dream big; dream BIGGER. The sky is the limit so reach for the stars" (Randi D. Ward, copyrighted 2012).

I grew up as a shy, small town West Virginia girl. Even though I was an intelligent person and an excellent student, I never felt I fit in. My abusive, alcoholic father did his best to demoralize me by whispering to me daily, "You are so ugly; no man will ever love you." As a young girl, I believed him. Even though he was cruel, he was still my father, so why would he lie to me about this. My deep scars still surface to this day and haunt my soul, but thankfully I have learned to handle these dark emotional moments better.

Besides this mental abuse, I also suffered a left knee injury at age fifteen that caused serious problems for the next five years and beyond. I could not walk and was forced to use crutches to get around. Corrected surgery at age nineteen resulted in a pinched lower leg nerve and paralysis for over six months requiring muscular electrical stimulation treatments three times a week. Doctors told me I would probably never walk again. Being stubborn and believing I would find a way to walk, I developed my own physical therapy program and was walking at the age of 20 although not perfectly. Throughout the next forty-four years, my knee continued to create problems. I have had to learn to walk too many times, but I was determined to keep moving. I never give up. On June 26, 2014, I had a total knee replacement at last—something I had refused to do until I could no longer overcome my horrible knee situation.

Six months after my successful knee replacement, a near fatal automobile accident occurred on December 29. I broke eight bones, including my neck, four left-side ribs, two fractures on my left pelvis, and my left lower arm. My left lung was collapsed; my spleen was lacerated. I had to be cut out of the car. I was treated by four trauma doctors, spent three days in ICU, fifteen additional days in two hospitals, and eight months of physical therapy on various body parts; wore a neck brace for 93 days; and now have an eight-inch plate with six permanent pins in my arm. The pain I endured was agonizing. I could have felt sorry for myself, but instead I felt blessed to be alive. To keep from going crazy, I chose a different path. On my laptop, I typed my 400-page world adventure novel Random Wanderings with my right hand, and my mind traveled the world in my imagination as a young female veterinarian. This novel will finally be published in 2021. Once again, I refused to give up. I had experienced my second physical miracle, according to my many doctors.

As I reflect on my childhood, I was so different. Of course, I had friends but always hid in their shadows and prayed they would not discover my deep insecurity. Graduating as my high school class valedictorian forced me to put myself in that unwanted "spotlight" when I had to give a fifteen-minute graduation speech in front of thousands of people. To my surprise I performed well as I spoke about the power of believing in oneself to achieve one's dreams.

When I started courses in Language Arts at Marshall University's teachers' college, I decided to begin my transformation—to find the confidence I lacked. To some degree I was successful, but it was not until I met the love of my life, my wonderful husband Bill, the summer immediately after receiving my B.A. degree that my life changed forever. Bill became my "earthly savior". His undying love, encouragement, and never-ending support helped to mold the woman I was meant to be---the kind of woman who dreams bigger and believes she can do anything if she works hard enough. No longer was I that shy girl afraid to be seen.

I spent the next 37 years of my life as a secondary Language Arts and Gifted Education teacher and leader in seven schools in West Virginia and Georgia. I was a West Virginia pioneer in the creation of the Gifted Program and the teacher courses for Marshall University in the 1970's. Bill and I raised our son Mark; cared for our four St. Bernard dogs, our beagle, and two cats; traveled around the world during many summer vacations; and enjoyed a comfortable upper-middle-class lifestyle. Retiring in 2008, I thought it would be great to have time to do whatever I wanted---continue to travel, sleep in late, do volunteer work, etc., but none of that was enough. I became totally bored and disillusioned. I had no purpose now. I was not ready for the "rocking chair" lifestyle.

In 2011-12, I got the opportunity to teach young adults English as a second language in a language center in Cairo, Egypt. My husband and son were totally opposed to this. The Egyptians had overthrown thirty-year dictator Mubarak on January 25, 2011, and things were still unstable politically, economically, etc. They were convinced Egypt was unsafe which turned out to be true. However, something happened I could not ignore. I started having dreams night after night for three months. This majestic voice I interrupted as the heavenly voice of God repeated the same message: "I want you to go Egypt. The young students need you. Egypt needs you. I will protect you. Go to Cairo and teach." I rarely remember my dreams, but this dream was so vivid—so profound. I did not share this with anyone at the time—not even my family---for fear people would not believe me. Against my family and friends' advice, I accepted the position. I was determined to follow God's "command" to me.

On November 3, 2011, I fearlessly boarded the first plane in Atlanta, Georgia, and headed to Cairo with my sincere desire to make a difference in the students' lives there. Little did I know Egypt's second revolution would begin one week after my arrival, and I would be living three blocks from Tahrir Square, the violent revolution center. Bill needed to stay home so I went alone. I knew no Arabic and was unfamiliar with Egyptian and Islamic culture, so the first few weeks were challenging. My friends and students did their best to support and guide me, but I knew I must become self-sufficient. Before I left, I had transformed into Egyptian Rere (my new nickname), a lady who could handle almost any situation even though I still did not know much Arabic. I could always find an English-speaking local to assist me in the tremendously difficult situations. The Egyptian people became my second family. I am still close to many of them.

Returning home in early February 2012, American Randi had been reborn. In Egypt, I discovered an even more independent Randi. As always, I had dreamed bigger. I had journeyed to Egypt to teach and to bring hope to young adult students, to create new memories with old and future friends, to live the unique and unfamiliar life as an Egyptian in this exotic culture, to explore the magnificent city of Cairo, to expand my knowledge and understanding of Islam, and to my unwanted surprise to witness firsthand the constantly changing political climate in Egypt's revolutionary period. It was the most spectacular and captivating adventure and another unforgettable life challenge.

A few days after returning home to Georgia, the dreams---more life-changing words from God---returned. "I kept my promise to keep you safe. You helped so many people. You made a difference. I am proud of you. Now you must write your story and the story of the Egyptians and their revolution. Begin soon." I had always wanted to write a book but never had the time. As a teacher, I had always been too busy evaluating student papers. I had traveled to forty-eight countries at this time and had amazing stories I could have told, but this was the most important one. Three months from the day I wrote the first book word, my memoir *Because I Believed in Me (My Egyptian Fantasy Came True)* was born with 153 photos included. The cover was designed by a real Egyptian artist friend, and two other Egyptian friends named my book having won my Facebook Book Title Contest. I wrote this book using words easily translatable into Arabic and other languages. I wanted my reader to feel as if I was sitting beside him/her and telling my stories. Readers tell me I succeeded which pleases me.

After the book was on the market in November 2012, I returned to Cairo for the launching of my book as well as for my first English center in January 2013. At the end of 2012, I opened an English-German Language Center in Cairo called Rise Up with two former male Egyptian students. My debut book talk was proudly conducted at this amazing center. Two Egyptian magazines and two newspapers also interviewed me while I was there. In early February, I had to return home. My partners worked hard at promoting our school, but sadly we were forced to close one year later due to the continued poor Egyptian economy.

Still hoping to provide quality English instruction in Egypt, my friend Samar Farouk and I opened 6 October Nursery School in 2014. I was teaching pre-school children and their parents English via Skype. I even wrote short stories and nursery rhymes to use as lessons. Things were going well, but Samar became ill for many months. This school closed in 2015. I do not consider either school closings as failures. I learned much about becoming an entrepreneur. Being a part of both schools fulfilled one of my dreams—owning my own schools. I attempted to tutor my international friends English online for free for the next several years, but time differences and poor internet quality in many countries forced me to stop. Now I just send helpful free websites I have found to them and answer random questions if needed.

My passion as a writer, my second career, grew to include many genres: short stories for children and adults, poetry, blogs, magazine articles, motivational or entertaining YouTube videos, and novels. Since I consider myself as an idealist, my writing must be positive with happy endings. We need more happy endings in our world. Sadly, I became disillusioned with the publishing world after disappointing experiences with my Egypt book and have not published any of my numerous, personally completed books although some of my work has appeared in magazines, newspapers, anthologies, and of course, my website and YouTube channel. I have won two writing contests for a short story and a poem. In 2020 I was in an International Best Seller book in six categories entitled *Quarentena and Beyond* with 47 authors from 32 countries. In 2021, I plan to begin self-publishing my books at last beginning with my novel *Random Wanderings* mentioned earlier. This year I am also scheduled so far to have stories in the following books: *Global Achievers, Volume 1*; *Finding Joy in the Journey, Volume 2*; and *World Leaders Experts Book*.

I am a "People Person" and an "Adventure Seeker". Because of this, I have been fortunate to have traveled to 60 countries in four continents. I have walked on the Great Wall of China; searched for the Loch Ness Monster (unsuccessfully); climbed the Eiffel Tower and the Tower of Pisa; and ridden on a camel in Giza, Egypt, a donkey in Santorini, Greece, and an ostrich in South Africa. I have happily and freely sung South Pacific songs along the coast of Bali, Indonesia (much to my husband's embarrassment). I have cruised many rivers, oceans, and seas: the majestic Nile, the blue Danube, the Rhine, the Thames, the Seine, the Atlantic, the Adriatic, the Indian, the North Sea, the Mediterranean, etc. I have been on numerous game drives in Kenya, South Africa,

Zimbabwe, Botswana, Swaziland, and Zambia; have been thrilled seeing beautiful African animals in the wild; and have even flown in a hot air balloon over the Masai Mara, Kenya. I have petted two adult cheetahs and walked with two lions in Africa and held a panda in China. As a serious animal lover/advocate, my animal encounters were moments I will treasure forever. This is just a small sampling of all I have experienced in my world travels. I pray I will add more in the future.

Throughout the years, I have been blessed to be recognized for my hard work and genuine dedication to help others. I continue to be humbled and often shocked and overwhelmed by these honors. I share them to demonstrate how this ordinary woman (me), once shy and unsure of herself, found the strength to achieve my dreams. I was named "Entrepreneur of the Year 2014 in the Education Industry" by Worldwide Who's Who and was profiled in the month of March in the 2015 Worldwide Branding calendar. In 2015 I was honored as this organization's Distinguished Worldwide Humanitarian of the Year and as 2014 Top Female Executive as well an Inductee, Elite American Artist (2015). My other awards and credentials include the following: 2014-15 VIP Woman of the Year by National Association of Professional Women (now IAW), an elite member and 2015 Delegate of the International Women's Leadership Association (IWLA), a 2014 Pinnacle Professional Member of Continental Who's Who, an elite VIP member of Strathmore Worldwide Who's Who, 2015 Professional of the Year with International Association of Who's Who, and 2016 Editor of the Year by International Society of Business Leaders. I appeared in a YouTube interview video with President Beth Johnston of IWLA and was featured on the cover of its May/June 2016 edition of *Inspirational Woman Magazine* with my article "Taking the Needed Risks". In an October 2016 edition of *Women of Distinction Magazine*, I was featured in a four-page article as an Author/Entrepreneur and in a 30-minute podcast interview on its website. I was named 2017 Top Professional in Language Arts, 2018 Top Female Executive of the Year, 2020 Female Visionary, 2021 Educator of the Decade By IAOTP, and inducted into its 2019 Hall of Fame. I am an elite VIP member of both Strathmore's Who's Who and its sister P.O.W.E.R. (Women of Excellence). I appeared in *TIP* magazine and *P.O.W.E.R.* magazine in the spring of 2018. In August 2019 I was featured on the cover of *Marquis Millennial Magazine* with a one-page article and will be in its 2021 upcoming book of entrepreneurs. In August, I was awarded with a 2021 Women Rock Global Red Blazer of Excellence Award from Carl Wilson and will Co-host the 2021 Award Ceremony in California. I will also receive a crown from Carl Wilson and Robbie Motter in a special ceremony. On December 18, 2020, I was given two awards by IYBC---a Certificate and an Award of Excellence---and spoke at the Awards Ceremony on December 17, 2020. My article "Imagining" appeared in the first edition of its "Global Influencers Magazine" on January 10, 2021, and I spoke at the zoom magazine launch. In 2020 I was honored as a Beautiful Survivor and Inspiring Global Change Maker and "She Inspires Me" award. I was the Spotlight Feature Story in the September 2020 Marshall University Newsletter and the Fall 50 Years Later Magazine 2020 honoring the 75 who died in our 1970 football team plane crash and was one of the featured videos for the Virtual Homecoming Series with my lesson on "Telling Your Story-Helpful Hints". On June 19, 2021, I will humbly receive an Honorary Doctorate in Humanitarianism by the accredited Global International Alliance and People of Choice Award Program. I have been interviewed on over 25 USA/International interview platforms. My short story "Isabella's Undying Love" is in the anthology A Cup of Love.

I am now a Visionary Book Consultant Coach and Master Editor (Career #3) after acquiring 4 coaching certifications, including

NLP, in 2020. I serve as the chief editor/contributing author for online magazine Morocco Pens, Honorary President of World Peace Forest (Africa) in Egypt, USA Director of Africa Nomads Conservation in Kenya, USA Advisor for International Youth Society, supporter of Lion Encounter in Zimbabwe, editor for Unity in Service, and Mentor for International Youth Business Communities. I was honored as a Service Hero, serve as one of the editors for the *Tour of Love* magazine created by chemo buddies 4 life, and assisted in the third annual 36 hour live telethon *Tour of Love* hosted by Tamara L. Hunter and many celebrities to raise money for cancer victims. I am a member of We Are the Change and LOANI, World Women Conference and Awards, four writers' groups, and Women's Prosperity Network. I keep busy because I get bored easily.

Currently I share my home with my Saint Bernard Savannah and my "adopted" Egyptian family the Abdou's. Tragically, my wonderful husband Bill died from lung cancer on December 15, 2019. The year 2020 was extremely difficult, but I am "fired up" and so ready for what 2021 has to offer. I dedicate my story to my beloved late Bill who always taught me never to give up and to dream BIGGER. I promised him on his deathbed I would move forward and find my joy again, and I am doing my best to do that now.

https://www.youtube.com/channel/UCPgbMr0GXsP-eZFmkAU1O6A

https://www.facebook.com/randi.ward and
https://www.facebook.com/AuthorRandi

https://www.linkedin.com/in/randidward/ and
randiteach@yahoo.com

Robbie Motter

The Color Red is Powerful
By Robbie Motter

Did you know that Red is the color of passion? It radiates strong and powerful energy that motivates us to pay attention and to take action.

Thank you, Dr. Carl Wilson, for your vision of presenting these red blazers to women around the Globe for their dedication and accomplishments to the world. Every woman who has received the Red Blazer and the award and those who will be receiving them in 2021 already have a passion for what they do and take action. They have strength and energy to step out and step forward to motivate and create positiveness, courage, and desire to commit and to go for their dreams. Read their stories and learn about their accomplishments. I am so honored to have been one of the first to be presented the Red Blazer.

The "All Women Rock" logo on the blazers to me instills the message: dream bigger and surround yourself with other positive and dedicated women and men who also step outside their comfort zones, dream bigger, play bigger, and accomplish things greater that one even imagined.

Last year I wore Red when I did my "Sue Talk" on the stage in Orange County, California, with over 300 women in the audience for the Connected Women of Influence. Although I had spoken for audiences as big as 10,000, I never had to memorize anything. For "Sue Talk" which is like a "Ted Talk" but for women, you can have no notes and no props, and the timing is tight. I decided to wear Red because I felt it is such a powerful color that would help me to stay on track, be seen, and give me the courage to deliver the talk.

In my life it seemed whenever I wore Red during my life, people would always compliment me and say "Wow, that color is great for you and looks great on you." I always remembered that, and in my career which was over 25 years in Corporate America, if I had an important meeting or training or a TV or Radio interview, I always wore red, and the results were always amazing and successful.

In fact, in 2018 when I met Dr. Carl Wilson of Wilson Events, it was at one of his "All Women Rock" events in Riverside, California. Dr. Cherilyn Lee, one of my GSFE members, had nominated me for an award. At that time, we were N.A.F.E networks, and the NAFE color was red, so I invited lots of my members to come to the event. They all dressed in Red. I believe we had two tables, and it was powerful. When we took a photo, it was even more powerful. At this event I saw the opportunity to form a collaboration with Dr. Carl Wilson and his events and have been working with him on the collaboration ever since. I have recommended many of my members for awards with his various events, and they have been thrilled; he has recommended individuals for my GSFE events. We know that together we can do more, touch more lives, and make a difference.

My network is now GSFE (Global Society for Female Entrepreneurs). We selected Cobalt Blue as our color. That color is perfect for our mission---the 501 c3 nonprofit whose mission is to Inspire, Empower, Mentor, Train and Connect Women, so they become successful entrepreneurs.

Cobalt appreciates and respects creative pursuits. Cobalt understands the passion and patience that goes into creating things which is why it admires creative minds. If you are looking for inspiration, cobalt will provide with deserved encouragement. I also am most grateful to Dr Carl Wilson as he has presented me with a Cobalt Blue Blazer with the "All Women Rock" logo on it, and I love it also.

Women are champions, wives, mothers, workers, house engineers, and so much more. They step out in their communities, they lead the way, they make things happen, and they take action. Thank God for individuals like Dr. Carl Wilson who have the vision to see Globally and see the work women do and step up and honor them for making a difference and touching a life.

I want to take this opportunity to congratulate all the women whom Dr. Carl Wilson has selected to receive the Red Blazer and the award as each is amazing and doing amazing things to make a difference and to make the world a better place. Also thank you, Dr. Carl Wilson, for your Vision and for honoring women for the work they are passionate about doing. I wish much continued success to you as well on your projects.

Robbie Motter can be reached at 951-255-9200 or rmotter@aol.com. Her website is robbiemotter.com, and her nonprofit website is www.globalsocietyforfemaleentrepreneurs.org.

Sue Phillips

The Power of Perfume, Reflections and Remembrance of Times Past

With apologies to Proust

"Confessions of a Fragrance Queen" – drop by drop!
By Sue Phillips

I was born in South Africa, became a singer and actress, and as a young girl immigrated to New York in late 1978 and through sheer persistence, passion, hard work (and serendipitous career moves) landed in the Fragrance Industry. I had to put my singing and acting career on the back burner as I didn't have a green-card and neither a SAG/AFTRA union card. However, the 'show-biz' energy of the Beauty Industry appealed to me, and eventually after receiving my green-card, I entered the Cosmetic Industry. Because of my ability to speak and perform in front of an audience, Elizabeth Arden management realized what an asset I would be to motivate and inspire department store beauty associates about the magic and mystery of fragrance. Thus, I began a life-long love affair with Fragrance. After six years at Elizabeth Arden in Training, Product Development, and Marketing, I was then hired by Lancôme as Marketing Director on Women's Prestige fragrance and Men's Skincare, and after four years, I gained expertise in marketing, branding, and product development and then the iconic Tiffany & Co. hired me as Vice President, Fragrance Marketing, to develop and launch the first TIFFANY perfume for their 150th anniversary. In twelve years, I had gone from not knowing anything about the fragrance industry to becoming a leading Marketing Expert and leader in the Fragrance Industry. After rising through the corporate ranks of ELIZABETH ARDEN, LANCÔME & TIFFANY & CO., (to become VP Fragrance Marketing) and creator of the iconic

TIFFANY Perfume, I became an International Fragrance Expert! *(Who would have thunk it!)*

After leaving Tiffany & Co. to have my first child, I established my company, Scenterprises, Inc. in 1990 to share my passion and knowledge of fragrance. Scenterprises became a global branding company and developed fragrances for Avon, Burberry, Diane Von Furstenberg, Trish McEvoy, and many others. I believe everyone's life can be beautifully enhanced through a personalized scent. Hence, Sue's Bespoke Fragrance Service - where scent lovers customize a fragrance as unique as themselves. I consulted regularly for celebrities, executives, and private individuals looking to ensure they create their ideal signature scent. After a proliferation of Celebrity Scents that dominated the industry over the last decade, I realized that this trend would soon be passé, and the bloom was off the rose. Consumers were tired of wearing what everyone else wears, and CUSTOMIZATION and BESPOKE are now the fastest growing trends. Think about Social Media – everyone is on Instagram, Facebook, Snapchat, Twitter, LinkedIn, Tiktok, now Clubhouse, and everyone is now reflecting their own Brand Persona! I recognized this and began to develop Custom Fragrance initiatives. I opened THE SCENTARIUM™, a beautiful bespoke perfumery in trendy Tribeca, where I had celebrities like Jamie Foxx, Katie Holmes, rapper Won-G Bruno, and Zendaya seek me out to create their own Custom Scents. My passion for perfume is well documented. I have created a deluxe Custom Fragrance kit, innovative, interactive 'experiential' Scent/Wine pairing events, SCENT DINNERS and fun, interactive custom Fragrance events for clients such as AOL, BULGARI, COTY, DIGITAS, DUFF& PHELPS, JOHNSON & JOHNSON, METLIFE, MERRIL LYNCH, SC JOHNSON, WELLS FARGO, ZUIRCH FINANCIAL and hundreds of other fortune 500 companies.

Scenterprises' Perfume Bar has been featured in the Oscars

(2020) and Grammy's (2019) Gifting Suites. Corporations hire us to create innovative events for brand development and team building & client appreciation events. Every special occasion imaginable has become an original with a Scent Event from bridal showers, engagement parties and weddings to parties, corporate holiday parties and customized celebrations. Clientele are always thrilled by how unique their event becomes with a lovely custom scent event. My experience and love for fragrance led me to become an Adjunct Professor at FIT College and LIM College and am frequently retained as a Legal Expert for trademark, copyright, and distribution infringements for Fragrance disputes. I love to speak about fragrance and authored my new book, The **Power of Perfume**, which debuted in March 2021.

To say that 2020 was a year like no other is to say that in 1969 a man just stepped foot on the moon! Both were monumental, global in impact, memorable, and life-changing! The moon landing, however, didn't claim 600,000 innocent victims, but it changed the trajectory of our future and opened the exploration of space and other galaxies in the same way that the global pandemic has forever changed our daily lives, and medical research and technology advanced at the speed of light to deliver several vaccines that were heretofore impossible to consider launching under twelve months or less. Everyone dealt with the pandemic in their own unique way, and thankfully, on one hand, my story was uneventful (in terms of not experiencing personal loss or covid illness), and yet, on the other hand, it has been life-altering.

As a single, woman-owned entrepreneurial custom fragrance business owner, March 2020 saw the corporate, team building, and in-person events (which were the lifeblood of my business) screech to a halt! Business dried up! In addition, the building in which I had operated The Scentarium, my lovely Fragrance Studio in Tribeca for close to twelve years, closed, and all tenants were asked to leave as they contemplated renovating or putting the building up for sale. (Good luck with selling the building, I thought, as downtown had become a ghost town!) Ever the Entrepreneur, I was undaunted and thought it would be a good time to write my book, and as a self-proclaimed Scentrepreneur* I put pen to paper and started work on my first book, which I renamed several times, but finally settled on **"The Power of Perfume" – How to Choose it, Wear it, and Enjoy it"!**

My fragrance 'experiences' begin as I invite my clients to take our Scent Personality Quiz and explain why fragrance is so powerful and introduce a brief history of fragrance. I take my guests on a fragrance journey, and present "Fragrance Through the Decades" and explain why certain fragrances define the social, political, and economic mores of the time. I explain how 'personalization' is the new metric and how people are reflecting their personality and individuality in all walks of life. Social Media has become the ultimate barometer for self-branding, and everyone now can be a 'brand'. How we look and sound and how our social media reflects our persona is a way for us all to be unique. In addition, I explain how a signature fragrance can help one identify one's persona and help people understand how powerful fragrance is for personal, home, and environmental use.

As background, I have been in the Fragrance industry for many years and created Fragrance brands for iconic companies: **Tiffany, Burberry, Avon, Lancôme, Lancaster,** as well as for thousands of fragrance lovers and many celebrities, Jamie Foxx, Katie Holmes, Zendaya, Susan Sarandon, Marcia Gay Harden, Laurence Fishbourne, and the late Cicely Tyson.

However, never has it been more apparent as to just how POWERFUL our Sense of Smell is until COVID struck!

A tragic symptom of the Covid pandemic is the loss of Taste and Smell which has affected thousands, nay, **millions** of people and has accelerated awareness of our most powerful sense. The symptoms of Anosmia (loss of taste and smell); Parosmia (smell distortion); Dysgeusia (person's perception of taste is altered) where everything seems sweet, sour, bitter, or metallic. Taste disorders are common in adults and studies have shown that over a 25 million people have suffered from Anosmia, and a study performed on adults in the US indicated that up to 17% of those tested had some impairment in taste.

An ironic and breakthrough moment occurred around mid-March 2021 when NBC TV wanted to do an interview and profile of my new book "The Power of Perfume" and inquired if I had a way of helping Covid "long haulers" rediscover their Sense of Smell? I said I wasn't sure, but I would try, and they brought in a woman who was desperate to regain her sense of smell and was a 'long-hauler'. What ensured over the next few weeks has been quite remarkable, emotional, and life-changing for so many people.

They brought in a woman who had suffered from anosmia for almost thirteen months, and by taking her on a 'scent-healing' journey, she was able to smell something, and she said: *"I smell something, and it is beautiful"*. The interview was aired, and suddenly so many other 'long haulers contacted us to help them, and Inside Edition, New York Post, AmNY, Reuters, NBC TV Chicago, as well as Good Morning America, Voice of America, and news stations around the world have all profiled different stories of people who have been helped. It has been so emotional to see people rediscover their sense of smell and a joy to have helped people realize how important our Olfactory sense is. Everyone has told me that they never paid attention to it before and now are so thrilled that they can smell again.

An interesting fact is that from the second we are born we instantly breathe and smell, and infants recognize their mothers because of their powerful olfactory sense. No one teaches us how to smell, and so we go through life taking it for granted and even ignoring it UNTIL IT IS LOST!! As it turns out, the title of my book was prophetic as people are now finally realizing the power of perfume, and I am truly thrilled to be helping so many depressed, anguished people, rediscover how life can be joyous again, through the small yet mighty olfactory bulb that connects to the limbic system, and to encourage them to 'smell with their brain'! Thanks to the W&WW group, we will be able to get the word out about our most powerful sense!

More on the Power of Perfume

Have you ever walked down the street and suddenly stopped in your tracks because you encounter a familiar fragrance? Perhaps a scent wafting in the air reminds you of the memory of your first kiss? Or the whiff of baby powder immediately takes you back to a beautiful newborn? Do the iconic perfumes of Chanel #5 and Shalimar remind you of your grandmother? Unlike our other senses, we cannot turn off our sense of smell, and it is the strongest link to memories, even more than sight and sound. So, during an event that is emotionally charged, what you smell at that moment becomes intimately intertwined with the experience. Scents can bring back the past or can set the mood for new experiences. That is because the limbic system houses the olfactory hub, the part of the brain that allows you to smell. When you process a smell, you're also processing the event or the emotion that goes with it.

This has happened to me several times where I live in Manhattan, and every now and again I will have an 'olfactive moment', and suddenly I smell an aroma that takes me back to my childhood in South Africa (many decades earlier!) where for example, I encounter a certain scent that reminds me of our annual trips to the Game Reserve---in the pre- dawn 'safari rides,' the confluence of the aromas of the rich red earth scorched from the previous day's burning sun melding with the crisp aroma of the early morning dew on dry blades of grass … ah! So fresh, intoxicating, pungent. and memorable! One day I'll bottle it!

"A woman who doesn't wear perfume has no future"

I believe, as many women in the beauty industry that fragrance can change your life. I know it sounds a bit of an over-promise. But it isn't. Having had over forty years of experience in this industry, forty years of studying, marketing, and creating memorable perfumes for iconic companies, and presenting innovative, interactive, fun, educational, and scentertaining bespoke perfume experiences, I can say, with some certainty, I know the power of perfume. I have been involved in the creation of major perfumes for iconic brands such as *Tiffany* and *Society by Burberry*, as well as *Trish McEvoy*, and home fragrances for *AVON, Diane von Furstenberg*, and I have witnessed, up close and personal how fragrance notes and the alchemy of mixing them can change moods, emotions, and realities.

Every time you experience and wear a fragrance that suits you, one that elevates your mood, that adds to your pleasure, that fascinates you, that expresses you, you are having a magical experience. That magical experience is subconsciously inspiring you, beautifying you, and strengthening you by increasing your happiness quotient and celebrating the goodness and wonders of life. In other words, you are gaining self-confidence in your powers of creating magic and beauty, simply by expressing yourself through a 'scentual' accent… drop by drop.

Perhaps your grandmother dabbed on Chanel No. 5 when she went out on Saturday evenings, and probably her friends did, too! It is hard to believe that this iconic 'parfum du jour' is 100 years old. Even though the actual formula has changed over the years, this eternal scent is still the symbol of luxury and femininity, but at the time it was launched in 1921 it revolutionized the way women would smell, embodying the 'modern woman' which Coco Chanel epitomized.

Women then began wearing perfumes daily and using them to suit their moods and now; perfume has become a staple of one's beauty regime. Every designer has a range of perfume offerings; celebrities endorse all kinds of perfumes, their own and designers', and a variety of smaller, niche perfume companies are bringing an assortment of perfumes and fragranced home products to market, quicker and sometimes more creatively than the large corporations like Estee Lauder or L'Oreal, and these smaller artisanal brands are eventually bought out or acquired by a larger entity to gain more widespread distribution. Perfume is big business now, upwards of $40 billion per year.

Perfume is the silent, invisible accessory that has become as important as the fashion outfits we wear, and that those interested in being original and unique are searching for their signature scent---one that reflects their individuality and personality, and that reminds them of who they are, never mind those who meet them informally. If a piece of jewelry visually communicates our aesthetic, a scent does the same, even more clearly through smell, one of the most powerful and emotional of our senses.

Since our sense of smell is so developed and evocative, I have noticed that women and men who **really** know themselves, who are confident and who want to be respected, want to wear fragrances that authentically reflect who they are, and to leave a scent trail that makes others stop and think, "Oh what is he or she wearing? I would love to know that person." Those people are not looking for the latest fad or celebrity scent or the cheapest priced perfume. No 'flavor of the month' for them! Even though perfume is intangible, it is powerful in its delicacy and distinctiveness; it is an elixir that creates beauty and lifts our spirits. If you are discerning and an arbiter of taste and one who understands the power of fragrance, you will agree that quality ingredients in a perfume are what you are constantly searching for. That does not necessarily mean the most expensive perfume, but it does mean the perfume that reflects the best part of you, that enhances you, that makes you feel alluring, beguiling, and seductive. There is no doubt in my mind that Delilah who mesmerized Samson, and Salome who danced the Dance of the Seven Veils, and Cleopatra and other legendary women throughout history wore scents that were part of their allure. I don't believe that will ever change. As long as men and women continue to enhance their lives by making themselves more desirable, passionate, sexier, and vibrant through all the senses—through harmonious music, through vivid paintings and exquisite clothes, through indulging in aromatic wines and feasting on savory delicacies, luscious edibles and experiencing the tactile hedonistic pleasure of attraction, they will enhance their lives through the poetic and meaningful power of scent. Those are the people who know how essential and necessary fragrance has become.

The world is moving more towards personalization in products since we all now want to express ourselves individually, and technology enables us to do more and more of that through the ubiquitous taking of 'selfies and the ability to develop our brand persona. A significant part of my work is creating personalized fragrances for those who understand the power of a signature fragrance that represents their psychological and spiritual profile. They know it will enhance themselves and complement those around them.

The human nose is a sensitive organ that can sense up to 350,000 different scents. It is our most powerful sense after our sense of sight and is directly connected to our memory through scent receptors in our nose, which are linked to the part of our brain correlated with memory and emotions. Research on scent aroma is being done to examine the productivity of the workplace and to assist with health and medical issues. Businesses from all over are examining different scents to trigger their customers to engage in an emotion that attracts them; to return to resorts and hotels, to purchase more products, and more importantly to label their brand with a certain scent, also known as scent-branding. Perfume is both a Science and an Art, and it continues to fascinate and intrigue.

"My mission is to create magical fragrance experiences and products…. drop by drop"

Scentfully yours,

Sue Phillips
Scentrepreneur™, Scentwhisperer®, Scenterprises.com
www.suephillips.com
www.scenterprises.com
www.thepowerofperfume.com

Sarifa Alonto-Younes

Transform Your Pain into Power
Sarifa Alonto-Younes

The unfortunate truth is that there are millions of young women who get deprived of opportunities from the moment they're born. Abject poverty may prevent them from seeing the potential that they hold inside. A lack of education may mean that they're not even aware of a life beyond what they know. The world is not always how we see it on television or even how we remember it for ourselves. Not every child has the perfect start in life. But no matter the circumstances, every child has within them the potential to do something amazing. Every young woman has the ability to succeed despite or even because of their painful experiences.

I am the living proof of this. I have risen up from the depths and fulfilled the potential that every woman has. Moreover, I have dedicated my life to helping orphaned and disadvantaged children.

I am now a Serial Entrepreneur, International Speaker, Best-Selling Author, and a Philanthropist. Due to those various forms and layers of obstacles I am shaped into the person that I am today.

At the age of ten I lost both my parents. My father died of a mix of a car accident and sickness when I was threem. Then few years later, my mother lost her battle with a stomach cancer. In my first book, Love Your Obstacles, I shared details of my life story, journey, and experiences to the readers.

I vividly remember on April 27, 1974, when my friends and I were playing hopscotch, and we decided to change our game to hide-and-seek underneath our stilts home. Our sweet carefree giggles soon became overturned by the sound of painful crying.

The cries came from inside my home. Neighbours and relatives began rushing inside our home, the sound of their footsteps hitting the timber stairs at rapid rates.

I dropped the game we were playing and ran with the panicked crowd. My small legs manoeuvred me swiftly through the legs and waists of the crowd until I finally broke through and began frantically searching for my parents inside the house. My sister was crying uncontrollably on the floor. My other siblings were crying, and relatives were wailing. All what I saw was crying bodies circling my dad. I looked around in disbelief as the house kept filling up with more people. I was lost amongst the mourners.

Before I could understand the surreal scene that was occurring, my father's big family began funeral arrangements almost immediately. In our Muslim culture, we believe in an afterlife and that an individual's soul gets freed from the physical body. So, funerals and burials are held quickly after death in order to free the soul from the body and before the body decays.

My father's body was taken out of the house wrapped in pristine white cotton. That was the last time I saw him. I didn't get to say goodbye. It was just like a ripping separation, being immediately torn apart from the man that I loved, respected, and adored.

From that moment, loneliness and emptiness filled every corner of the house. Sadness engulfed the rooms and grief lined every wall. It was as if the house was also mourning. A huge empty bore gauged into my heart; a little girl was lost.

Our home didn't feel like a home anymore. My siblings slowly started to move out of the house one after the other. The house saw too many changes in too little time. Over time, my siblings grew more restless and disturbed and stopped going to school. I quickly lost that playful childhood that used to fill my days, the innocent joy of playing underneath our large home with my friends. Instead, I had to find ways to cope to understand and navigate our new stage of life; the tragic curveball thrown on us by nature was beyond our control. Then, we moved to the city of Marawi so my mother could fend for us. **This is how I learned my first lesson, acceptance.**

At three years of age, I was too young to go to school, but my older brother Nasroding went, and I found an ingenious way to learn through his education. Perhaps it helped me deal with the grief, but for me it was like a ray of sunshine that cut through the dark looming clouds.

Every time my brother was studying or reading books, I would sit next to him or behind him listening intently to how he pronounced words, how he read them. I tried to mimic the way he read, and often he'd push me away or ask me to leave because I was often copying him out loud instead of in my head. That's how I learned how to read although he sometimes yelled at me and told my mum that I was distracting and disturbing him.

When I was old enough to go to school, I felt that school was my second home. I felt at ease and truly confident and enjoyed every moment of each day learning. While I was busy learning and enjoying going to school, life was busy making other future plans for me---plans I didn't want nor was prepared to handle.

My mother developed stomach cancer, a cruel and devastating disease. Every day was a battle for her. I could see her physical pain, and I could feel her emotional pain inside my own heart every time I looked at her. She would desperately be trying to shelter me from her struggles and sufferings, but my heart knew the truth.

On the 7th of December 1982, I made a decision not to attend the school as I had a deep strong feeling that it would be my mother's last day with us. That day, I prepared myself psychologically and emotionally. I remember sitting next to her bed with my grandmother.

While she was lying down, I was trying to make conversation with her in case she had an important message to say before she went. In a serendipitous moment, my mum reached for me, and we clutched our hands together. Her familiar deep brown eyes looked straight into mine, and she squished my hand. A delicate teardrop in the shape of a small pearl sat perfectly on her cheek as she closed her eyes one last time. Her hand rested in mine, but her final signal, that loving squish of my hand, still pulsated through me.

My mother was gone. I knew deep down that we'd taken a unique journey together. That as we held hands, she had entered a new life, and so had I. Part of me did not want to disturb her soul's journey because I knew that she had suffered enough. Yet, the child within me only wanted her to stay. My inner cries pleaded for her to stay with me to watch me grow.

At ten years of age, my fate was sealed. I was an orphan. Life would never be the same. I had to grow and learn to cope emotionally. I felt that I had lost everything. My parents were my everything. Losing one was hard; losing two was unbearable.

What could life possibly hold for me now? At ten years old I felt that the worst had happened. My parents had died. They would never be here to see me grow up, to help me grow up, to be proud of my achievements, or to share in a simple family gathering. Emptiness and insecurity knocked at the door of my soul every day. Would I be strong enough to push it away?

I soon learnt that when in grief many people's well-meaning words fall short---not because they aren't filled with support and love, they certainly are but because they can't fill that deeper void within.

No matter how hard people tried to offer me solace and comfort through their kind words — I didn't find my way out of misery that way. But one sentence did circle my mind like a longing seed floating in the wind seeking a warm place to germinate and grow.

Words my mother had said played over and over in my head. "Education will drag you out of misery. If you want to succeed, you need to understand the power of education." The sweet remembrance of her guiding voice flooded my consciousness.

After the death of my mother, something transformative dawned on me. This time my acceptance skills began to develop better. I quickly realised that I had the power within me to accept my circumstances, and in doing so, I was able to control how I was feeling and thinking. Learning to accept would help me stop fighting and resisting what had already happened. When I began to accept the harsh fact that my parents were no longer there for me, it somehow eased my pain and suffering. It soothed the wound little by little and allowed me to focus on my studies.

Before the death of my mother in Marawi City, we used to live where the Padian (Market Place) was. Usually, early in the morning, without my mother's knowing, we used to go to the Pantalan (wharf) to play and check on those people coming from different places around the largest lake in Mindanao, Lake Lanao; the Maranaos called it Ranao.

At that time, the wharf was called Pantanal where the Lansa (boats) from places around the lake used to dock. My friends and I enjoyed watching those people as they rushed out of the boat when they reach Marawi.

In the morning the Ranao is so beautiful, majestic, and irresistible. Children would just jump into it as soon as they arrived Pantalan. Literally, Ranao was just another big playground for the children at that time.

As those Lansa start to approach the Pantalan, the children would merrily wait for those Lansa to be docked and impatiently would swim around and under them. Initially I would enjoy watching those children as they frantically rejoice jumping into the water. I did get tempted to join them, but my brother (who was seven-years old at that time) would warn me not to dare and would give me an angry look. He used to scare me that I could drown as I'm too young and too small (I was five-years old by then) and that if a big wave would come, it may carry me away to the deep end. Though I enjoyed watching other children having fun, playfully swimming, I would go home with a heavy heart.

Not all the time, Ranao is calm and serene. There are times it's rough and furious! The waves would roar and come in different sizes, but the children would still jump on each of the wave and have more fun in the rough waves than when it's smooth and quiet.

It made me wonder what was so special with those big waves as the bigger the waves were, the more excited and happier those children become. Now here is where I learned my second Lesson, DECIDE. One day I just jumped into the water and started to surf on those small waves and then into the medium waves and to the bigger waves. Once you ride on the big waves you would no longer go for the smaller ones.

Which wave would you ride on? The small one or the bigger one!

One thing I learned from that experience is if I didn't make the decision to dare jumping into the water to ride on those waves, I would have missed out for the rest of my life not knowing and understanding how it feels to ride waves. If I just stood every day at the edge of the lake and waited for the right time to come, I would have missed the opportunity to surf.

Sometimes, you need to make decisions. You may need to start to ride on a small wave and then to a bigger wave. Then one day you will be the one creating those waves for other people, and that's what I call a LEGACY.

Like the previous empowered women such as Margaret Thatcher, Indira Gandhi, Eleanor Roosevelt. Mother Theresa. and the like paved the way for us to create waves for other women and the generations to come; that's their legacy to humanity.

While you are strong, you need to create the waves because a time will come that you no longer are able to create them, and someone will create them for you when you are unable to ride the waves. Therefore, jump in and participate in making waves.

The sea was rough, stormy, and unwelcoming, but I rode the breaking waves. Now, I'm authoring a chapter of this book for a reason. I feel the need to share my journey and what I learned along the way.

Becoming an orphan has had a profound impact on how I perceive the world and life in general. Some of the challenges I overcame may resonate with you. Ideally, they'll inspire you to take on a different perspective.

You know – we're all kind of boxed in by our perspectives. Of course, our living conditions and experiences shape our worldviews, but there's one exciting thing.

Each person is a unique temple faced with specific challenges, obstacles, and pains. Indeed, these are very personal but, at the same time, they're universal.

So, what did I learn after my parents passed away?

People have the capacity to learn different life skills. You can learn how to be confident and resilient. You can learn acceptance, decision-making, and courage – to name but a few.

If you don't learn, you can acquire the skills and build upon them through experience. The critical thing is that we need those skills. Otherwise, it's next to impossible to change the society and the zeitgeist we live in.

Women now have more opportunities in the workplace than they've ever had before. But we need to help and support each other. As Sheryl Sandberg once said *"there's a special place in hell for women who don't help other women."*

Last thing that I want you to remember is nothing is impossible if you truly believe in your potential and have a support system you can lean on.

Caprice Crebar

Advice For a Graduate
By Caprice Crebar

My youngest child is a 2021 high school graduate. As I write this, I'm on a plane to Fort Jackson, South Carolina, to see him graduate from Army Basic Training. My husband and I are preparing ourselves for the rewards of empty nesting as his two older brothers will soon be spreading their wings and flying the nest as well!

Our three sons have completely different personalities, skills, and ambitions. Their paths to success will be different, yet many of the tools for success are the same. My greatest prayer is that they each find a path that serves God, makes a positive difference in the world, allows them to feel personally fulfilled, and to be happy and enjoy the financial freedom to live comfortably and give back. This to me is the definition of success.

I have witnessed several graduations this year. I have shed tears watching the pure joy of kids having "made it" and sent many heartfelt messages to graduating friends. At that milestone ceremony, we get that "send-off" into life via speeches containing profound advice filled with belief in our success, inspiring us to launch into adulthood with the best laid plans. Shortly thereafter, we begin "adulting", and all that excellent advice becomes a distant memory when we in fact, we need it even more as we grow through life.

My dear friend's daughter also graduated this year. In her announcement she asked for advice for succeeding in life. Thank you, Cameron. It made a perfect outline for this chapter.

Don't Be Afraid to Be YOU

According to the National Forensic Science Technology Center, **"no two people have ever been found to have the same**

fingerprints"— including identical twins. Sit with that for a moment. YOU are the only YOU that exists among more than 8 billion human beings on Earth! Embrace your uniqueness! Trust that beyond a shadow of a doubt, YOU have been created to leave your fingerprint on the world. You don't have to be a celebrity or a genius. You just have to be kind. What you have to say is important; the love you have to give is needed. Never hold back because you worry about what people will think. You don't have to be perfect. In fact, it's best that you're not! Be kind in your approach and be willing to let people get to know you for the value you add. Everyone has value, including YOU! When you make a difference in the life of just one other in the eight billion, it could simply be flashing a smile to someone who desperately needed one. You have made a positive ripple effect in our world. Thank you for being the only YOU!

Be Prepared to Have Setbacks Disguised as Blessings

I sometimes pray that if turmoil may come in my next fifty years, it will not include sudden death or disease, and I will come back stronger, allowing me to leave more with my fingerprint here. I have observed in others who have experienced major setbacks and loss that those who survive are resilient, and they lean on God for strength. In life, there will always be peaks and valleys. There will always be rain and then rainbows. Focus on the peaks and rainbows as you confront the valleys and rain. Have you heard the phrase there are only three certainties in life, Birth, Death, and Taxes? Add a fourth, setbacks. We all will have them. When you turn lemons into lemonade...when you trust there will be a silver lining even when it seems impossible, you will experience blessings on the other side.

Always Keep Learning

You've probably heard the phrase if you're not learning, you're not growing. I will enthusiastically admit that I will never know it all. I will always have more to learn until my last breath. I'm not much of a reader, and I've always heard that readers are leaders. Luckily, we have audible books now, so I believe I still qualify! Choose informational sources that help you grow as a person intellectually, personally, and professionally. In this digital age, we have so many other sources for stimulating our brains and growing our knowledge base, including podcasts. webinars, clubhouse, workshops, coaching programs, and more. As you continue to learn, you will acquire more thought material to express your perspectives and be uniquely YOU! P.S. Thank you for being a reader and reading this book!

Don't Allow Yourself to Compromise Your Values

Do you know what your personal core values are? I believe core values are a description of your backbone. That phrase "you're spineless" doesn't ever apply to you when you have unshakeable core values. My core values are love God, hold family close, serve others, live with integrity, and prioritize health. I have many secondary core values although these top five are non-negotiable. When you are faced with making choices in life, you measure these choices against your core values. If they don't match up, you make another choice. Take a moment and write down your top core values now. Refer to them often.

Be Open to Growth Opportunities

Over your lifetime, you likely will have thousands if not millions of growth opportunities that present themselves to you. In my business, my number one goal is to provide tools you can use about living life to the fullest with health and vitality. From there, someone can make his/her own decision about whether it applies to him/her and if he/she feels ready to take advantage of the solution. Maybe he/she doesn't feel ready and is closed to receiving a growth opportunity in that moment. I do believe that timing is everything. A person might accept the same opportunity later, when he/she is more desperate for growth or a solution to his/her problem. In the seventeen years I've been a health coach, I'm certain I've asked thousands of people "are you open?". Whatever messenger you meet, a friend offering a referral or possible solution, an invite to an educational event, a workshop, a networking event, or a mentor wanting to come along side and support you, opportunities for growth are abound. We live in a day and age where we can scroll mindlessly on Instagram, wishing we had other people's success, or we can invest our time into building our own. You have major potential when you use the tools for growth. Be open and take action whenever you can.

Always Believe in Yourself

This ties closely to number one above; don't be afraid to be you. It's deeper though. It's one thing to walk into a room feeling good about expressing yourself authentically. YAY YOU for accomplishing that feat. I, too, sometimes feel judged and nervous. Usually that's all in our own heads. So right now, let's stop making up stories about what other people think about us. OK? OK! It's another thing to truly believe in yourself. Believe in the fact that you are here for a reason. You are special and unique. You have a purpose that no one else has. You are strong. You are courageous (it doesn't mean you have to skydive or jump off black rock!). You believe whatever it is about yourself that you want others to believe. The more genuine you are the better. When you have an aura of belief around yourself, others experience that aura too. When you believe in yourself whole heartedly, others will, too. It's the energy you put out. It's contagious in a great way!

Don't Forget to Call Your Mom Frequently

Of course, I wrote this one because I'm a mom who wants to hear from her children frequently. It's a given. We earned it. Even though our job is done (it really never is, we are always going to be mom) we want to hear that voice, and we want to be there to celebrate the peaks and rainbows and comfort in the valleys and rain. I'll never forget visiting my cousins who have operated a barber shop in Union Square, San Francisco, for more than fifty years. I happened to be on a girls' trip and stopped in to say hello---brothers in their 70's. At the same time, the phone rang and their mom, my Great Aunt Gladys, called to inform them to take a different route home because of a traffic accident on their normal route. It was one of the sweetest moments displaying a mother's eternal love and support. Maybe it's another non-maternal mom in your life; dad's get in on this, too, or a mentor, a brother, an aunt or uncle. "Mom" is synonym for anyone in your life who holds the dearest place for you. Call them frequently or email, or instant message, or DM, or even snail mail. Just K.I.T.

Always Make Time for Fun

You may not know it yet, but we are entering the age of Self-Care. It's something that we got away from in the urgency to get ahead and create success. Surprising we have to focus more on having fun these days. Stress and anxiety are all too common these days. We weren't created to go to work, come home, go to sleep day in and day out, and then die. Sounds morbid, though finding ways to have fun, even in your small cracks of time, will contribute to your health and longevity. It can be feeling amazing after a facial or massage. It can be spending time alone reading, listening to music or relaxing in hot bath, or it can be going out with friends to dinner and live music, which is one of my top fun activities. It could be having a picnic or snuggling with your honey for a movie and more if you know what I mean. As a leader of a networking group for entrepreneurs, I see how people invest so much time, energy, money, blood, sweat, and tears into building their dream business while they neglect their health. Make fun a priority as much as possible to help fuel your health instead.

Eat Your Fruit and Veggies

This might be the best advice you ever receive. If you didn't listen to your grandmother or your mother, please listen to me. A healthy person has 1,000 wishes. An unhealthy person only has one. You can guess what that is. Your body literally runs on fruits and vegetables. Every organ will operate better and last longer when it has this fuel. Please prioritize plants.

Let Go Let God

There will come times in your life when you feel there are no answers. At these times, I encourage you to trust in God for the answers. Whenever we feel helpless, we give it up to God. There's a plan. It's your purpose. Trust.

Clarisa Romero

Inspiration
By Clarisa Romero

I have a message for women around the world. It is a quote from Napoleon Hill, and it goes like this.

"Anything the mind can conceive and believe, it can achieve."

Now, I would like to share a bit of my story so that you can understand why I live by this understanding.

Ten years ago, I experienced what I now understand to be a dark night of the soul. Within nine months I got divorced, became unemployed, lost my home, and lost my father to cancer. I became extremely withdrawn, and I felt hopeless. I shut myself out from my friends and family. I felt lost and stuck and struggled to find clarity.

My life was in a rut, and it was a very dark time in my life. My toxic thoughts and emotions were having a direct impact on my capacity to feel confident and to possess my overall well-being. It became so severe, I had a phobia of going back to work, to network, and to speak in public. I used to spend many hours trying to figure out what should be my next step in life.

One day I heard someone ask:

Do you create your life? Or do you think life happens to you?

Then I heard someone else ask: What will it take for things to be different? It was my big ah-ha moment!

I had a big revelation. I realized that up to that point, I was living life as a victim! I treated life as if it was something that happened to me, and there was nothing that I could do to change it. Once I started to question how things could be different, I began my quest to find out how I could become an active participant in my life.

Things have a way of being synchronous once you ask the right questions. I kept coming across experts who helped me further understand how I had been trapped in a victim mentality. As a victim, you are more likely to believe that there is nothing you can do to change your circumstances. It will lead to you feeling completely lost. I started reassessing the things that happened in my life and questioning whether I could see them differently. I wondered if there could be a meaning to the things that happened to me. I realized the reason I felt stuck and unclear had to do with my thought processes and how I was showing up in the world. I started to pay close attention to how I showed up personally and professionally. It led to a shift in my belief system. I started changing my perception that I was a victim of life. I started to learn how to become the creator of my life and to explore what that would entail. When you realize things can be different, suddenly, a whole new reality opens up. I discovered that feeling lost without a clue as to what was next had been necessary to find the true me. To uncover who I am meant to be in this life, I had to first lose myself to find myself.

Moving forward, I religiously crafted time every morning and evening to become a better version of myself. I cultivated present-moment awareness by learning about mindfulness. In particular, I studied the brain science associated with your thoughts and how that influences how you think and behave.

I discovered metacognition, which helps you analyze your thinking by observing what you think and feel. It brings awareness to your emotions and thoughts---how they impact your life and show up in the experiences you are having.

I changed my daily habits. I started listening to self-empowerment and professional growth videos, webinars, and classes. I adopted the habits of successful people such as thinking positively and being productive. I learned we are living in a time called the Golden Age of Brain Science. I became fascinated with how the brain works and how your thoughts and emotions shape the way you see and experience life. I became fascinated with the pioneering work of Dr. Bruce Lipton, who demonstrates how the new science of epigenetics is revolutionizing our understanding of the link between mind and matter and how you influence it. It was a turning point. I had to learn how to let go of old programming that no longer served me. Like any other muscle in the body, your brain must be exercised to best serve you rather than work against you.

You do not need to be a victim of how your brain developed. New science opens up a whole new way of looking at your capacity to reprogram your brain to serve you better. My quest incorporated a deeper understanding of positive psychology, emotional intelligence, and the phenomenon called neuroplasticity. Now we understand the brain can be molded by practicing mindfulness. I started diving into additional research in quantum mechanics and quantum physics---specifically, how you can manifest your reality and create the life that you want.

"Everything is energy and that's all there is to it. Match the frequency of the reality you want, and you cannot help but get that reality. It can be no other way. This is not philosophy. This is physics."

— ALBERT EINSTEIN

What I'm outlining here isn't new information. It is ancient knowledge that has been secularized in modern-day society thanks to advances in science and technology. We are fortunate to reap the benefits of present-moment awareness of how to retrain the brain.

When I adopted and started to understand that you get to

choose the way you experience life, I had to deconstruct the unintentional self-imposed limitations that were hindering me from pursuing my dreams. I began to live my life consciously. All of this inner work led to the creation of the 4 Step Brain H.A.C.K., a process that involves hacking your brain and reprograming your mind to design your life with intention.

The steps provide you with the brain hacking tools not only to survive but to thrive in life. Life will be life. Things will always happen, causing unpredictable changes. There will be constant highs and lows, good and bad times. Life is always unfolding. How you cope is what will make the difference. I was unclear and doubtful about my capacity to start my own business because I allowed my inner chatter and external distractions to get in the way and dictate how I was feeling. I allowed it to prevent me from making smart decisions. Understanding brain science and being equipped with tools to hack your brain so that it does not sabotage and work against you is critical.

Hence, my slogan: "A healthy mind equals a successful life." This is when you get to unlock and unleash your full potential.

The 4 Steps provide the brain hacking tools to reprogram your brain to operate out of a success and growth mindset and not a fixed autopilot mindset. Not having brain hacking tools is the reason why a lot of people do not achieve their goals and dreams. Having a brain hacking tool kit like the 4 Step Brain H.A.C.K. method will prevent obstacles from getting in the way. The steps will help you to become resilient in life. Resilience is your capacity to bounce back from hardship and uncertainty. Life will always have ups and downs, but these four steps will help you develop the skill of equanimity, mental calmness, composure, and evenness of temper especially in difficult situations.

Following these steps, I not only started my own business, but I also achieved clarity on what kind of business to pursue. Fast-forwarding to today, I have a thriving six-figure business that I love!

I am here today to tell you that because I consciously designed my life; I am now considered a Thought Leader in my industry. I am an Award-Winning Business Mindset & Transformational Coach Founder & CEO of Mindful Consultants and International Best-Selling Author of The Fearless Entrepreneur: Break Through the Corporate Mindset and Start Your Dream Business. I am passionate about helping women thrive in their entrepreneurship by helping them overcome the limits that come with starting a business, allowing them to grow into the fearless leaders they were born to be.

I am also honored to say I recently became the Face of WOHA 2021. The Women of Heart Award (WOHA) is a platform spearheaded by an empowered and heart-centered soul sister, Desziree Richardson. The Face of WOHA's message is for women to work from their hearts. Because when you operate this way, there is no competition. There is only love and collaboration.

Your life can be a masterpiece by unlocking your brain's inner power to heal and consciously design your life.

You see a caterpillar is a very vulnerable creature. It crawls on the ground, moves very slow, and may seem that it's at the lowest point. The whole world is above her; anyone can take advantage or even step on her. She seems hopeless. Until one day, she goes within, takes a step back, and becomes a cocoon. In that alchemical transformation, she is growing and discovers that she is more than a caterpillar. One day she wakes up and starts pushing her way out. At this point no one can assist her; only she can break out of her shell and when she does, she opens her wings and realizes she can fly and bring beauty into the world.

So today I ask you.

Do you create your life?

Or do you think life happens to you?

What will it take for things to be different?

Will you always stay a caterpillar? Or will you break out of your shell, spread your wings, and never be looked down upon again?

"I choose to make the rest of my life the best of my life!!"

— LOUISE HAY

It is time to train your mind to know that you have what it takes to accomplish your dreams and discover your life's purpose.

It is time that you determine how much you are worth, not leaving that to others to determine. Remember that you are living in the golden age of brain science, and with all the understanding of the greatness you possess, you have the power to transform. It is time to invest in you.

It's time to stop being the caterpillar and transform into a butterfly. Spread your wings. Allow for the alchemical transformation because it is non-negotiable. You know in your heart that you no longer want or need to play small to be safe.

Alchemy represents your attempts to refine and improve yourself. The goal of alchemical transformation is to attain a higher state of consciousness and access your true self. This is the perfect time for you to do the inner work and become resilient. You can face the changes in our society and stand out in life! It is an amazing time for growth and expansion, to connect inwardly and be introspective, and to shift and align according to your dreams and heart's desire.

"From this instant on, vow to stop disappointing yourself, separate yourself from the mob, decide to be extraordinary, and do what you need to do – Now."

— EPICTETUS

You are now equipped with the knowledge and tools to hack the fear-based mindset and embrace a growth mindset. The present moment is always the right time to reinvent and transform. This is true no matter how old you are or where you might be in life. It is time to face your fears, to face the resistance that shields you from greatness. As Lisa Nichols says, "It's like you've been about to jump into a double-dutch game, wondering is it the right time? Can I do it? Should I jump, or should I play it safe?" It is time to hold fear in one hand and passion in the other and leap. It is time to defeat the enemy of your mind and turn your mind into your ally. You are in control of your destiny. You are not a victim.

It is time to slow down and work on yourself. Reflect and implement the 4 step Brain H.A.C.K. and you will find that in your slowing down you will move forward faster and further than you ever imagined possible. You will find yourself shifting and aligning with the higher calling of your life's purpose.

You will finally know how to make decisions based on your intuition and what your heart tells you from an emotionally intelligent place without doubt and with complete clarity. I am so excited about your journey, and I am looking forward to hearing about your progress. Please share with me at MindfulConsultants.com or on social media @MindfulConsultants.

Robbie Moss Manning

Just Robbie
By Robbie Moss Manning

My name is Robbie Moss Manning, and I am beyond grateful and blessed to be writing this chapter on my story in this incredible book! I am a Performer, Writer, Producer, and Director. I am a Sister, Daughter, Auntie, Niece, Mother of three, "Gaga" of two, and Girlfriend!

My love of the theater began with my very first performance on the live stage. It took place at the Riverside Municipal Auditorium in 1959 at the ripe age of three in a Children's Theater Production. At four years of age, I began studying traditional ballet and excelled in acrobatics… (I was bendy). I took as many classes as my parents would allow and ended up on "point or toe" by nine years old. Today this wouldn't be encouraged as we know that this is way too young for developing bodies, but that's what I did. Dance was my passion!

Although no one in my direct family followed a career in show business, they all played a large part in influencing me. My Mom held season tickets to the theater in Los Angeles and always took me along!! I was mesmerized by the sets, the lights, the colorful costumes…it was all so incredibly beautiful to me… and the music!!! We would go see a show and then buy the record of the soundtrack. Mom would play it daily at home until we knew all the words, singing and dancing around the house… performing just like the stars on stage!

When I would visit my maternal grandmother "Gama", we would dress up in her dresses from the roaring 20's and choreograph dances on her stairs. My paternal grandfather "Papa" was our biggest fan.

My father was a Car Dealer in the auto-mobile business and

really didn't have any theatrical experience. But he sang me a lullaby to put me to sleep every night…and I thought he was a famous celebrity!! When I'd spend time with my paternal grandma "Mema," she would play her organ, and we'd sing hymns and classical music by the hour. She grew-up playing piano in a movie theater, back when there were silent movies. My paternal grandpa "Pepa" loved to sing and talked about his dream of becoming a professional, but for him it was only a hobby.

Then came the preteen years. Dance recitals started to become monotonous, and boys who played guitar became way more intriguing! My heart was shifting, and I lacked the discipline and drive for dance to become a true prima ballerina. In middle school, I continued to become restless and needed something to sink my teeth into. The Vice Principal of our Middle school called me in to speak with me about my lack of attention in school. I got good grades but was bored and sometimes disruptive. He recommended I take theater classes at the local high school. He even arranged for me to take a bus there for me to attend… HHHMMMMM!!

In my first year at Poly High School, I tried out for A MIDSUMMER NIGHT'S DREAM and landed the lead role of Hermia. It was the most amazing experience, and I was completely smitten! Yes, I was bitten by the "theater bug," and it has my life's devotion ever since.

Hanging out at garage band rehearsals, I discovered I could sing and was soon asked to join my boyfriend's Rock Band. I enjoyed performing songs from Jefferson Airplane, Linda Ronstadt, Janis Joplin, and any other hits by "Chick Singers," that the guys were willing to learn.

By my senior year I was getting restless to get out of my hometown and experience some real adventure! I graduated early that year and at seventeen moved to Malibu to pursue a Theater Degree at Pepperdine University. I played the lead in every major performance there…and had to learn how to balance school, rehearsals, performance, and relationships!!

Of course, love was just around the corner, and he was an extremely well-educated aristocrat…a handsome young man from the Middle East. His sister became my roommate and best friend…so they encouraged me to take the opportunity to travel to Kuwait (in the middle of my studies) and live with them and their family for nearly four months. It was a life changing experience that I will never forget! It was such a transition for a young girl from Riverside, California!! I was the only single-white female allowed in the country at the time as their father was an international diplomat who helped me obtain my visa. I learned to speak a little Arabic, belly dance, and sing the songs of Fairuz…their version of Joni Mitchell.

After my return to Malibu, I completed a four-year program (in three years) at Pepperdine. I packed up and made my next adventure a move to Hollywood. I soon needed a job to sustain myself and landed a position at Chasin-Park-Citron, one of the most prestigious talent agencies in the industry. They were the first three agents to break from the studios and took every famous (and willing) actor along with them. It was there I met my husband to be, John Baer.

John was an amazing musician and music producer. It was love at first sight, and we married in 1979. I was 23. He was already creating great music, and we quickly discovered that I was the lyricist of the team. After having done our first film score for the movie CRUISING with Al Pacino, we realized we were a musical match made in heaven and built our first recording studio.

John and I worked around the clock, writing original songs and music for such movies as *WEEKEND PASS, HUNK, HAMBURGER THE MOTION PICTURE, BEACH FEVER*, and *PRIME EIVAL*. We also wrote for television with famous and established musicians from 1979-1992. Although we divorced in 1989, we still collaborate on music projects and perform together to this day. John and I share two beautiful sons, Chad and Jonathan, as well as two perfect grandsons, CJ and Aidan Baer.

To further develop my writing skills, I took a Story Analyst Class at UCLA. My professor was impressed by my ability to understand, synopsize, and relay a story, so he offered me an opportunity. Being single with two boys, my desire was to work from home, and I happily accepted a job as a subcontractor for Disney, analyzing scripts. It's here where I fell in love with story structure, development, and the telling of it.

Not loving the single life, I went on to remarry the next "love of my life" in 1992. Another musician named John (Manning), and magically we shared the same passion for music. Although John's past was deeply rooted in music, his "day job" was working as an Electronic Engineer. He was hired as a director for a large Pacific Bell operation in the Bay Area, so after the highly anticipated birth of our daughter Chelsea (I was 36), we packed up the family and moved to San Ramon, California…just outside San Francisco.

While getting to know my new digs and wanting to keep my hand in entertainment, I created a Karaoke Show that John and I ran together on Tuesday Nights. At the same time, wanting to keep my boys busy (and get back in shape), I got involved in Martial Arts and trained for four years in Shito Ryu Kai, a traditional Japanese Karate.

I eventually returned with my three kids to my family in Riverside. Full time work was required, and "in these parts" showbiz was scarce…so I became the Executive Producer for Riverside Children's Theater. Soon after I created shows for the Riverside University Health System (previously RCRMC) Foundation's

Festival of Trees, I was offered a position as Musical Theater Director for Jump Dance Performing Arts. Because philanthropy and the arts go hand in hand, I was then hired as Executive Director of Parkview Hospital's Foundation.

I then became Director of Development for Family Service Association and ran KARAOKE FOR A CAUSE while working there. I followed that with a five-year run at Riverside University Heath System as Director of Volunteer Services and Vice President of the RUHS Auxiliary.

My live performances over the years have included a variety of clubs venues: The Whiskey, The Rainbow, The Troubador, The Coconut Grove, to name a few. Throughout the years, I have had the extreme privilege of performing for dignitaries across the globe at private parties and major events. I continue to teach vocal performance and sing and perform on a regular basis.

My love for the arts has become stronger, more now than ever… and after a lifetime of experience, I've embarked on the most exciting project to date! My best friend, Alyce Berard, who also has an extensive resume in the arts, has joined me in writing a full-blown musical!! This has also led us to develop our company… Born to Sparkle Productions.

We are now under full sail and committed to our dream, vision, and mission to bring this "feel good story" of colorful entertainment to the stage…and after a thrilling seven-year journey…it's almost showtime!! PALM SPRINGS THE MUSICAL: Born to Sparkle, is a one-of-a-kind script with twenty original show-stopping tunes… and is sure to be a "must see" musical masterpiece!

Our story begins in the jewel of the sprawling Coachella Valley desert - Palm Springs. While famous for its climate and ability to attract and cater to celebrities, it also embodies a gorgeous cultural heart, beating with diversity and promise. A unique cast of characters comes to life in this desert oasis, and their story has not been told until now.

PALM SPRINGS THE MUSICAL is a love story – between two faithful friends among aa devoted family throughout a tight-knit community – a love empowered in unity that lights their path to self-discovery.

We are currently developing the ultimate dream team of collaborative professionals to help us bring this exceptional enterprise to fruition! Fingers crossed, and prayers to the heavens…we'll see you there in the audience with a smile on your face and a song in your heart!

Some life lessons and words of encouragement:

Know who you are, where you want to go…and who you want to go with!

My Grandfather used to tell me "Show me your friends and I'll show you who you are." If you have a strong moral compass, good for you! Hang onto it and let it guide you…It will always serve you well! Make good choices!

The men you choose in your life need to be trustworthy and have integrity (a sense of humor helps), and they need to know God!

Share your future with someone who has the same values and vision for life that you have. Watch, listen, and learn. A man who seeks you out and then offers you the opportunity to really get to know him is a gift. Remember, his word is his bond.

Your girlfriends will help you every step of the way, but the greatest relationship you will ever have is with yourself…be kind to her!

Be your own best friend. Be disciplined in the things you tell yourself…remind yourself of how valuable and special you are on a daily basis. Your uniqueness will open doors if you let it. Hold your head high and go fulfill your dreams!

Negative head talk is destructive. Just as you would talk to your best friend…talk to yourself.

Constantly telling yourself that you're not good enough, better known as a "self-defeatist attitude", is contrary to any positivity that you have worked to create in your life. Take compliments from others (be humble) but let those kind words nurture you… you deserve them!

Set boundaries; learn to say no!

It is so important to be clear about your goals, your views, and your ideals. It is important to protect your life, health, and happiness by never giving yourself away. Don't expend all your emotional oxygen on other people's drama. Be mindful of your energy, and don't over-extend yourself…learn to strike a balance!

Learn to listen to your gut instinct…and talk to God!

He's listening…and if you are patient and listening, He will guide you through it all!! Trust in Him, always!! Pray about all your decisions, big. and small. He's also given us a special detection device to work with! You know the phrase "woman's intuition…?" Well, it's built-in and it's God given! So, more times than not, if it feels right, it is…and if it feels "icky", it is!!!

Don't be afraid to ask for help when you need it. Reach out to your trusted family and friends and let them know what you need.

The people in our lives are put there to share in our journey. We can't do it alone! Lean on them when you need to and let them in. It will create a life-long bond and will allow true intimacy into your world.

Help others where you can...it's a great feeling to give to those in need!

When you get away from your own worries and focus on helping someone else, you get your power back. You remember that you have great gifts to offer, and it will fill your heart to do good for someone else. Have the "attitude of gratitude" and share it with everyone!

No matter how many times you may suffer a broken heart...keep your heart open!

Be smart but love hard! If you have spent some time getting to know someone and you admire their qualities...allow yourself to trust as it is earned. Anyone worthy of your love and attention will reap the rewards of knowing you and you them.

And the piece of advice that my children always quote me saying is, "FEEL THE FEAR AND DO IT ANYWAY!!"

Be brave...when you don't want to do something because you're afraid like...speaking in public, making yourself vulnerable to others, being afraid of heights or the dark, or doing any new experience that causes you stress but is not a real danger..." FEEL THE FEAR AND DO IT ANYWAY!!" You'll amaze yourself with how strong and capable you really are!!

You are unique...You're it!!

There isn't another one like you!! Be your authentic self. Your individuality and incredible gifts will sparkle, sizzle, and shine when you allow your God given light to be seen!! Trust in him... then trust in yourself...and live the greatest life you can possibly imagine...After all, this isn't a dress rehearsal!!

Thank you for taking the time to read my story...I look forward to reading your story one day! Maybe our paths will cross, and

I'll be lucky enough to get to know you! Always remember… each and every one of us was **BORN TO SPARKLE!!**

Traci Jeske

UNAPOLOGETICALLY ME
By Traci Jeske

My story begins 51 years ago in a small town in Alberta, Canada. I was born into a big, beautiful family to two incredibly giving, generous, and fun parents who love and adored me from the day I was born. I was the youngest of six, and as my siblings say, I was probably one of the most spoiled one of the bunch. Our home was always filled with family, friends, laughter, and a whole lot of music.

As a little girl and growing up, I was always the super sensitive one in the family. It did not take much to make me cry or hurt my feelings, which was very hard to deal with. I always felt as if I was weaker than others, and that something was wrong with me. I found myself growing up having to deal with these emotions on my own as I felt like no one understood me; showing emotion or talking about it was not ok in my family. I learnt at a very young age that showing emotion, especially tears, was something you just didn't do as it made everyone uncomfortable, and so I had to soon learn how to mask those feelings, which meant crying in my room alone only coming out with a smile on my face. This also led me to be a complete people pleaser as I myself did not know how to deal with tears or be sad. I wanted no one around me to have them as well. So, I did all I could to have those around me happy, especially my mom and dad. I saw all they did and wanted for me, and I just wanted to see them happy and pleased with me. If they weren't, I automatically thought it was my fault, and I didn't do whatever it was I had to do well enough, so I blamed myself for those around me not being happy and smiling, which is a heavy load to carry around. But this act of having to be happy all the time and not being able to express my feelings or be comforted when I had those moments led me to be very insecure with myself, my body, and my overall level of confidence as I labeled my sensitive soul and weak, not strong and not worthy and that others would only like and love me if I wasn't so sensitive so basically if I was everything but me.

Going through my teen years, I found comfort by numbing my emotions through food. Filling myself up with food was like a drug for me. It left me feeling satisfied. I enjoyed it, and I could eat as much or as little as I wanted. Food became my best friend or so I thought! But eating food had me gain a lot of weight going through high school, and having such beautiful, skinny friends had my self-esteem, which was already low, go literally under the ground. I started to hate even more than before my body, the way I looked; everything about me was wrong, and not being able to talk about it and having to keep it all in was leading me to my breaking point. I still remember that day I broke. I was visiting home from the university; I was extremely unhappy; it was Easter break. I was 17. I even remember what I was wearing. After another meal of eating until I was way too full, I went into the bathroom and looked at myself in the mirror; those horrible voices just overtook me so much that I purged for the very first time. Little did I know what I was putting myself into and what my life would be like for the next 23 years, the battles and demons I would have to overcome before finding freedom, inner peace, and joy.

During those years I would binge and purge eight to nine times a day---sometimes more. I literally never kept anything down so family and friends were pushed away. In those years, sad to say, I had little or nothing to do with them. I was embarrassed and knew that everyone knew once I got up from the table and went into the bathroom what I was doing, and I could feel their anger and frustration. Then I would have to try and make them happy, so I had to work even that much harder at pleasing them; it was just much easier to be alone with no one judging me or seeing what I was doing. I wanted nothing to do with anyone. I had to keep everything so hidden; it became a job for me to fit them into my schedule from work and binging and purging. No matter where I was or what I was doing I just could not wait to get home and binge and purge. It was a vicious cycle that consumed my life for far too long. But the one thing that I know to this day that probably saved me even in my darkest moments was the fact that I never let myself look the part of being sick. I always made sure I looked good. I dressed well. I always had makeup on, and my hair done because I knew that if I let that part of me go, I literally would not be here today. If I started looking the part of being sick, then I knew it was game over for me. So no matter what I made sure I looked fabulous from head to toe. My personal style and love for fashion literally helped me fight one of the biggest battles of my life.

Getting my first job in retail after quitting my first year at the university, I found for the first time I was doing something that lit me up and brought me so much joy! I always loved playing dress up from the time I was a little girl; I loved fashion and style. I was very creative and expressed myself through what I wore, and I always made sure never to wear the exact same look twice. Working in retail was like playing dress up all day and helping my clients find outfits and create looks that they loved came so easy and natural to me. I just knew that somehow this is something I would be doing for the rest of my life.

At the age of twenty-two having two attempts at committing suicide and after losing my father to cancer, struggling terribly with losing him and the emotions that were inside me, and dealing with my eating disorder, I decided to quit my job, hit reset, packed my suitcases, and moved to Australia. I had no job and knew nobody there, but I had to get away. Within a month I found my apartment in Surfers Paradise. I got a job in the fashion industry and lived there for four years. I got engaged to a man twice my age and then went back to Canada to renew my visa and organize my wedding. My girlfriend introduced me to this Italian man that was working in Canada at the time, and to make a long story short, I never went back to Australia and never married my fiancé at the time but moved to Italy and got married in Italy to my Italian husband and have been living here ever since.

At the age of thirty, I gave birth to a beautiful baby boy. God only knows how I ever became pregnant with me being as unhealthy and thin as I was. I did have complications with my pregnancy; my son was born premature and extremely underweight. but he soon gained the weight necessary to be a strong healthy boy. I loved and still do love my boy more than anything else in the world along with his sister, but even he was not enough to have me stop binging and purging. After putting on weight during my pregnancy, I had to lose it. I felt so uncomfortable, and the voices in my head got louder and louder. I did binging and purging even more, but my body had changed, and I never returned to being as thin as I was no matter how hard I tried. No one ever realized what was going on. It was much easier to keep it and hide it from everyone around me, including my husband as I didn't look sick like I used to. My teeth were literally rotting from purging so much; my skin was a terrible color, and my hair would fall out into the strands. By my late thirties I was becoming tired and fed up with being sick and living like this. I loved being a mom and wanted another baby so badly but did not want to put my second child at risk as I did my first.

By the Grace of God and desperately wanting a little girl, I finally broke the chains of my eating disorder three months before my 38th birthday. I had tried over and over being in and out of hospitals for years but never managed to let it go. Three months before my 38th I gave my heart to God completely. I gave my illness to him. I prayed and asked for forgiveness, and I know to this day it was a miracle from him as I went from purging day and night to literally overnight stopping and have never looked back.

That was fourteen years ago! When I was 39, I gave birth to a beautiful healthy baby girl!

Being finally free of my demons, the woman that little girl dreamt to be but was too afraid and insecure to become finally came out, and she exploded out. Looking back now, I know my eating disorder was a way for me to keep myself hidden and small as I was afraid of me and my dreams. I was going against who God destined me to be. When I got to my 40's, I literally made a promise to myself that I would never hide again, and fear or no fear I would do what it takes to walk into becoming and being that woman. It was stepping up to the plate, stopping to please, and making everyone around me happy but me.

Working already in the fashion industry for so many years but never being seen, it was time for me to become known, stand out in a crowd, be that bold woman I was, have my center stage moment, and start creating my very own successful personal styling business---not only transforming women's wardrobes but their lives as well. I want to inspire them to be all they can be and look absolutely fabulous doing so! Age is just a number and should never define how we dress, look, or feel. Working with so many women, especially in their 40's, I noticed and saw time and time again the struggles they were having no matter what continent they were from. The message I heard and saw was women not feeling worthy of being seen, the fear of becoming invisible due to their age, not feeling confident, nor loving their bodies---so many things I had been through at a younger age. It was there and then that I had my ah ha moment, and I understood why I went through all I did. It was so I could serve and help these women through style to build up the confidence, have them stand out in a crowd, and look absolutely fabulous while doing so---thus, the beginning of my successful styling business and me becoming an international style expert!

When I think about the woman I was before starting out on this adventure and the woman I am now, I always get extremely emotional. This is what success means to me. When I think about that woman I was, that little girl inside of me, who had a dream but was so afraid of going after it, my insecurities and fear of how amazing and how big I wanted to become had me on such a self-destructive pathway to hold me back. I hurt myself and my body everyday telling myself how ugly I was, how fat I was, how unworthy I was, what a failure I was, and that I didn't deserve to live, but then the incredible transformation of the woman I am today began. Full of confidence and self-love, I followed my dreams and stepped into that woman I was destined to be. It is such an incredible blessing, and my biggest success story in my life so far. I thank God all throughout the day for the blessing and favor He put on me and my life as I know that if it wasn't for Him, I wouldn't be here today. I wouldn't be the amazing, strong, determined woman I am today. I know I had to go through what I did to help other women and to show them that no matter what their past is, no matter where they come from, it is NEVER too late to live the life of their dreams. They can and will have their center stage moment looking and feeling fabulous doing so. Age is just a number and does not define how we dress, look and feel.

I can honestly say now more than ever in my 50's I have never felt better, felt more alive, and loved life and myself more. I love my job, I love my business, and I love styling women. Every day is like a new day as every woman and every client is unique. They are all so different but all dream and desire to look beautiful and feel good in their own skin. Yes, it was and is not always easy running my business. Yes, at times I felt like a horrible mother and partner doing something for me. But my children are my number one fans, and I am determined to leave a legacy for them. They push me to do more and inspire me every day to go for whatever makes my heart sing. I am such a fulfilled and much happier woman now than I ever have been in my whole life. I literally have to pinch myself at times to see if I'm dreaming. I thank God each and every morning, afternoon, and evening for the strength and courage He has blessed me with along with my dreams, I have always wanted to work and style women travelling around the world and never dreamt I would have worked and styled women in Dubai, London, New York, and all across Italy and many other beautiful cities. I have met so many amazing incredible women in my journey and know I have touched and changed the lives of so many of my clients and the women I have come across just as they have touched and changed mine.

About Traci Jeske

Traci Jeske is the director of En Vogue Stylist and an internationally certified personal stylist, known as Italy's style icon and style motivator. She helps women forty and beyond up level their glamour game to unapologetically create and live their best and most stylish second act ever. No stranger to wrapping up for winter, Traci was born and bred in Canada before establishing her stylish, stiletto-sharp brand in Italy, where she has been living for the last twenty years.

Blending Italian *la dolce vita* with her flair for fashion and style Traci takes her personal life experiences, living in Australia, working in Dubai, London, and abroad, overcoming an eating disorder and her experience of over thirty years in the fashion industry to have women find their unique style, be bold, and stand out in a crowd looking and feeling absolutely fabulous in every season of their life.

She has been featured on WBOC CBS ,FOX43, NBC, ABC YCL, WFLA BLOOM TV, Sacramento Ticker News Australia. She has been seen on Looking Good with Daniella & T Coffee-The Show , numerous podcasts, and has spoken at various women summits and events. She has recently been featured in Authority Magazine and Thrive Global Magazine, Hollywood Beauty Magazine and has 47k followers on Instagram, where she gives women 40 and beyond tips and inspiration to be and look their best no matter their age!

Dr. Angelica Benavides

Conquer the Chaos Turn It into a Legacy
Dr. Angelica Benavides
B-Global Press Houston TX, 77064, USA

More and more people's stress is being amplified and they are facing uncertainty due to COVID-19. Many obstacles may get in your way but remember every challenge brings lessons. Telling your story can be cathartic and makes you grow as a person, gives you satisfaction, and allows you to increase your chances of success. It takes you out of that dark area that perhaps you thought ruined your life forever; it shows you the light. By doing this, you can clearly identify the steps you took to get ahead, detail the tools you used or developed, and you can share that light with others who await your life-transforming message. You will leave this experience with a feeling of dominance.

You matter and your stories will impact and make a difference! Everyone has a story to tell. We all have a period of "Dark Night of the Soul". I am sure you have lived an extremely difficult moment or experienced a painful moment in life. Most recently we have all known of someone who passed or lost a loved one due to COVID-19. We all have either gone through a divorced, had financial struggles, diagnosis of a life-threatening illness, or experienced some life challenge.

I know this because I experience all of the above. I went through a divorce and bankruptcy and was diagnosed with two types of cancer. My whole life tumbled right before my eyes. There were moments of my life when I lost hope and had no idea what to do or who to go to. These difficult times helped me discover "what works" and "what doesn't work". I also realized that I was leaving this world with broken promises I had made to myself. I had many dreams I had not achieved because I put them on the back burner until I achieved other goals. The big "Aha Moment" was the feared being forgotten and not leaving a mark on this world. It is when I decided to write books that will outlive me and help millions of people to write their stories to inspire hope and steps people can take during life challenges.

You're going to have to step out of your comfort zone to excel in these tough times. Most entrepreneurs struggle to give their businesses visibility. The truth is that visibility is the only thing that will make you stand out from the masses if you believe that your contribution and service will positively impact people.

You are here to make a big difference in the world. The best way to do this is to use your story, experience, knowledge, and advice to help others be successful. This strategy that I share with you will guide you in a process so that through your story you can package and share advice, systems, tools and processes, and create a lucrative business that impacts lives. You will not only offer hope and inspiration but need to discover how you can generate income sharing your message to the world.

One of the most remarkable gifts that life gives us during our difficult times are lessons. Life is our earth school. We win or we learn. John Maxwell says, "Sometimes you win and sometimes you learn". Every story has a lesson and "Aha Moment". Make sure to write about your learning and your wins. Always include four or six steps that you took during that time to help others navigate life if they are experiencing similar life challenges.

One of the strategies that I use with all my clients, especially with writers, is to help identify an experience that has been very difficult for them and guide them to reflect on how it impacted them---if it pushed them to find their passion, or if as a result of that experience, they have had new ideas that can germinate into a new or better business. I help entrepreneurs find that story and tell it to overcome the wounds of the past.

Leading and leaving a mark on this world is important as leaders. Leaving your mark on this world means you need to do something that is important that has a lasting effect on people. Leave a legacy that inspires people to take action and become a better version of themselves. You leave a legacy to never be forgotten. You need to live your passion. Life is not easy and brings many challenges that shape who we become. Unfortunately, life challenges, not just depression, lead to suicide. Research has shown that mental health issues lead to suicide.

There are many businesses like yours but remember that there is only one person like you who has an impressive message and there is someone who is waiting for it. You have the potential to make a difference in a person and to generate income with what you know. Your advice and your life experiences are more valuable than you have ever imagined.

You will need to gain clarity on what legacy you will live and leave that has a greater purpose. Focus on what you love and do it! Don't wait because life is shorter than you think. You will need to live a life as if you matter. Most of the time we forget about ourselves and rescue the world. You matter! Live as if you matter by doing what you love most. Then serve others after you practice self-love and self-worth. When your cup is full, you can fill other people's cup. If you don't live and leave this legacy, people will not reach their desired outcomes and a gap will be left on this world. It is not easy to leave a mark in the world, but it is necessary. It will take patience, dedication, and commitment, and it will come with failures. Remember your failures are only feedback and lessons that need to be shared with the world to guide them on how to navigate life when it gets difficult or chaotic. Look at the word "Message" ME SAGE, so you will wisdom during difficult times and will become the sage that will inspire and give hope to many waiting to hear your message.

How can you leave your mark on this world? Write a memoir or participate in an anthology such as this book. What is an anthology? An anthology is a collection of writings from various people. I focus on helping entrepreneurs refine their message, telling their story and sharing their knowledge. When you participate in an anthology such as this book, you cross promote each and make strong connections with other leaders who have overcome challenges in life. Writing with other experts is a faster way to grow together, generate more profitability and gain more visibility because it gives access to new markets and distribution networks. **Joint ventures** offer the benefit of every entrepreneur bringing its share of knowledge or experience to carry the product or service to the market, making marketing is a minor challenge.

Writing your story and sharing your wisdom can become a source of income if you offer practical information to help people succeed. With this you can build a lucrative business and a deeply meaningful life. Every entrepreneur has a story; yours will allow you to reach the hearts of your prospects faster. I'm going to show you how to position yourself as a hero so that your potential customers have a deep interest in everything you offer.

Sharing your hero's journey is power! Every hero decides to achieve something in life and every hero embarks on a journey in which he discovers his power, potential and transformation. Your clients or prospects need to know that you also have struggles and achievements, that nothing was easy, but that anything is possible. I will help you discover the hero or heroine within you.

Nobody makes decisions just because. People only act after a challenge or because of an outside force. Challenges or external forces push us on the journey of achievement and transformation. All people with an entrepreneurial spirit want to know the maps, processes, or tools that have worked for other people or businesses.

Something in your way made you come to this business you want to create or reinvent, prompted you to seek more information, and to read this book. But no matter how many books you read or what courses you take, you have to implement everything you learn and the way to keep growing is to help more people. Your growth and satisfaction will come when you begin to put all your discoveries, gifts, talents, tools, and processes at the service of other people. Your message and story have the power and ability to change lives, of course, only if you know how to reach those people who are waiting for your message.

I know you have a great story within you. I also wanted to write for many years and for many years I could not. Now I have another five books ready to publish with entrepreneurs like you who dared to write an anthology.

What's more for a long time I didn't feel capable of writing. When I was a child, I not only hated writing I also hated school. I was shy and did not have the confidence to ask for help and even less to speak in front of an audience. I was born in Nuevo Laredo, Tamaulipas, Mexico, and grew up in Chicago. My parents spoke Spanish, and at school the teachers only spoke English. I was confused with that language that was strange to me. The saddest thing is that the teachers did not know how to educate me or six other students who only spoke Spanish. We were all different grades and ages.

I was in kindergarten. I remember being taken out of class with the other six students who did not speak English. I did not feel that the teachers challenged or taught us according to the grade that each of us was in. They made us draw letters and numbers; most of the time we spent playing with puzzles and coloring. I think the lack of high-quality instruction made me lag behind my peers.

Writing was always my worst subject; I hated it. But I was left with the curiosity to understand why I struggled to learn and write when it was made easier for others. For this reason, I studied Learning Theories and how the brain works, and I got my doctorate; writing my dissertation was not easy, but I did it. Do you feel and think that writing a book or an anthology is not easy? You may be right, but it is possible especially if you follow my writing template that I teach all the authors who join my **"The Spotlight Author's" program.**

The first reason writers fail is that they don't believe they can succeed. Without a doubt, a lack of self-confidence is one of the most common obstacles that prevent us from moving towards our goals. If you don't believe in yourself and your writing skills, you will never reach the goal. One of the main reasons why many writers do not believe in themselves is that they have never written before and do not have someone to advise or guide them in learning to write. Like many, you probably have no idea where to start, how to start. We all have an author within us. We should all write a book that will outlive us so you can leave a mark on the world.

BIOGRAPHY:

Dr. B's is supercharging women business owners through storytelling, delivering the right message to the right audience. Turn your life story into a legacy for future generations.

Build trust by connecting with your clients at a deeper level, your story shares the real you. Elevate your business by using the power of storytelling to connect and establish authority! The right story is an opportunity for those who are dedicated to changing the world...

Dr. Angelica Benavides is known as Dr. B. She inspires women worldwide to share their story. You have a special talent, a gift to be shared that will impact and have influence on those it touches. Storytelling is an important social aspect of life, and your life should be remembered. She is a Badass Influencer, an Ultimate Legacy Builder, A World-Class Storyteller & Best-Selling Author and Publisher.

Dr. Angelica Benavides is known as Dr. B and the Ultimate Legacy Builder. She increases visibility, exposure, and influence helping entrepreneurs be all they can be. Dr. B's, [Angélica Benavides (Underwood) Ed.D.] story is being written and shared worldwide by the exposure in the Women's World Conference and Awards. Dr. B is the Marketing Director and Publisher for Face of Women of Heart Awards (WOHA) for 2021. She was recently invited to be on the International Advisory Board for the 100 Successful Women in Business Network. She has been featured on NBC, USA Today, Fox, and recognized as an Amazing Women of Influence. She shared a Global Virtual Stage with Forbes Riley, Bill Walsh, Ragne Sinkas, and Dr. Freddy Behin.

After healing from two types of cancer, losing two homes, went through a bankruptcy, a divorce and her world tumbling down around her, she discovered she has a bigger purpose in life. She now shares her impactful story and influences women around the world to never give up. What she loves most is listening to people's stories on how they overcome hardships, how they inspire purpose, become unstoppable and unforgettable, with stories that must be told. When she is not working, she loves spending time with her children and grandchildren.

I help entrepreneurs to write an anthology, design a mini-course, and participate in a summit with other experts so that they have more visibility and exposure. Even more, I will help you design your message and story so that you not only succeed in transforming lives but also make a fortune sharing your message.

We all have an author within us, and I will help rescue yours. Several of the authors he joins with at El Autor Spotlight not only intentionally impact and transform lives, but even heal areas of their own lives. By recounting and writing about the moments of this very difficult challenge in their lives, they discovered that it really helped them achieve their dream and business. With Author Spotlight On, I reveal exactly how you make a difference and make a profit with your advice, experience and expertise.

The strategy that I use to help entrepreneurs to position themselves as experts, have more visibility and exposure to increase their number of clients and money is to use the technique of co-authorship. It's a great way to save time and publish a book with more authors. The benefits you get from writing a book with other business-building authors include opening the door to more presentations or attracting more ideal clients. By writing an anthology or book you will transform yourself as a speaker, *coach,* consultant, and of course you will create online marketing. Connect with me!

Godella Mary Petty

From the Fire to the Gold Purified Vessel
By Godella Mary Petty

My name is Godella Mary Petty. I was born in Gary, Indiana, at Mercy Hospital to Zenobia Sandra Bell and Milton Swanson on October 19, 1973, in Gary, Indiana. I was born to an offspring of Bishop Laselle Clark of Memphis, Tennessee. Clark, my great grandfather, and great grandmother lived in my hometown Gary, Indiana. My mother moved my three sisters and me to Milwaukee, Wisconsin, in 1976 and with my mother's entire family and life was very good; we were a very close family. My mother loved me in a very special way. I was her child that connected her to God. That's why my name is Mary for Jesus Christ's mother. I was always destined for a deveined life and service to God.

I didn't like my name growing up because everyone teased me. Once I understood who God was, I didn't want to have another name. My life didn't seem to be starting out as very meaningful. Life was totally opposite from my God-given name. I started out with a strong mother who enjoyed partying and having a good time. She liked going to concerts of all the greatest R&B groups. She went to all the best night clubs in Wisconsin. My mother was a very outgoing lady, but life as I knew it would change. My mother went out like any other night, but when she returned, she was never the same even until this day. My mother had a mickey slipped into her drink and completely lost her mind. I no longer had a functioning mommy but a journey with my mother's mental illness which would forever stain my beautiful life as a three-year-old now without a protector over my precious life.

My sisters and I had to go live with our relatives in a house filled with drugs, sexual immorality, cursing, fussing. and constant fighting. I had no training as a child. I was just growing up hurt, lost, and very confused. God was not in the house. Because of all the abuse from the relative I lived with who was so drunk just about every single day, I hardly ever ate. Starvation was so hurtful to my little young mind and body. I developed a serious disorder to hoard food even as an adult because I vowed never to go hungry again and never have to eat tissue and toothpaste to be full from a desperation to eat. Not long after living with this relative, the close friend began to sexually abuse me from three years old to six years old. I became very aggressive, angry, and violent with my words to control my surroundings and stop the constant abuse. This led me down very dark paths in my life. I joined three different gangs in my city for protection.

I began smoking weed at the age of eight years old, and by the time I was twelve, I was pregnant. At thirteen I was a mother and with no guidance only to go from relative to eventually landing in foster care until I turned eighteen years old. My journey in foster care was very awful. I was in seven foster homes in one year. I then dropped out of middle school homeless and with a child looking for the life I saw other children have. My view on life was very distorted and confusing as a teenage mother not understanding where God was and good people to help me and how to have welfare in extreme poverty while living in ghetto housing conditions. I was an uneducated teen mother with no help whatsoever. The tables in my life turned once again after God blessed my cousins to be saved, and she began to teach me about Jesus Christ.

I truly didn't embrace her conversation about God. I was very upset because I felt as though it was too late from too much hurt and bondages. I felt that there was no way I, Godella Mary Petty, could possibly have an amazing future---let alone a blessed life. God had a plan for me while I was in the foster home. I was told in order to live in this great woman of God's house, I must go to church or to continue to move from home to home in foster care. Due to my situation, I was desperate, so I agreed for the sake of my baby who was now almost two years old. I then was told by my foster mother that I had to attend school, so I obeyed only because my victim attitude or any of my excuses were not flying by in her house. My journey began to change when I met my foster mother, and she also made me get a job as a housekeeper in a nursing home.

My foster mother told me having a job was better than being on welfare, and God requires us humans to work. I began to get my life in order but not because I wanted to but because God gave me a willing mind to accept corrections and new directions, so I stopped getting in trouble. I gave my life to Jesus Christ at seventeen and pregnant with my second child. I allowed God to begin a wonderful work in my life. I graduated from high school in 2007. I became a foster parent at the age of nineteen in the state of Wisconsin which is not the normal process. I defied the odds; you're supposed to be twenty-one years old. There was an expectation for me.

Here are Some things I've accomplished throughout the years: I was a foster parent for seven years. I then started a daycare in my own home for eighteen years. I've been a community advocate for over twenty-one years presently for the mental ill, and foster children, homeless people, veterans, and the elderly in my city. I am a guardian to my mother and a guardian for my two disabled granddaughters. I'm an ordained evangelist since 2014. I have a non-profit our reach ministry named Sons and Daughters of Virtue Outreach, Inc. I'm a notary in the state of Wisconsin and a global speaker. I am in the movement of popcorn and movies and clothing for all children across the globe through the Johnny Regan organization. I was nominated for positive direction for outstanding community work. I am a face for rap mothers of an organization located in California. I am also a third time best seller for the twelve books I've written. I am a co-author with eight beautiful children in the inner city of Wisconsin.

I'm a mother of five adult children and a grandmother of nine children. My name after God's is forever my blessing

Ava Fang

Invisible Heroes
By Ava Fang

"The key to immortality is first living a life worth remembering," Bruce Lee once said. When I woke up in the middle of my life, I was struggling to free myself, own my worth, and take charge of my voice. My mother's attitude of service sang from my heart, "Help whenever you can even when no one's expecting." With those words, I remembered to start living, to find the keys, and to be myself again.

I grew up in a big household in a little city in Northern California, filled with family, multiple languages, and traditions from a bouillon cube of culture. As a first generation Asian American, I lived with my parents, younger sister, grandparents, aunt, uncle, and cousins, all in one house. Life was busy and noisy, it was organized chaos, and as kids, we were carefree.

My earliest memories had a house full of people and delicious food. I remember thinking my family was huge; everyone was aunt or uncle, grandparent or cousin, coming and going, some staying for months, and others just a few days. Having limited means never stopped my parents from helping someone in need, especially my mother, who turned strangers into friends, then friends into family.

My mother helped everyone, whether they asked or not. If she was down to her last twenty dollars in her wallet, first she made sure we ate, and then she willingly gave the twenty dollars to someone else in need. She was the youngest of eight, born during hard times, so she had a very different lens of life than some of her siblings. She knew what it was like to have very little, to be the last in line, and to struggle for everything. No one knew that about her, just as no one knew she would give the last few dollars in her purse, smiling as if she had plenty more when her wallet was bare.

We lived simple and practical, and she taught me that sharing was everything. Although I wasn't aware then, that was the first key I received in life, the key of contribution, which she deeply engraved within me. Speaking up, giving, or doing something for another were built into our nature.

Being immigrants, my parents gave everything to make sure their kids spoke English and mastered American culture. As the eldest, I became the translator for my family. My parents worked arduous, long hours in their corner store seven days a week, so I spent most of my early years with my grandparents.

When I was in first grade, I asked my dad, "How come Grandpa doesn't speak English?"

"What do you mean Grandpa doesn't speak English?" my dad said incredulously. "Grandpa speaks English so well; you just don't understand yet."

I believed him completely until I got to second grade and was still translating restaurant menus.

But that didn't stop me from continuing to translate for my family. In fact, I had become the official translator for my elementary school, too. When teachers and Chinese students needed to communicate, or a non-English speaker visited the office, I would get that call of duty, and I loved being of service. Actually, back then they called on me to help any Asian person, never mind if they spoke Korean, Japanese or anything other than Chinese, I was still sent to translate. I was so proud to help, that it never even occurred to me that sometimes I didn't speak the same language; I just figured it out through keywords, gestures, and big smiles.

Sometimes I was overly zealous. That second grade year, I was in the same class as my cousin. At home, she was fun and loud, but in class she was quiet and hardly spoke. Whenever the teacher called on her, she would freeze until giant tears rolled down her cheeks. I couldn't bear it, so I spoke up for her.

"Is your name Mina?" Mrs. Pumma would ask me.

"No, I'm Ava," I answered confidently.

"That's right; put your name on the board," Mrs. Pumma would say, and I'd obediently get up, feel guilty, and write my name on the chalkboard, all while Mina cried.

There were days I'd speak up for Mina, Michael, and Jenny, and end up with three check marks behind my name. At the end of that week, I'd go home with my report folder and a note, "Wonderful model student, very helpful, but talks too much." My mom would ask me what happened, tell me "Good job" and "stop talking in class!"

I watched my parents enough that I wasn't afraid to step up, whether it be translating, communicating, or speaking up for someone who was struggling. I wore those check marks as a badge of honor not because I was a rule breaker but simply because they meant I helped others. My first achievement was that pink slip my teacher awarded for "talking too much."

Whenever there was a school or community activity, I was a helper. If there ever was a chance to lend a hand, I raised mine. Together with my mother, we helped out at countless functions from local fundraising events for school districts to community service and cultural charities for our beloved little city and businesses. Everyone knew my mother; we had amassed wonderful friendships.

When I started high school, my immediate family moved into our own home, and my mother continued to take in friends and family. Decades later, when I returned from a month of travels, I visited my parents and found that my friend Raina had moved in. By chance, Mom saw Raina in the grocery store, heard about her divorce, and invited her to stay. Over four years later, Raina remarried and left my parents' home.

By my early twenties, being of service was ingrained into my lifestyle. I spent my time working, attending classes, and helping people along the way. I took friends to appointments, translated when someone didn't understand, picked up groceries and prescriptions for neighbors, and babysat kids and fur babies when friends went on vacation. I even got ordained, and I'm honored to have married six couples! No matter who, a friend, co-worker, mailman, or stranger – if someone needed help and I was capable and available, I would do my best.

I had become the "YES Person," building the muscle of helping, supporting, and cheering others so much that I became a champion of people. I solved issues, gave hugs for comfort, listened when someone was in need; eventually, I spent so much time with people that I started to understand their essence and truly believed in their greatness. Anything to do with helping, I had the confidence to figure it out. Belief was the second key, and by repetition my whole life, this muscle was so strong that if someone was in need, I would find a way to help. \

Several years ago, a good friend felt a calling to bring ancient wisdom back to humanity and shared there were so many sacred places around the world, like Machu Picchu.

Immediately, my championing muscle flexed.

"Why don't you take people to Machu Picchu to experience that wisdom?" I asked.

Patrick looked at me in surprise, "Well, I haven't thought about it."

"Why not?'" I asked.

"I can't. I have some health constrictions now," Patrick answered as if it was something he already accepted.

"Can you find out from your doctor?" I asked.

Patrick paused.

"If you take a destination plus a learning, you seal in the experience. I'll help you plan everything," I said confidently.

I could see the wheels turning in Patrick's mind; physically he already looked different, as if the possibility had somehow opened a new door.

A few months later, Patrick, his wife, the team, and I landed in Lima, Peru, making the trek through Cuzco, one of the highest elevations in the world, and all the way to Machu Picchu, defying his health conditions. Because I was confident that I could help him, I believed I could do it, and because I believed in him, he believed he could do it too. Now we continue taking trips around the world, collecting and spreading wisdom gems.

Sometimes it takes someone else to believe in us first to remind us that although it's pitch black at night, the sun will rise and light up the sky all day. Just beyond belief was my next key, perception.

In my mid-twenties, I met a man who took over my whole world, literally. We opened a retail franchise together. The hours were long, and the work was grueling; I operated the physical storefront, hiring, training, and serving, which was still my absolute favorite thing. I loved people, so I brought along the championing mentality.

Very soon, my retail store became more than just a place of business. People stopped by to get hugs, share good news, chat, bring food, and take breaks. They dropped in when they were nearby, when they felt happy or sad, and when they needed help. My store became a central hub that was a resource to the local community, and I knew everybody.

But there was a disconnect in the perception between my work and life.

At work, my life was fun, fulfilled, and complete. At home, I was distraught, unworthy, and miserable. Even though the business thrived, my partner and I shared a very different vision of life. Since I allowed him to control every aspect of our life, I was constantly berated, under pressure, and stressed by his dissatisfaction. Everything was my fault, and nothing was good enough. Living for the few good days, I gave everything I could and did my best to do things his way to preserve the relationship and my sanity.

One night, I woke up gasping and thinking of my mother. What had I been doing? How did I become so unhappy? At that moment, I understood that I was happiest when giving my all freely, openly, and unconditionally, without constraints and limitations of someone else. In my relationship, I had lost that perspective – I was giving while hoping for another's happiness. I'd forgotten myself, and changing my perception was the key - I was not responsible for someone else's happiness or dreams – I was only responsible for my own.

As Steve Jobs brilliantly said, "You can't connect the dots looking forward; you can only connect them looking backward." When I realized I was in control of living my own life worth remembering, I trusted the dots would align, and this began my discovery of becoming the truest, most authentic version of me.

I walked out of that life renewed with a sense of purpose to spread joy, love, and abundance, owning my power and voice with a heart to serve as a ray of sunshine to brighten someone's day because everyone deserves to be happy. Now in command of my keys – contribution, belief, and perception – I'm grateful everyday, take nothing for granted, and feel truly free.

I started in the travel space helping people visit destinations of their dreams and curating experiences of a lifetime to create memories with loved ones. I began building personal brands and helping people discover, define, and showcase their most authentic and beautiful self to the world. I mentored people in business and daily life, living fun, free, and fulfilled, so they could become who they were meant to be.

Beyond my work, I volunteered at a myriad of events, helping various organizations across differing cultures, backgrounds, even faith; although it may not be popular to say or easily understood, I was never bound by category nor limited by system. For me, it was always about the people - the people involved and helped, loving, caring, and doing everything in service, making our lives worth living.

Today, I continue to live in service. I'm a translator of life, guiding people through interactive programs that focus on getting clarity in the life they want to live and building that into reality while having extraordinary experiences, creating memories with family and friends. Yes, whenever I see someone struggling to communicate, I immediately help, whether I speak the language or not!

Although this story is about my journey, it's actually not about me. I've never won an award or been given recognition for anything I've done in my life that shows I'm in service to others, yet every day, I live in pure gratitude I get the chance to help whoever I can, whenever I can, and feel blessed by the work and the appreciation I get in return.

When my dear friend, Starley Murray, nominated me, my initial reaction was, "I'm not worthy; I don't have any accolades, so I don't deserve this."

But then, I thought of my mother, the invisible superhero, who taught me by example, living her life in service, that sharing is everything, to live is to give, and it's all about the people we get to be with in this lifetime.

My mother is my Invisible Superhero. Long before the days of purpose driven living, my mother was already living her life on purpose: to care for and give someone a bit of relief during their hardest times, always believing that if they came across her path, they were there for a reason.

"Ava, you're worthy. In honor of your mother's lessons, accept this recognition to share your light, you and the world deserve it," Starley said wholeheartedly.

Eternally grateful for her vision and support, I knew then that she had already turned the spotlight on me.

Like my mother, I'm an Invisible Superhero. You might be one, too. Sometimes it takes another to believe in us first, to believe that we are all worthy.

Thank the stars for the extraordinary women who have rightfully earned their place in the spotlight. There are countless more women, who have equally earned their place and who stay in the invisible light. I'm honored to cast a ray of sunshine upon anyone who has a heart to serve, a mind to care, a body to take action, and a spirit that will keep on giving.

You can make a difference in the world without being noticed, so never underestimate your worth and the power of your impact on another human being. You never know who's in need, so do something every day to bring sunshine and hope to brighten someone's world.

I believe that success is using our keys to unlock the doors so that we live the way we're meant to. Living a life of contribution is believing it starts with us and having perspective can change everything. I'm proud to be an Invisible Superhero. There's magic in being behind the scenes because without the crew, there's no movie. Just as we don't always see the rainbow, but the colors are always there.

Once I asked my mother why she felt compelled to help. She said, "When I was young, I was powerless, and somebody helped me. Now every time I help, I'm thankful it's my power to give." That might just be one key to immortality.

Isabelle Stephenson

Success Comes in All Shapes and Sizes

by Isabelle Stephenson
International life coach, helping women to
achieve their goal of healthier relationships

What does success mean to you?

Is it a satisfying career, a fat bank account, a happy family, being featured in Forbes magazine, or running a business?

Success to me is like a multi-faceted diamond, where each side reflects the light in its own wondrous and unique way. Let me explain by sharing a few stories. Sit back and relax as I pull back the curtain and you get a glimpse into the lives of some amazing people.

These people did not receive any accolades in the public eye, but they won a gold medal in successfully transforming their lives.

I am Isabelle, a life coach who helps women in midlife achieve their goal of healthier relationships.

"Anne" was open to hear what really triggered her. Anne's struggle appeared to revolve around constant bickering with her husband over small things like not completing projects around the house or leaving dishes in the sink. To help her get to the root of the problem, we uncovered that she had a strained relationship with her sister throughout her life.

The pattern of her behavior of reacting with hurtful words was triggered by seemingly innocent marital behaviors. Now that she realizes her quick retorts had nothing to do with her husband; she is now able to pause and respond in a more appropriate manner.

I call this success through releasing old patterns from your childhood.

"I started out talking about things that were on my mind and my reactions to things around me. Before you know it, we were talking about something else about my past and came to the realization that my current reactions were totally based on these other factors from my past. Who knew?" Anne

"Beatrice" shared a personal thought with me that I could see was not serving her well. Her job required her to cold call clients and offer them medical insurance services. In this type of career, the potential to feel rejected is real. My goal was to reshape her thinking to reaffirm that she was indeed helping people to better their lives through the service she was providing. Once she realized that she was improving their lives, rather than disturbing them, she had a rejuvenated outlook about her career.

I call that success by renewing the mind.

"Isabelle gave me the tools to work through a work-related mental stumbling block. Results always prove our thoughts. Changing one thought made a big difference." Beatrice

"Cara" has a medical condition that does not allow her to speak loudly, so we conversed through texting. Cara was vulnerable in sharing some old beliefs that she had that were instilled by her mother. She would berate Cara with negative words, such as suggesting that she is a failure and nothing she tries will ever work out. These derogatory beliefs had been embedded in her subconscious throughout her childhood and well into her forties. Her texts flowed, revealing a person who had been damaged by her mother's demeaning words.

Perhaps, those words were spoken to protect Cara from failing and getting hurt in life. However, to counteract her mother's negative words, I just presented Cara with simple questions about her life. Is it true that you have never succeeded in anything? Do you feel that you are a good mom? Once she was able to answer these questions truthfully, she was able to reinvent herself with renewed confidence. Although she did not have a literal voice, her new-found attitude speaks volumes. She started building her business, because she started to believe in herself again.

I call this success by constructing a new belief.

I've been in therapy most of my life on and off for many issues. Just a few texting conversations with Isabelle and I had sorted out a whole slew of issues. She really asks the right questions to get me thinking about where I'm struggling. Cara

"Dana" was excessively texting her boyfriend because she was afraid of losing him. By asking her how he responded to her texting, I was able to show her that her actions were pushing him away rather than strengthening their connection. She refrained from texting which gave him space to reach out to her.

I call this success by using self-control.

Isabelle has such a kind heart, and I liked her approach to see things from a different perspective. Dana

Georgia shared with me that during a car ride with her teenage son, she was able to apply what she had learned in my workshop. She said "You were so fun to be with this morning…" Then she zipped her lips because she wanted to say" BUT….", but she didn't. Without the added criticism, he was able to say, "I love hanging out with you, too, Mom."

I call this success by respecting our teenage children.

She helped me understand my children's personality types and how to work with them. She taught me that one of the best tools is to just keep my mouth shut and listen! The result was Life changing!! I am working on ending the "crazy cycle" of constant yelling. One thing I liked most was her practical solutions. Georgia

"Joelle" was going through a difficult divorce in her seventies and receiving much criticism from family and friends for doing so. Her mind was clouded with trepidation whether to step out on her own, go back to her ex, or begin a new relationship. I was able to abstract positive aspects of her character and life experiences, which allowed her to see her self-worth and make the decision that was best for her. Through our sessions she gained the fortitude to begin a new life alone. She is a testimony that it is never too late to leave an abusive marriage and build your life back up again.

I call this success by having courage to start over.

Regardless of the magnitude of the storm, she helps one to understand and to know it's a storm and storms do pass. Joelle

Karina came to me feeling overwhelmed and small in this world. Slowly, she was able to see all the good she was doing in her life and in her community, such as educating her children and facilitating classes for other students. I vividly remember one day where I introduced the tool of using a metaphor, and she could see herself as the mansion in her neighborhood of common homes. It was she who raised the value. What a transformation.

I call this success by faithfully implementing small steps and by being willing to see your true value.

Isabelle helped me to see the beliefs that were behind many of my emotional responses and has supported me in rewriting them to reflect the truth about who I am. The result was that I found new confidence in my role as a parent. I really appreciated that she helped me in starting to discover my highest values and supported my desire to instill these values in my children. As I have continued this practice, it has transformed not just my parenting, but my life. Karina

"Lisa" came to me because her marriage was on its last leg. She went to work and implemented everything I shared with her.

Lisa was able to focus on the now and on the future. She started filling her needs and was able to understand her husband on a whole new level. Lisa took time to see friends, plan dates, and say yes to outdoor adventures. They are both less stressed and are better able to stop and redirect the spiral that has brought them so much heartache and despair before. She created more peace in her home and is able to sustain the marriage as she had intended to.

I call this success by implementing a future focus.

"After 4 plus years of on and off counseling, we were about to give up. She helped me realize the power/control/responsibility I have for my happiness. We both now have a better view of our relationship. We have had more success in two sessions with Isabelle than with the last four plus years of counselors prior. Isabelle's technique brings actual healing to our marriage, not just a band aid till the next blow out." Lisa

"Heather" came to me because of anxiety that was interfering with her everyday life, especially at work. Her husband was addicted to alcohol, and she was addicted to fixing him. She had made the decision to stay for the time being. By observing herself, she was able to learn to detach from the daily situations and not to let them control her. Heather understood that her fear was causing her to manipulate and yell. By focusing on herself, instead of trying to fix something that she had no power to fix, she was able to stop beating herself up. That allowed room for Heather to see her needs and to start filling them. One tool that helped her gain more confidence was to write down daily, something that she acknowledged herself for. Self-regulating practices, like meditation and processing emotions, became a positive habit in her life.

I now am busy reminding myself that I have control over my thoughts and my feelings. I have tools to calm my body and mind, instead of beating myself up all the time. Heather

"Bob and Susi" came to me because of recent tension in their long marriage. Susi felt that she couldn't approach his recreational drug use, and Bob felt spied upon and criticized. Susi learned that her expectation of how married life should be and how she expected him to behave caused her much pain. I helped them build trust again by encouraging them to return to things that they enjoyed doing together. Bob also learned to be more transparent with Susi, because all she wanted was honest conversation. She was able to see that her thought of "he is being sneaky" didn't help at all and she replaced it with just focusing on the facts. For example, "he is just going to the store". They also learned to see that they have different needs. For example, she needed safety and security while he needed adventure and freedom. They found a good balance by doing some activities together while also doing other things separately. Susi implemented the phrase I taught her, "I feel… when you…." and Bob learned to listen and validate her feelings by saying "I understand." They started celebrating the good times again.

I call this success by rebuilding trust and celebrating life again.

Isabelle helped me understand my husband better and work through issues in a positive constructive way. Susi

She reaffirmed our love for each other, and we have more trust in our relationship. We are communicating better. Bob

And last but not least, my story.

In my forties, I was struggling with managing six children and my marriage and just feeling frustrated and lost. I had given up everything to move to the States and marry my husband. People thought I was living a fairy tale, but deep down I was hurting. Every day, I yelled at my wonderful children and knew in my gut that this was not me. One day, I reached out and hired my first coach. This was a life changing experience because she gave me hope and the tools, I needed to practice peaceful parenting. I stopped taking things my teens or spouse said too personally, and I was able to ground myself in a way that allowed me to respond instead of react. Then, a dream was born in my heart, and I knew I had to pass this magic on to others. The magic of transforming your life and being excited for each day. Now, I am honored to help people to increase their self-awareness, create more happiness, and take control of their lives.

With three children married, one in college and two in high school, I get to learn how to connect with young adult children. For example, I am learning not to give advice unless they ask me. That is difficult sometimes. I remind myself that I do not want to control them; I need to respect and accept them as they are. Learning life lessons is as imperative as making mistakes and learning from them. My intention is to be there for them with a listening ear and zipped lips unless I have an encouraging word to say. The best thing to say when your teens or young adult children are struggling is "Yes, I hear you. That's hard." We can't always fix it for them. You show love by letting them go through the painful moments, so they have a chance to become more resilient, which is a skill that is highly useful in this world.

I am growing and stretching out of my comfort zone daily to allow for bigger dreams and goals to manifest in my life.

It was important for me not to give up because my six children are watching, and I want to inspire them to pursue their goals and dreams.

I call that success by role modeling.

Success has no age limit. It is multi-faceted.

Dear reader. If you have a dream, listen to it. Be aware of it. Write it down and let it take shape. Ask how your talents can bring this dream alive. If your dream will benefit the world, then you are meant to pursue it. Size doesn't matter. You start with one step and then another. Believe that the right people will support and uplift you along the way. God gave you these talents and dreams. Use them for good in the world.

When you start out remember that failing forward is the way to go. Success in any area of your life requires you to take imperfect action and to try different things. Try Them. Do them and fail. Failing forward is better than standing still and doing nothing. All these actions and perceived failures are actually bringing you one step closer to your dream. Success doesn't happen overnight. The seed for my dream was planted in 2014. I was in my mid-forties. I let it take root. I let it grow. I took action. I became certified. I hired the wrong business coaches. Twice. I lost money. I earned money. But this dream to help other women achieve their goals was becoming louder. I would wake up with my heart beating anxiously. It keeps pushing me to take action. You know it is a God given assignment when it just doesn't let you go.

Your success will inspire and empower other women. That's why I am delighted to help ministries like Terri Savelle Foy who rescue girls from sex trafficking and Shamila Ramjawan who helps girls in South Africa with her invention of the reusable menstrual cup, so they can pursue their education.

Sharon Martin

LIGHT BULB ON!
HOW I WOKE UP TO WHAT I DIDN'T KNOW ABOUT WORKING A JOB AND MAKING MONEY!
By Sharon Martin

By personal invitation, I invite you to take a glimpse into my personal journey of how I woke up to what I didn't know about working a job, making money, creating wealth, and designing my life. However, to truly understand my journey and the woman I am today, I must take you to a major event that occurred in my life when I started to understand the impact a lack of money can have on a life. My journey has felt like that feeling I get when I am dreaming about something that's scary, and for a moment I can't tell if it's a dream or real. I am having an adrenaline rush, my breathing is panicked for a split second, and then I realize it's just a dream. Thank God! Have you ever had that feeling? This is exactly how I felt when I realized the underlined deception regarding the direct correlation of a job versus creating wealth.

My name is Sharon Martin; I live in British Columbia, Canada. I am divorced and a single mother of two. I was raised by my mother who passed away when I was only fifteen years old. I recall that day so vividly. You see the day she died I was in a car accident and rushed to a nearby hospital. While waiting for the doctor in emergency, I got the news my mother had been rushed to another hospital across town. Needless to say, the news of my mother being rushed to the hospital was frightening. My mother was diabetic, it didn't look good, and I needed to get to the hospital immediately. By the time I arrived at the hospital I was too late; she had passed away. I ran into the room where my mother was being kept, and when I saw my mother lying there, her body still warm, I was devastated. I was beside myself, crying, sobbing uncontrollably, and clinging to my mother. She was my everything, and now she was gone. At that moment I felt so lost and alone. Then something else happened that day. When it was time to leave the hospital, the staff gave me my mother's belongings which included her wallet. Desperate to hold on to anything that belonged to her for some reason, I opened her wallet, and what I saw was my mom's last five dollars; my heart broke even further. As a fifteen-year-old I didn't really realize the financial hardship and sacrifices my mother faced until that moment when I opened her wallet and saw only five dollars. A flood of realities was racing to my mind, my poor mom; this deepened my sadness. Unbeknownst to me on a conscious level, my relationship with money was formed on a subconscious level that would motivate me for a lifetime. This was a life changing event, which planted a seed in my heart to strive for financial success even though I didn't understand it as such. Knowing my mother only had five dollars in her wallet really bothered me. As a result, the connection I made with money with my limited knowledge and as a fifteen-year-old was sketched in my mind like nails scratching on an old chalk board. Can you hear that sound? I will never forget it. My journey has been rocky with lots of ups, downs, twists, turns, and beauty at the same time, which has made me the women I am today. I am grateful, and I am reminded of the words of Maya Angelou. I quote,

"You may not control all the events that happen to you, but you can decide not to be reduced by them."

I decided not to be reduced by them, and neither should you!

When I graduated from high school, I knew I had to have a good career to take care of myself and make money because a good career/ job was a key to climb the economic ladder, right? What are we taught from childhood? Do well in school. Go to university. Get a good job. Work for a good company and this will equal your dream life, right? But how many of you know life just doesn't always cooperate on our timeline. It didn't in my life. Follow me as I link my education, my jobs, and my own business together like links in a chain that revealed to me the deception and direct correlation of a job versus making money and creating wealth…

My Education

As a Christian I believed in putting God first; therefore, I went to Bible College for two years and graduated. Then I decided to go to a university for my professional career. But before starting university, I took a little detour. I decided to get married. I was nineteen and had my first child at twenty-two. Life got interesting. Juggling married life, a child, work, and university was a lot to manage. As a result, I stopped school because we needed more money, and we both couldn't afford to attend university at the same time and support a family. However, I supported my husband at the time by working full time; he worked part time and completed his university degree. By this time, I had my second child. Sounds familiar? Money challenges, all too familiar! Working but not enough. My dream of getting a university degree fell by the wayside. Even though I wasn't taking classes towards a university degree, I started to work on myself, my mindset asking myself the question: How could I get better, do more, create more? These thoughts plagued my mind, drove me to read, and seek for answers. The connection started to appear, money, an average job, lack! I felt as if someone tripped in a room, banging on the door for me to open it. This is how I felt. Can I break this cycle?

My Jobs

Even though I didn't complete my degree, I decided I would pursue my dream to earn more income by working my way to the top, which I did! I worked for the Toronto Stock Exchange on the trading floor, and I was one of the top trainers. I worked for CIBC, Royal Bank, and JP Morgan Chase in their Call Centers and worked my way up the ladder as Customer Service Agent,

Sales Trainer, and Supervisor and became a New Hire Corporate Trainer. I was still living from pay cheque to pay cheque. My pay cheque determined my lifestyle---job, hourly wage versus creating more money. I wasn't getting ahead financially the way I envisioned. The connection again---not enough income to create wealth. There was a ceiling on my income if I continued to exchange my time for an hourly wage. The connection-average job, average pay, lack! I was seeking answers. So, I continued to work on my thoughts, my expectations, trying to find a solution that would break the cycle? As I continued to seek for answers it felt like I was looking for a needle in a haystack. Should I try and finish my degree? What should I do to make more money? Have you ever felt that? How to break the cycle?

My Self Employment

Start my own business. So I did. I started my own business in 2001---Venture Marketing. I worked early mornings on my job and ran my call centre business in the evenings from 3 p.m. – 9 p.m. Monday to Saturday. It was a lead generation company for the Time Shares Industry. My eyes were opened to the differences between working a job earning an hourly wage and generating money from a business. I went from earning under $100,000 per year to over $100,000 per year. Light bulb was on! My financial situation started to improve. I generated more income than I had ever made on a job. Just when my financial situation started to improve life hit, 9-11 happened and severely impacted the Time Share Industry; my business came to a halt and so did my income and my marriage and my morning job. Can you image all this happening at the same time. it was a gut-wrenching experience. I cried myself to sleep at night. How was I going to survive? As Vince Lombardi said, **"Winners never quit and quitters never win."**

So I had to go back to square one-a job! Valuable lesson learned;

owning my own business gave me the ability to generate more income and change my life! I was hooked! The light Bulb was on! Meaning I understood that even though running your own business has its ups and downs. Even though I had to get a job, I never stopped looking for a part business to generate additional income. This was a major eye opener for a woman who lost her mother at age fifteen, no mentors to speak of in my life, just figuring it out on my own as most of us do. Now divorced, a single mother of two---what should I do and what could I do? Being the optimist that I am, I always strive to see the glass as half full rather than half empty I continue to push forward. Which brings me to where I am today. I finally went back to school, obtained my Life Insurance License, Mutual Funds license, and am currently working on my Branch Manager's License. I am a very successful entrepreneur running my own business in Financial Services. I love what I do. I coach, empower women, families, and young adults about how money works. My passion in life is to help as many people as I can to eventually become financially independent through financial education, consistent investing, and proper financial planning. I now conduct local investment seminars, train, and develop leaders in my own business, and I am on track to generate a $300K to $500k by December 2022 and beyond. I just started my journey in the Financial Services Industry in September of 2018 just a little over three years ago. If I can change my life, so can you! The Light Bulb is on forever! Just stop for a moment; look around; opportunities are all around you. You can create more income by finding something you're passionate about, and if you can generate a six-figure income or more by doing what you love and passionate about-Why not? Just DO IT!

Lesson learned and still learning---life doesn't always go as planned or envisioned. and the road to success may look different than you thought but when life gives you lemons, make lemonade.

Remember this in the words of Robert Kiyosaki:

"All depends on how determined we are to be successful."

And finally...

"The journey to financial freedom starts the MINUTE you decide you were destined for prosperity, not scarcity—for abundance, not lack. Isn't there a part of you that has always known that? Can you see yourself living a bounteous life—a life of more than enough? It only takes one minute to decide. Decide now." ~ Mark Victor Hansen

Mom

The Light Bulb is On!

Jo Wiehler

You Have a Purpose
By Jo Wiehler

It was a heartbreaking day... too heartbreaking for words! I was barely 37 years old! I was a mother, a single mother of two beautiful children, and a business owner of a very large and fast growing cleaning company that I had just proudly spent the last five years pouring my blood, sweat, and tears into to make it work, and now it was flourishing, so proud of my accomplishments knowing that I had created my company due to my own grief, and agony of losing my oldest precious child in a custody battle due to the lack of financial means to continue to go against my ex-husband and their unlimited resources.

I waited until the doctors and kind sympathetic nurses left the room. I had even thanked them in my "Jo Wiehler funny way" ... I had actually thanked them! I stared at the wall, and when the door quietly closed, the silent tears started to fall. I couldn't breathe! They have to be wrong! As I lay on my side, I watched the heart monitor and listened to the drip of the IV. I had never heard a more painful and deafening sound than that Bloody awful IV drip!

Is this it? Is this what my life is reduced to? My dreams and goals and visions for the future my children? My life? Shattered by the sentence of the doctor and the strength of the compassionate nurse's hand firmly holding mine as I felt that I had been sucker punched.

NO!!!!

Drip...drip...drip with every drip it felt as if my heart was going to be ripped out of my chest! Drip! Another dream-gone! Drip! Not seeing my children grow up! Drip! Not seeing my daughter in her special moments, prom dress, wedding dress, or becoming a mother, and me a grandmother ...Drip! Not buying a home by myself or taking the trips we had planned to take. Drip! Or seeing my son again...Drip! Drip! Drip! What about all my plans for the future? My murals that I had put off for so long to raise my children---and now never? Drip! What about my mom and brothers and sisters and their kids? Drip! My Birthday, Christmas! Drip! What if I don't have the strength to close my eyes for the very last time? What if I can't say goodbye?

...DRIP!!!

My tears were like silent prayers---I couldn't even talk. I couldn't breathe-all I was capable of doing was lying in my cold hospital bed shivering---not quite sure if it was from the cold or the shock of what I was just told. I felt as if I was already dead---like a lifeless zombie-or a rag doll, a lifeless zombie rag doll! Me the person with the most energy, joy, and laughter despite what my circumstances were! The tears slipped down my face, and the drips were deafening!

I was told that I had stage 4 breast cancer, on both sides, rapidly spreading, and the size of mandarin oranges, and the 3rd bomb drop was that it was genetic BRCCA-1 cancer gene ...Drip!

DRIP!!! They told me I was dying! DRIP! That it was too late! DRIP! That they didn't think I would make it to Christmas! DRIP! That I needed to gather my children and family together to tell them that I was dying---that I wasn't going to make it! That all my dreams and hopes were over – that my life was over!....................NOOOOO!!!..............DRIP!!!!!! DRIP!!! As one more of the thousands of tears waiting to fall slipped silently down my cheeks! ...DRIP!

No! I will not yield! "Lord," I silently prayed, "if this is my time to come and meet you, I am ready... let me be ready; let me have the courage to close my eyes for the last time!" another Drip, another tear,

"But **IF NOT,** let me live! Let me see my children grow and be blessed with their special moments that those precious memories be given to me. I have so many dreams and goals and such hope for the future that you gave me which would be promises unkept. Let me live! Let me share my love for others. Let me impact this world for good. Let me be a mighty tool and testament of You and Your greatness!" **DRIP!** Let me impact this world for good and empower others to become their greatest self and their highest potential... **PLEASE... LET... ME... LIVE!!!**" I silently begged. Another silent tear, another deafening drip... as I slowly drifted off to sleep.... **DRIP! DRIP! DRIP!**

I woke up on a Monday morning to a beautiful day in Sabbioneta, Italy... "RISE and SHINE", I said enthusiastically to myself. The gorgeous sunlight streamed in. The smell of homemade bread and pastries baking in the ovens nearby permeated the air. The glorious church bells were ringing---the birds were chirping, and the neighbors were bustling by to get to work.

"Buongiorno e tutti!" ... proud of the few phrases in Italian that I had learned and said with the most excitement and all the oxygen in my lungs-I smile as I go to the center of town to get the produce for the week. Never in all their lives have the citizens of Sabbioneta ever known a more joyful, optimistic, energetic person as I am. I had so much love and joy to give to others; it just radiated from my every being. I loved life, and I cherished every beautiful moment of everyday.

What was my secret? It's simple---God!

Opportunities were all around me; being in Italy and living here was an incredible opportunity and so many miracles in between-Thank You! It's been eleven years! Eleven years since that heartbreaking moment in my life... I was ready to accept the outcome-if that was the outcome! But there by the Grace of God go I! Luckily, I chose to be living out-loud every day! I vowed not to waste the second chance that I was so freely given, that other precious souls had not. To live freely, to love freely, to drink life like it's a Big Gulp! To be joyful, and cheerful, to love with all her heart. To take the risks that I was afraid of and the opportunities that are presented to me---to have a bucket-list so long that I have to be a very old lady before I 'Go Home'. To be an impactor to others to rise and accomplish their greatest potential. To Get Up! Wake up! Rise up!

Do I have bad days? Do I get tired? Yes! I went through a total of 28 rebuild surgeries, complete removal of both breasts, and all chest muscle, and two implants. Yes, they are prosthetic-but not removable-so when tired-there is no escape. So of course!

But I choose love in all things and to smile as if my life depends on it. I choose to be happy, hopeful, and joyful, to keep going when others tell you to quit, to press forward when you are faced with adversity, to dream big, and then bigger, and bigger, and then much bigger until the only way that you can accomplish them is with God as well as taking my eyes off myself and focusing on the needs of others, serving others, and putting them first. With that I even more so poured love, kindness, and service into work and business-a very unexpected quality to have in the business world. But I cheerfully decided to do things differently and not worry what others think but poured myself into creating the "Back-Door" Sales techniques.

What was my turning point? Every day I choose to dream scary dreams and put the needs of others first. The law of success is the more you sow into others, the more it easily flows back to you. If you want more time, serve, and give of your time. If you want more energy, give more energy. Same thing goes with love and money; give more, and you get more. It's like breathing...

Breathe in-Breathe-out! Let it flow easily and freely! Give more than what is expected. Love as if your life depends on it... you never know it just might your last day.

There was a lot of emotional work to be done; I had to reprogram my mind---so much work that had to be done. I had to clean house and take the garbage out! It was a long time not only to rebuild me physically...but now just as much or more so emotionally! After all of my treatments-and surgeries, I felt as if I was worthless-I couldn't even button up my pants-I had to relearn everything! Everything!

I had worked so hard to rebuild my life from my last heartbreak. Now with all my surgeries and the 2 ½ years fighting to live every day, wanting to quit everyday...watching all I built slip away, feeling as if I was a failure day in and day out and so helpless, I felt so ugly and disfigured...that no longer would I ever be lovable.

There is a really great saying from Albert Einstein that rings true: "Stay away from negative people. They have a problem for every solution." Sometimes we are that 'negative people' to ourselves. We have to guard our minds as if we would guard our most valuable possession. Be extremely cautious about what you say, think, or allow in your mind, read, or watch TV...even yourself and self-talk!

Learning to love yourself is sometimes the hardest thing to do but the most important person that you can ever love. I had to remind myself that I had worth and value. I didn't feel that, but I was the computer programmer for my mind so I refused to allow ANY NEGATIVE whatsoever that could destroy what I was trying so hard to rebuild!

So, when I wanted to say the negative, I held onto the vision of the woman I saw in my mind that I wanted to be! It was the daily reminder that I had a purpose and that the lord had given me a second chance of life-the decision was made. I was going to come back better, stronger, kinder. I was a Champion! I was love! I was light! I was going to win. I held on to those thoughts! I refused to lose. I was the Queen of my own story! In my lowest moments I had to remind myself that the scars were sacred--- those were my battle scars we had all fought hard to make it. Even though the new normal was a new normal, I was the Hero in my story!

You know what? I was still whole!

You are still whole-you are still beautiful; you are still lovable and worthy to be loved. What helped me to rise was the simple truth that I was my own mountain. I was my obstacles, and I was the decision maker, and I had a choice! I...You...We...All of US are the computer programmer of our minds. We are all worthy, but on our journey our light gets diminished along the way by our circumstances, others, ourselves---especially ourselves. The value doesn't change because the of a few scrapes and bruises. We are all still worthy; we are conquerors in our life. It was not an easy feat to conquer myself or especially my mind; your mind can take you to some very dark places...IF YOU ALLOW IT.

I had to refuse even a crack of what I did not want to enter my mind. I chose to speak victory. You are a failure...I had to say No! I am Fantastic. You are not ugly. You are beautiful beyond belief. Stop saying no man will ever love you again with those scars... Girl, the right man is not going to let you pass him by. Do not think you are useless or what purpose you have now? You are Powerful beyond measure---you are going to not only own the business, but God is going to use you for good, and you are going to be prosperous beyond your wildest dreams! I have physical limitations now...Honey your body has changed; you need to make adjustments and maybe take a rest, delegate...but don't you stop-you stay focused. It's going to hurt... yes, it might, but the prize will be that much more worth it, and yes, you may cry, too, and that's OK! Just get back up! So many of the trials and hardships I went through became my strengths and the courage I needed to get back up and try again, but more than anything I had to clean out my mind and get rid of the trash inside. I had to know deep down especially on my darkest days that we were going to win, and we could get back up. That failure was not an option, and I had to really treat and love myself like my own best friend. I was accountable to myself. So many wonderful friends treated me as if I were encased in bubble wrap. I had to release that in order to find my strength and purpose again, and I had to start dreaming big scary dreams again, but first I had to fully love myself scars and all I had to conquer myself! **...And SO DO YOU!**

I had to really decide how I was going to live and what I was going to do and what my purpose was, and for my own healing I had to do the things I was afraid of. I had to take the risks again- especially to show myself that I CAN, but more importantly what I was still capable of in my mortality. I had to rebuild, repair, and renew, but this time to do it with an even greater love and joy and zest and determination to be my best... I had to jump! ...and JUMP I did!

The Lord blessed me with a window that opened for me, and as scared as I was to do it, I closed my eyes and jumped all the way from Pennsylvania, USA, to Sabbioneta, Italy--- a chance to turn a long awaited dream into a reality to combine my love, kindness, and servitude for others into my business, La Belle Sabbioneta B&B for the Retreats & Coaching industry & International Global Leaders, to encourage, empower, and truly have an impact in their lives, to put my Sales, Marketing, and Branding skills to use while beautifully blending it with my heart, soul and love for others, creating the incredible International Powerball Team to become a greater force not just locally but globally and to become a strong and powerful force to do good, love, serve, and impact this world in such a powerful way---to truly step beyond myself, encourage others to do the same, and prosper in all that we do.

Shoulder to shoulder, hand in hand, I created a Global impact while helping others to do the same and Rising together, Bruised, Broken, Scared, Scarred, Rebuilding, Repairing, Renewing, Flawed, Fallen, Forgotten, whatever the case may be.

You, My Darling Friend, are WORTHY! ...You are ENOUGH! ...You are INVINCIBLE!

You CAN DO THIS! ...You are POWERFUL BEYOND MEASURE!

DON'T STAY DOWN! ...FIGHT! ...GET UP! ...RISE!!! ...BLAZE the TRAIL!

...AND YOU ARE A RED BLAZER WOMAN!

11 years ago...

Drip! ...Drip! ...Drip

Dr. Shamila Ramjawan

Action Packed Personal Growth
By Dr. Shamila Ramjawan

When I was 34 years old in 1998, my husband was struck with a sudden heart attack and passed on. This left me as a young widow to fend for myself and take care of my two young children. Although distraught and enduring this tragic and sudden loss, I decided that I needed to continue studying to be able to support myself and my children and the only way to face the real world and take care of them was to further my education.

I believe that we are the masters of our destinies. Nothing is given to us on a silver platter, and we have to work hard to achieve successes.

My most prized asset is the knowledge I gained over the years, and I am a firm believer in the saying "knowledge is power". I've earned several qualifications and currently at the tail-end of my doctoral degree. Acquiring knowledge through these qualifications and life experiences has equipped me to become a powerhouse entrepreneur.

Honoris United Universities and MANCOSA provided me with a scholarship in 2018 worth R500K to study for the sought after Doctor in Administration (DBA) doctoral degree. I was the only South African on the African continent to be chosen as one of the Women In Africa (WIA) 54 Laureates to proudly represent our beautiful country. The WIA initiative is the first international platform for economic development support for African women leaders with high potential. Its two main goals are to reveal the potential of the new generation of African women leaders at all levels of civil society and state and to network African and International women leaders in the service of an innovative and inclusive Africa. I was humbled to be chosen as a Laureate, and I didn't come back home with just an award and making South

Africa proud, I came back with a scholarship so that I could study for my Doctorate in Business Administration (DBA). I'm saying this again 'I'm unstoppable' Tata Madiba's words 'Education is the key weapon you can use to change the world' I'm doing just that! This is a remarkable achievement for someone that could not afford to go to the university, but I never stopped and achieved all my degrees through distance learning.

I'm so honoured and privileged to be at the tail end of the doctoral degree. Some dream of having an MBA, but I will have a DBA, too, in a few months' time. Of course, I am a proud holder of my MBA degree through UNISA SBL and Open University in London. When I started my MBA in 2008, UNISA SBL did not have the accreditation for MBA degrees and partnered with Open University, so I proudly hold an international MBA.

You are wondering where this is going ... you are never too old to study or achieve your goals. Work hard, study hard, and persevere to achieve what you can.

I appreciate the recognition and accolades that are bestowed upon me, but I also work hard to achieve them. That said, my academic qualifications put me in good stead as a lecturer at one of the largest universities! I am so passionate about learning that my current full-time job is in academia where I am a Business Management Lecturer at the University of South Africa (Unisa).

I have two registered companies, Famram Solutions (marketing and communications solutions) and Famram Foundation, a self-funded family organization that empowers, uplifts, and provides CSI solutions to enhance socio-economic development in the deep impoverished areas.

My companies, Famram Solutions and Famram Foundation were conceptualized from the realization that the development of a better way of life for the less fortunate in Africa is a step in the right direction for the betterment of our beautiful continent. I encourage funding and sponsorships for educational programmes, resources, and products from government and corporates that decisively impacts the quality of lives in rural communities. Famram Foundation is a family self-funded non-profit organisation. I am instrumental in empowering, uplifting, and providing CSI solutions, enhancing socio-economic development.

I am the former Mrs Johannesburg 2019---definitely a pageant that is beauty with a purpose, owned by the Role Models Foundation. I scooped all the special awards and was the first person in the Role Models Pageantry to receive the Lifetime Achievement Award for raising the most about of funds.

From humble beginnings, I know what it is "not to have". I believe that my purpose is to give back to the impoverished. My philanthropic interests lie in changing lives and making a sustainable difference and an impact, regardless of how small the gesture is. It's all about putting smiles on faces.

As an unstoppable woman of substance, I debuted as an actress in two South African movies.

I was recognized as one of the global Ambassadors by U.S. bestselling author Dr Larita Rice Barnes, for "My Pink Stilettos" a book available on Amazon, that is co-authored by seventeen women from across the globe which was released in October 2020 in view of breast cancer awareness month. My chapter in the book is "Keep on, Keeping on" where I talk about my life as a young widow and single parent, raising two young kids.

With my continuous and admirable work in communities, I earned the "Play Your Part" Ambassadorship for Brand South Africa.

Continually searching for the silver lining and making the best of any situation I find myself in, I started my own talk show

"Red Corner Show" during Covid 19, where real life stories are shared by people from across the globe, focussing on empowerment. Challenging situations and obstacles are a part of life; your story will help others to overcome their challenges, too. For Women's Month 2021 and celebrating the Red Corner Show's first birthday, I am showcasing 31 inspirational women on 31 days in August from across the globe to share their stories of resilience, endurance, and success on my show. This has taken up lots of my time and resources, but there is no better feeling than to sit back and listen to these phenomenal women share their journeys of inspiration to people across the world. To date, over 150 people from across the globe have been featured on my show which is co-hosted by my daughter Daksha Ramjawan.

I am the newly appointed Africa Chairperson for Ladies of All Nations International (LOANI UK), the largest women empowerment platform in the world with a representation in 155 countries. I am the Country Director (South Africa) for the International Youth Society (IYS) with a representation in over 140 countries and is the President of the IYS in South Africa.

As Mahatma Gandhi states: **"The best way to find yourself is to lose yourself in the service of others." This resonates with who I am as a person. I believe that my passion and purpose is to serve those around me.** One of the most common motivational factors I have come across is the desire to give something back and help others. For me it is sense of fulfilment.

Not having the second pair of school socks to wear when I was in high school taught me a lot about not having. I used to go to school wearing my precious pair of socks and get home after school wash it, and if it wasn't dry by the next morning, then I would iron it so that I had socks to wear. Even my friends at school didn't know

that because I was too embarrassed to tell them!

Having worked with communities for over a decade, I realised there was a dire need to research the menstrual cup as a sustainable solution for menstruation because girls in deep rural areas miss school for up to 5 days in a month. Due to unaffordability of sanitary products, girls are leaving their menstrual products for longer than three to four hours which results in infections. I researched menstrual cups for about 2 years, and since they have been around since the 1930's, I felt it was time to create my own brand and introduce it to the market. Early in 2016, I launched my own brand of the menstrual cup, the PrincessD Menstrual Cup. I named the product after my daughter, Daksha, whom I used to call PrincessD from an early age. At first my focus was on rural and impoverished areas, but after launching the product, I found that its's an essential product for girls and women everywhere because it is cost-effective, eco-friendly, and hygienic.

The aim for creating the PrincessD Menstrual Cup, which is reusable for ten years, a "green" alternative to disposable tampons and pads, was to help disadvantaged rural girls, but we found that all girls and women who menstruate are able to benefit from this healthy, hygienic, environmentally friendly, cost-effective, and sustainable solution. Other benefits are they are comfortable for sports such as athletics, cycling, scuba diving, swimming, yoga, dancing, or any type of physical activity as it offers safe, secure, discreet, and leak-free protection for up to twelve hours at a time. It alleviates the embarrassment for schoolgirls from having messy dresses and the school principals love it because it ensures there are no messy toilets or blockages in toilets.

One menstrual cup is equivalent to approximately 3000-5000 sanitary pads/tampons over a 10-year cycle. Take a moment to visualise the landfill chaos (sanitary pads/tampons take approximately 500-700 years to biodegrade). Our combo pack comprises of a menstrual cup and a compact, foldable silicone steriliser cup (only supplier with the compact foldable silicone cup that is safe to use, especially with the younger girls being exposed to boiling water). At the end of the menstrual cycle only 200ml of boiling water (less than one cup) is required per month to sterilize the PrincessD menstrual cup for 15 minutes! In most rural areas girls fetch water from the river, boil it, and then sterilise their cups.

With my extensive humanitarian work across the globe, I am grateful and blessed to have received an Honorary Doctorate in Humanitarianism from the Global International University in the USA. I also received the Lifetime Achievement Award from the President of the United States, Mr Joe Biden. It is awarded for outstanding vision, dedication, and commitment, for my outstanding contributions in making a societal impact in the lives of people not just in South Africa but across the globe. Receiving this award via courier from the USA got me in tears as I could not believe that I was holding a certificate that came from the USA Presidents office and signed by him! I made history---a first for SOUTH AFRICA. Accolades such as these remind me of my persistence and perseverance throughout my journey, mainly as a young widow and single parent.

Not many people will understand what I do or how I do it. Being a single mum, a full time academic, a businesswoman, and a final year doctoral candidate are surely not for the faint-hearted. At times life throws massive curveballs, but I believe in myself, and I believe it's God's doing and God's Plans. God gives the hardest battles to his strongest soldiers.

Some of my accolades in the last 5 years:

2017: Winner of the OWAMI Women's Award. Global Awardee: Centre for Economic & Leadership Development (CELD) :

Global Female Leadership Impact Award 2017 Dubai; Induction: Global Women Leaders Hall of Fame (GWLHOF) Dubai; and featured in the January 2018 special Edition of Amazons Watch Magazine as the Top 100 Most Influential Women to watch in Emerging Economies.

2018: Woman of Stature Awards: Entrepreneur of the Year. Women Economic Forum (WEF) Global Awardee: Iconic Woman Creating a Better World for All in New Delhi, India. Identified as one of South Africa's Top 50 Entrepreneurs to Watch. Rotary Club Paul Harris Fellow Awardee, awarded by the Reservoir Hills Rotary Club. One of forty Honourees for the 7% Tribe Foundation, Steyn City. The only South African Laureate in the Women In Africa (WIA) Summit in Marrakech.

Invited to judge the Elite Miss India/Mrs India Pageant in New Delhi, India and scooped another award as a Global ChangeMaker.

2019: African Leadership Persons' of the Year and induction into the CEO's Hall of Fame. Humanitarian Award at the Miss India Gauteng Pageant. Recognised as the Pan African Awards Most Influential Woman in Business Country Winner in the SME sector of CEO Global. Black Management Forum (BMF) Manager of the Year 2019.

1 of 8 "Thrivors" for Season 1, Real TV Docu-Series (recorded in 8-28 October 2019). The theme "a million dreams for the Win Wins" is right up my alley as I thrive on changing lives. I spent 21 days in a tent, ate plant-based food, fundraising and honouring community projects in Swellendam, Western Cape. The reality show will be released on Netflix in 2021.

2020: Women Appreciating Women (WAW) Honorary Award, London– 1 0f 100 most inspirational women in the world. 100 Successful Women in Business Awardee Global Trade Chamber, Miami, USA. "She Inspires Me" Award by a UK organization.

"The Best Humanitarian" award Els Edification Plus UK. The Red Blazer of Excellence and Achievement Recipient by Mr Carl Wilson from All Women Rock, USA. One of 35 women globally for the prestigious "Crown" award from the USA. One of 30 Influential Women in South Africa. Global Changemaker Award from Ladies of All Nations International (UK).

2021: Princess Peace Award - Future Leaders Entity Egypt/ LOANI UK Appointed as the Country Director South Africa for the International Youth Society (IYS Global). President of the IYS South Africa. 100 Successful Women in Business Awardee Global Trade Chamber GTC (Miami, USA). Included in the book "100 Successful Women Across the World 2021" which has become an Amazon Best Seller. Global Ambassador for the Commonwealth Entrepreneurs Club. Member of the Institute of Global Professionals.

Received the prestigious University of South Africa (Unisa) Annual Award – Significant Achievements Category in August 2021.

I have been selected as one of thirty for the TEDx University of South Africa speakers for the event on the 2 October 2021. TEDx University of South Africa is a full-day event under the theme 'WE DEFINE TOMORROW' being curated by Kudakwashe Mazhetese a TEDx Talk Curator, with an audience of about 350 000 students in the UNISA community. I am ecstatic at this opportunity as there are 34.7 million TED.com subscribers and I envisage that millions will potentially watch my presentation.

The challenging entrepreneurial journey thus far, not forgetting the impact of COVID 19, has been rocky yet extremely humbling at the same time. The specific experiences during this journey cannot be justified briefly, but if I had to mention the highlight, I would say that it is knowing that I am making a positive impact whilst chasing my dreams.

I've learned that people will forget what you said, people will forget what you did, but people will never forget how you made them feel.
Maya Angelou

Contact details:

Email: shamila@famramsolutions.com

Facebook:	https://www.facebook.com/redcornershow
YouTube:	https://www.youtube.com/c/RedCornerShow
Instagram:	https://www.instagram.com/princessdmenstrualcup/?hl=en
	https://www.instagram.com/redcornershow/
Website:	www.princessdmenstrualcup.com
LinkedIn:	https://www.linkedin.com/in/shamila-ramjawan-a9550025/

Dr. Nephetina Serrano

Legacy is True Success
Dr. Nephetina Serrano

The great use of life is to spend it for something that will outlast it. - William James

Living in a world where a pandemic has seemingly changed life forever as we know it, many of us have suffered loss and the longevity of life feels uncertain. The contemplation of life and its true worth and meaning challenges us to reexamine our definitions of success. Why do we do what we do? Is success a thriving career, a happy family, fulfilling health and wellness, and the ability to move financially in this world at leisure? That probably sounds like a pretty good life to most. But when life is all said and done and we face the inevitability of our mortality, we have to examine if our possessions and our experiences on earth will be even remembered when we are gone. How will we live in a way so that after we take our last breaths those who succeed us can carry our torch of purpose and vision, extending our life's meaning into the years to come? We must ask ourselves: "What lasting impact do we want to make in the world?" By answering this question, we began a quest of creating a legacy of success and excellence that far exceeds death. It extends past our finite existence and reaches into the future with hope. Creating legacy is, indeed, true success.

As a woman of God and wife of 32 years, I have overcome many difficulties, challenges, and tragedies, including the more recent loss and sudden deaths of loved ones indirectly due to Covid-19. Building legacy has become more important to me now than ever before. It is absolutely essential for us to determine our purpose and establish success in that purpose while committing to building our legacy. We must be intentional in this quest because tomorrow is not promised.

A great man once said: "The power of a person's life is in the stories they leave behind." Our legacies are not just about what we've created but about the story that we are a part of and share. In truth, we are always part of a bigger narrative. Our story is never just about ourselves. There have always been events, actions, and people who intersect with our stories. Our challenge is to see the larger narrative, recognizing how others have shaped us and how we impact others.

We should not limit the pondering of legacy to old age or when our loved ones die. Every day we should reflect about the meaning of our lives, being intentional to live each minute towards that greater purpose. My life journey forced me to consider legacy at a very young age. Although I grew up in a loving home, the dysfunction of my parents' relationship weighed heavily on my teenage mind. My parents' relationship would later dissolve, but not before I left first. I ran away from home, leaving my last year of high school.

Walking away from being an A student to being a high school dropout was devastating, my goal was to finish high school and go away to college, never to deal with that life again. But things didn't quite happen the way I planned. I needed to secure a healthy space for me to live and be with the wisdom even as a youth to preserve and prioritize my own sanity and well-being. I solemnly promised myself in those low moments of confusion and transition that I would not be a statistic. My life would mean something, ensuring that the next generation that I would impact would not have to endure the hardships I had to survive. After securing my living situation, I wound up going back to school the very next year and finishing. I kept that promise to myself.

It was at this moment I had to make very adult decisions at a time when most youth my age were celebrating their impending independence, only starting to scratch the surface of their ultimate vision of life. I had to decide in those moments what legacy I wanted to establish on the earth. Who was I? Who was I to become? What did I have to do to survive and ensure that I was not labeled just another at-risk teen with a bleak and pre-determined fate? Renowned speaker Steve Saint says, "Your story is the greatest legacy that you will leave to your friends. It's the longest lasting legacy you will leave to your heirs." At a tender age, I had to direct my choices towards who I wanted to be on the earth and how I wanted to be remembered.

Being a teen who worked to support herself while going to school wasn't easy either. However, I persevered and was rewarded with opportunities for doing so. I had already started working at the early age of fourteen with the Philadelphia Mayoral Summer Youth Program. After that, there weren't many jobs that I didn't get on a first interview. My gift of articulation that I was once teased for by my peers, would actually take me far. From there, my first job was an assistant secretary position in the Counseling and Psychology Department of the elite University of Pennsylvania's Wharton School of Business. I built a life, step by step, brick by brick, of serving others, developing my skills and gifts and delivering those gifts in excellence. Years later, full circle, I am a now Dr. Nephetina Serrano, certified Marriage Counselor, Empowerment Speaker, and International Best-Selling Author, 4x Amazon Best Seller, Certified Counselor (NBCA) Mentor, Relationship Expert and Certified Life Coach.

I have been able to break generational curses of dysfunctional marriage with my husband of over thirty years, Dr. Richard Serrano. We both are co-founders of Covenant Marriages, Covenant Rescue 911, and Covenant Marriages Institute. We support couples in crisis and transitional phases within their marriage to achieve balance and stability in life and in business through Biblical principles. We also co-host "Your Marriage Matters" on Dominion TV which has aired in over 35 countries around the globe. In addition, we hosted the RISE Up Series airing via Zoom and streaming LIVE on Facebook. We went on to co-author the book, The Marriage Corporation which highlights the organizational needs of a covenant marriage.

I am the Publisher of Marriage CEO Magazine, a publication tailored to meet the relationship needs of couples, especially those leaders in the community, marketplace, and ministry. I am also co-author of and contributor to *Make It Happen, When Doves Cry: "Stories that Heal," The Price of Greatness, No Matter What You Can Make It* and the *RISE UP Women Who Lead Building Legacy Anthology*.

I have received many awards and certificates, including The City Council of Philadelphia Citation, recognizing my contribution to women. I have also received awards from The Echoes of Africa, The Mayor's Commission on African and Caribbean Immigrant Affairs, Women of Wealth, Publishers Golden Eagle Award, and ACHI Magazine's Woman of Inspiration. I was named one of Success Magazine's 100 Best Life Coaches in 2021. I also received both the California Senate's Recognition and Legislature Assembly Game Changer Award. In addition, I was awarded The Assembly Member 61st District Jose Medina 2021 County of Riverside Influencer Award. Most recently, I was recognized for Mentorship at The Lady in Blue Sapphire Awards of GSFE by Robbie Motter.

I have a life rich with accomplishments and honors--a life of pouring into others so that they experience success in their endeavors and relationships because I dared to commit to the legacy I envisioned. However, establishing a legacy of success is not just about the accomplishments and honors that one receives. It is not merely about money and assets as much as it is about you, your life, your impact in the world, the lessons you have learned, and sharing your personal story. It is about the people that we are able to truly invest in and touch during our journey. I recognize that I am and have always been a part of the bigger narrative. One day, the challenges I have had to overcome will be a source of inspiration to someone who feels the odds are stacked against them but still has the audacity to build their vision by any means necessary.

Here are 7 Key Steps in Establishing Success by Building Legacy:

1. Get clear on the woman in the mirror and what impact you want to make in this world.

My moment of clarity began when I was a young teen forced to provide for herself, find a place to live, and defy the odds stacked against my favor. Until you are clear on what you would like your legacy to be, you cannot start building it. Stop wasting time and start to build! Establishing success in this area is not something you happen upon, rather you must be intentional and understand your why.

2. Begin building your legacy today. Tomorrow is not promised; our days are numbered.

We must start now as we have seen in the most recent decade, time waits for no one and none of us know when we will cease to be no more. Start a family tree. Even begin writing out traditions so your family does not lose sight of the ties that bind you all together. What do you want your family, friends, and world to know about you? What words of wisdom, recipes, or experiences do you want to share that may encourage, uplift, or inspire the next generation in this lifetime?

3. Seek opportunities to serve others.

Part of our purpose on this earth is to serve one another.

Serving helps to build up others. Remember, you matter, your life matters, and what you do for others matters.

4. Discover creative ways to make a difference in this life, making the world a better place.

None of us are perfect. Oftentimes we experience failure along our journey; however, we don't allow those failures to get in the way of our success. We take the fall, but we get back up. We become the change we desire and the hope we need, first for ourselves and then for others.

5. Develop your skills. Find 2-3 things you're good at and explore them.

What are those things that you find yourself doing relentlessly without thought that bring you joy? It could be making pies for your neighbors, feeding the hungry, fostering children, teaching self-care seminars, coaching, mentoring youth, etc. Do those things.

6. Be the change that you are looking for by sharing love and kindness and providing hope to others.

Everyone needs to know he/she is not alone. We must inspire hope in knowing that no matter what, we can and will overcome any obstacles.

7. Never stop believing in the POWER of ONE.

It takes one person to make a difference. So why not be the ONE? Don't be afraid of those times when you must stand alone to establish your legacy. You can eventually find your tribe that will inspire you in your journey.

I hold my head high knowing that my legacy of excellence is established in the world to be a beacon of hope for the next generation and inspire them to be successful in their own right on their own terms. You, yes you, can make a difference in this world and in this life, here and now. See where you are making the most impact in life and do that more. This is true success. We influence people every day by what we say, do, write, create, and share. And all that influence adds up. It took overcoming and enduring many of life's ups and downs, victories, and hardships to be able to find my purpose, define my own version of success, and establish my personalized legacy of success on the earth. I share that with you so that you can do the same. May we use the power of our lives for the lasting good of those we touch to further impact our families, communities, and the world. Remember, Legacy is true success.

Dr. Nephetina L. Serrano
Relationship Expert
The Marriage CEO ™

Dr. Nephetina L. Serrano is an Evangelist, International Empowerment Speaker, Marriage Counselor,

Co-founder of Covenant Marriages, Covenant Rescue 911, and Covenant Marriages Institute. She supports couples in crisis and transitional phases within their marriage to achieve balance and stability in life and in business through Biblical principles. Dr. Nephetina and husband Dr. Richard Serrano Co-host "Your Marriage Matters" on Dominion TV in over 35 countries around the globe. Host the RISE UP Series airs via Zoom and Streaming LIVE on Facebook.

She co-authored the book, THE MARRIAGE CORPORATION which highlights the organizational needs of a covenant marriage. She is the Publisher of Marriage CEO Magazine, "For the Entrepreneur Who Leads, Building Legacy" a publication tailored to meet the relationship needs of couples especially those in leadership positions in the community, in the marketplace and ministry.

Dr. Serrano has received many awards and certificates including; City Council of the City of Philadelphia CITATION honoring and recognizing her contribution to women. The Echoes of Africa, The Mayor's Commission on African and Caribbean Immigrant affairs, Women of Wealth, "Publishers Golden Eagle Award" ACHI Magazine Woman of Inspiration Award 2019. Success Magazine named her as one of the 100 Best Life Coaches 2021, State of California SENATE Recognition in honor of GSFE Senator Richard D. Roth 31st District, California Legislature Assembly Game Changer Award, Assembly Member 61st District Jose Medina 2021, County of Riverside Influencer Award and more.

DR. NEPHETINA L. SERRANO
www.marriageCEOs360.com
DrSerranoministries@gmail.com
116 BALA AVE, SUITE 1B, BALA CYNWYD, PA 19004

Renee Huffman

I AM A CHAMPION!
By Renee Huffman

I learned early in life at a young age that I was born from a mother who battled mental illness and a father who suffers from a learning disability since his childhood. This created a lot of obstacles and roadblocks for my journey ahead. But I've always been a staunch type of person who strives to be the best in all aspects of my life. With a vigorous determination and strong faith in God, nothing is impossible to accomplish under his authority. In life we are presented with harsh multifarious of events, and I've discovered your reaction and response will determine how great you can become. Life is ten percent what you experience and ninety percent how you respond to it. Everyone is bestowed with a deck of cards, but the unknowing if a good or bad card is next is the mystery yet to unfold.

My mother was diagnosed with bipolar disorder, but she was determined to keep her children in church, greatly teaching us to have a forgiving heart and never to give up. Having a mother with a high caliber determination richly configured the woman I am today.

My memory flashes back to high school with me having a brilliant mind and wanting to excel, but I thought and learned differently from my classmates. As hard as I tried, my grades would always manage to average C's instead of A's that I tried so desperately to get. This brings me to the story of "There are more than one way to climb a tree." One day a fish, monkey, dog, penguin, and elephant show up for a race on land. Automatically the dog would win the race because it's within his element. Does this make everyone else slow or dumb? The answer would be no because if the race was in a tree, the monkey would win; if the race was under water, the fish would win. This is a great example of how each person responds and learns differently in life and how our school system needs a revamp to assist all students. I love the quote by Albert Einstein, "Everybody is a genius. But if you judge a fish by its ability to climb a tree, it will live its whole life believing that it is stupid."

I distinctively started to think differently and started to embrace every grade I received--good or bad. During my senior year of high school, I entered a writing contest to win a $10,000.00 scholarship for the first two years of college with Price Club Foundation (Now Price Philanthropies Foundation to help the community of City Heights, located in inner city of San Diego, California. The Founder Sol Price believed in utilizing his wealth to give back to the community and provide better opportunities for the working class). I was committed to being the first in my immediate family to go to college. I wrote my paper with my heart and eyes on my destiny and submitted my entry for the scholarship. Weeks elapsed, and I finally received the good news that I was chosen out of 100 stories to be a part of the Price Club Foundation family. This was a great accomplishment. Regardless of how hard your uneven road or path maybe, it's your road to show up and grind your way to greatness.

Some people assumed I would finish in last place in my life. But I'm adamant and decided to crawl, walk, jog, and run until I reached my finish line. I'm not in competition with the world but focused to win the race at my own momentum. My personal life quote is "Stay in Your Lane OR Be Disqualified." This why Dressed N Dignity is so important to our community because we help women who have different strides but the same goal (FINISH). Women can take heed to my story and decide to never give up and be all they dreamed to be.

I've worked in Corporate America for twenty years. I remember during my senior year in high school (21 years ago), a non-profit organization by the name of Dress for Success came to my school campus to help young women to transition from high school into workforce; they showed us how to select proper suit attire and colors and hair styles and to implement necessary accessories to enhance our looks. I am forever grateful for Dress for Success for providing me with the necessary tools to be successful in my career. Fast forward 21 years later, a young lady was inquiring about clothing to wear on an interview, but the nearest location for clothing was fifty miles away. In that moment I discovered there was a need in my local community, and I encompassed the tools to navigate and organize a non-profit to help women who need professional business attire, communication skills, resume building, interviewing tips, and business etiquette training. I decided to form Dressed N Dignity and place it within a 25-mile radius of any city within the Dallas-Ft. Worth area to shorten the commute for women who are currently looking for employment.

Dressed N' Dignity is non-profit organization established in the fall of 2017. Our mission statement is to restore and empower women to walk in excellences in business, community, and family life, providing adequate dress attire, communication skills, and necessary etiquette training. Our vision statement is set forth to transform and enhance the lives of each woman as she becomes a mirror that reflects the next generation. Since the existence of Dressed N Dignity, I'm extremely thankful and proud to say we have professionally made-over multiple women and transformed their lives by planting seeds of hope. During the spring of each year, we have our annual women's business conference; this year's theme was B.O.S.S Born Only to Strive Successfully. We also have a brunch during the winter called Restore Her Dignity; this year's theme is Restore Her Love Dec 14th, 2019. All our events present dynamic local speakers of the community who help the women of dignity to strive and thrive to be all they can be. We also have successful entrepreneurs to join the ladies at the table during our brunch to give business advice and encouragement.

These ladies by my term are called Sister Angels.

Since 2019 I have become a full-time entrepreneur. I'm the publisher of Women of Dignity Magazine and the publisher of books (Cover in Dignity Publishing).

I will leave you with my life quote: "Stay in Your Lane or Be Disqualified!"

Ilona Parunakova

Unleashing your Dreams through the power of Identity

By Ilona Parunakova

Every single girl in the competitive and brusque world we live is bombarded with the fairy tale fantasy of princes and princesses which the media and the world has shown her. This fantasy and false image disconnect us from the naturally innocent heart we are born with. The danger is as girls and women, we become obsessed with these false images and dreams, and we are eager to share with everyone around us; they become our hope for a better life but are actually a dangerous disruption that takes us away from our true identity.

I myself grew up wanting to fit into the role of Cinderella—the marvelous, elegant sweetheart everyone fell in love with at the ballroom party. I remember feeling excited when I imagined myself wearing an exquisite couture dress tailored just for me as Cinderella had worn. In our imagination we are superheroes who are the most important and valuable star of the story—our life story with the ability to shape-shift into any dream character we can imagine in our minds—and I was this in my mind. These dreams keep us intrigued because in our mind we can change them into anything, we can be anything, and always keep the final ending at bay, which relieves us of responsibility.

There was absolutely nothing in my life that held any possibility for me to be that Cinderella character. Nothing in a million years. It was only a fairy tale, especially living in a war-torn country. After our country had experienced the collapse of the Soviet Union, there was an unbearable aftermath from the impact. During those hard times, I missed the days I could turn on the TV and grab a cup of tea and settle in for an evening of comfort and warmth. Winter was usually the perfect time I could embrace this mood of coziness, a season that was filled with warm sweaters and snuggling in front of the TV enjoying Brazilian soap operas. I longed for those times that were marked with peace and happiness. Now our days were filled with strife and hardship.

In early September of 1997 my friends and I noticed the flyer on school's entrance door. It read *"Armenian Diaspora is hosting their first Beauty Pageant in Georgia. Anyone who wishes to enroll may stop at our office for the preliminary casting."* This began my journey entering a beauty pageant. I was on fire! I was also nervous.: 'Am I good enough?' This negative self-talk occupied my mind as I prepared to hear the words of rejection, 'You didn't make it." Instead, I did make it, through one cut and then another. Once in the Beauty Pageant I even became the People's Choice winner. The prize I received was a free trip to my Fatherland, Armenia. I was also given a bodyguard and private driver and had access to a personal jet. This was my Cinderella moment! It was also a turning point in my life.

Our lives consist of many small steps, each which always lead to something more. 'Perhaps I just have to move my feet and make a leap of faith, no matter how insignificant,' we can say to ourselves in those moments of fear if we remember to *always follow the call of our heart, which is God's heart when we tune in.*

During the Beauty Pageant, I returned to the childhood dream: I wanted to hear someone tell me just once, 'You are *breathtaking!*' At least once in my life I wanted to be pampered, spoiled, and the center of attention, just like Cinderella. Considering I had grown up during the war, I did not feel selfish, ambitious, or arrogant with these desires and thoughts. For the first time I wanted to really celebrate me and who I could be. I wanted to strive for something that felt purposeful, and this beauty pageant was that. I wanted to grow the flame within myself that made me get out of bed every morning. I wanted to feel a sense of accomplishment, and I did.

Sometimes we can turn what begins as an idea or false image into something magical and true. Sometimes what we dream—or what someone else dreams—can become our dream that we can birth into reality. When we do, we feel proud, especially when we look back and see all that we have accomplished—and as always with God by our side. Luke 11:9 reminds us: 'And I tell you, ask, and it will be given to you; seek, and you will find; know, and it will be opened to you.' Our dreams hold value, and when we see them as that, they become extensions of us. In this way our dreams intersect with our identity, especially when we do not give up. It takes courage, but we can achieve what we want even when it may cost us time or a false reputation, image, or status we have held onto. It is urgent we learn to follow our dreams. It is imperative we listen to God's call because it may be His whisper that is pointing us to dreams which we are afraid to go after and fulfill. It may be just what God wants for us.

Many times, on our journey to creating our dreams, we fall into the one thing that can stop us the most—the trap of low self-worth. We may assess ourselves from the positions of 'I am nothing,' 'I can't do anything,' or 'I am not as good or beautiful as she'. Some of us develop low self-esteem from childhood or from how our parents had treated us. Low self-esteem can manifest at any age. That is why it is important for us to work on improving it.

The fallen world we live in does not immediately value internal qualities and beauty and instead promotes broken and damaged images that are made up of external qualities that give pleasure to the eyes with seductive stunner looks. The world has figured out how to take advantage of the fallen sinful nature of humankind by making a profit out of the external images it has created. Where is the industry or institution that is willing to take on the role and responsibility to develop the self-admiration and confidence that the girls and boys in our world need? Where is the school our youth can attend that will teach them the importance and truth of our inner spirit and show them how prayer is one way to discover this?

Every day of our lives we must make choices, and there is no guarantee our choice will be the right one; sometimes the choices we make lead us down roads we do not desire. In those moments of adversity, it is important to ask ourselves what we can do to refocus our attention from the pain we feel and rekindle our joy—what can we do to come back to self-confidence? This begins in our hearts and in God's heart, which is brought home to us in Mathew 10:30: 'Fear not, therefore; you are of more value than many sparrows.' God believes in us, and when we believe in Him, all self-doubt can wash away.

When I was young, and before I found my strength in my faith, my mom was an instrumental force of encouragement and support during my hard times. What an amazing woman of God! I will always be grateful to her. Sometimes, we need support not only from God but also from the people we love who care about us.

I still question why I continue to attack my own self-esteem. Of course, I grew up being called 'ugly' by my relatives since I did not resemble them (Armenians), which affects me still to this day. Now I am working on breaking this bad habit of negative self-talk. Prayer does help and brings me back to the truth of my soul. When I read the word of God as it states in Song of Solomon 4:7: 'You are altogether beautiful, my love; there is no flaw in you.' Then I feel re-energized and reconfirmed in my strength and confidence. The gauge of our self-esteem affects our lives, and our level of well-being and happiness affects the way we perceive ourselves.

It is rarely possible to experience true happiness and joy when we are coming from low self-esteem, and the reasons why our low self-esteem shows up are very diverse. When I am in my feelings of low self-esteem, I am also feeling my own insignificance. Instead, we judge ourselves, and when we do, it is most urgent that we pull upon our faith and turn to the heart of God. As it says in 1 Samuel 16:7: 'But the LORD said to Samuel, "Do not look on his appearance or on the height of his stature, because I have rejected him." For the LORD sees not as man sees: Man looks on the outward appearance, but the LORD looks on the heart.'

My biggest realization is that when we are in low self-esteem, we often miss opportunities life has to offer us. We are not living to our fullest potential God intended for us. In this sense, one can say we may not even be honoring God. Is it possible for a person with low self-esteem to reach some heights in their life? It is although it is rare. Usually when someone is suffering from low confidence, they would rather keep their dreams as only 'dreams' and 'desires' than make an effort to turn them into reality.

If we treat ourselves as a little thing, unable to achieve anything and do nothing, we will not be able to jump above our heads and our thoughts that we are insignificant and not worthy of success. We may think that other people are happier and more fortunate than we are. Yet the only difference may be that people with healthy confidence are always striving to go beyond their capacity, to stretch their limitations, while a person with low self-esteem will draw conclusions about themselves and their life without doing anything or accomplishing.

Some may say it is better to have an inflated self-esteem than an understatement of low self-confidence. Of course, neither extreme is a true source of happiness, but when someone has inflated self-esteem rather than low self-esteem, they do have one advantage: an arrogant person achieves success in at least something while a person who considers himself insignificant usually does not achieve much, if anything, and thus may experience a general lack of happiness in their life.

Ultimately, our essence is not limited by any rules; every day is a new opportunity to create something new and to learn about ourselves something we were previously unaware of. We have come into this world to develop and create moments of happiness for ourselves, so it is important for us not to listen to the inner voice we may hear at times that tells us we are wrong, or that we are a fool who will not succeed. We cannot achieve authentic success by noticing only our shortcomings. The more we fixate on our flaws and weaknesses, the greater they seem to become.

The truth is every emotion we feel, every obstacle or closed door we encounter and every moment of weakness and doubt we experience will eventually become a thing of the past. All we can do is move forward in our faith. I have placed my past and struggle behind me, and now all I see is a future that I create. As we create our future, God stands beside us. In Ephesians 2:6 we learn that 'we are seated with Christ in heavenly places.' Knowing these awesome truths and living them will change the way we see ourselves and how we respond to different situations. Our circumstances may change but who we are truly remains forever the same. Our identity is eternally secure in Christ.

The main thing is for us never to forget who we are and who we want to be because we can still become what we dream of becoming. Dreams are not cheap; they are priceless. They are our most voluble possession, and they are uniquely and exclusively designed for us.

No one, *not one single person other than ourselves*—unless we give them the power to do so—is capable of taking our dreams away as it is only our responsibility to see ourselves as God does through His eyes.

Discovering Identity is the heart of my life journey. If you experience disappointments and setbacks, if you do not have a job or failed at an important task or have bad credit, it doesn't mean you have to be poor in spirit or live without identity. It does not mean your life is over. It can become your identity and is one of the biggest vacuums for joy.

I made my mission to empower one soul to truly know his/her own value and purpose of life. This is my dream to share wisdom, experience, and ideas, and inspire people to make a difference. It speaks to the warriors, the survivors, the determined, and bankrupt in spirit. I want this message to bring something valuable to whoever needs to hear it and change his/her life for the better.

Protecting our identity is like protecting our freedom. How do we find identity when it seems lost, so we can tend it and nurture it?

I   ***True identity is formed in the midst of our toughest challenges*** – the minute life feels tough, that is when we begin our journey to take back our power we have given away.

II ***Identity begins with hope***—not a static hope but a hope propelled by action. Map out your next step and then have the patience to see what shows up.

III ***Perseverance is priceless.*** Too often, we give up before joy of identity has a chance to take hold of us. If we take that one more step or action beyond what we believe we are capable of, then strength appears, and suddenly, we are propelled forward again.

I want to inspire people to make a difference. Whether you are a warrior, a survivor, have a determined or bankrupt spirit, my hope is to bring you something valuable, and I hope it can change your life for the better.

Through my journey what I've discovered is that when we hold God's hand and allow him to fill us with the strength to overcome what we believe are insurmountable obstacles—when we push through in faith, no matter how hard it may feel, we crack something open inside of ourselves where our hearts open, and our dreams can truly come alive.

If I could write a slogan in a public place, it would sound like this: "Do not build your identity on anyone's opinion. Know who you are. You are God's Masterpiece."

Madeleine Wober

"LIVING MAGICALLY"
by *Madeleine P Wober,*
aka Maddie Sparkles, America's Scottish Sparkle

Success is having big dreams and taking steps towards them without one thought of doubt or disbelief and having those dreams come true.

Success is having a focused and positive mindset. It's about the way we view ourselves, others, and the world. It's learning from our mistakes instead of feeling failure. It's knowing every challenge presents us with a gift if we stay open-minded, discerning, and grateful.

Many quotes have inspired me over the years and kept me on track for success, for example, "Leap and the net will appear" (John Burroughs). There have been many times when I have felt paralyzed with fear because I knew with every fiber of my being that I HAD to take the obvious next step even though it was excruciatingly terrifying.

Every time I took the risk, it paid off and made me feel extremely confident, resilient, and invincible. I have an intense fear of heights, so when I mustered up the immense courage to do the famous AJ Hackett Bungy Jump off the Kawarau Bridge in Queenstown, New Zealand, I felt as if I could do anything! Did my fear of heights vanish? Not at all, but to this day, I still feel proud of myself for accomplishing this feat and living to tell the tale!

Seven years ago in 2014, I was visiting San Francisco, and I decided not to take my connecting flight home at the last minute, forfeiting my return flight to the UK with only £100 left in my checking account. As a result of taking this risk, I ended up crossing paths with a woman who sponsored me to work and eventually live in America---my lifelong dream.

Daring choices open incredible doors of opportunity and give us the strength to trust our intuition.

I share these personal stories with you because just like you, I am a spiritual being having a human experience. Sometimes we need to experience great discomfort to give us that nudge forward in the direction of our dreams. When we have faith, our energy and path lead to meaningful coincidences, or 'serendipities'. I truly don't believe in coincidence. I know I am meant to meet certain people and be in certain places. Divine timing is never in my control.

Here's an example about the light-hearted movie "SERENDIPITY" starring John Cusack and Kate Beckinsale. Living in Hove, England, in 2013, preparing to close that chapter of my life, I was still obsessed with my childhood dream of living in New York City or California, trying to figure out how this would ever happen, and this movie came on TV. It was all about chance meetings and happy accidents, and New York City was one of the movie's greatest characters. I was waiting for the guy from the Salvation Army to drive over and accept my beautiful oak table as a donation. As I watched the credits roll up on the screen, I waited to see the name of the person that wrote this amazing screenplay 'Serendipity'; it was a screenwriter called Marc Klein. I said aloud to myself, "I'd LOVE to meet this guy someday!"

Moments later, my doorbell rang. It was the guy from the charity shop to collect my table. As he was leaving, I asked him what his name was. He said, "Oh I should've introduced myself. I'm Marc, Marc Klein!". I gasped in disbelief, "Marc Klein? Do you spell your first name with a 'C' or a 'K'!?". He replied, "Marc with a 'C". He had the EXACT same name as the screenwriter I was fantasizing about meeting only minutes earlier. This was SERENDIPITY at its best and a real sign for me. Six months later, I'd been offered a job and was living in California.

I mention 'signs' because while we are on our path to success, we can do everything in our power to make things happen, and they still may not. It has been my practice to do all the things I can, and then let go of the outcome, trusting what is for me won't go by me, and since we all have a Guardian Angel, we all have the ability to tune in to these signs or messages that point us in the right direction and whisper to us to continue

Success to me is being creative, productive, following my joy, and collaborating with like-minded people. I love this quote I heard from one of my mentors, and it has worked for me, so I'm passing it on to you. You don't have to believe in yourself 100%. Not even 80%. All you need is 51%, a little more than halfway, to take your first step towards success.

Sometimes things happen that are out of our control, and at the time it seems like a disaster or a roadblock, but I'm sure you get by now (if you're still reading) that everything is working out for your highest good. As a result of *seeming* obstacles, we are often forced to take a step back and reflect where we are in life, versus where we want to be.

During the Pandemic, I wanted to find a way to share positive energy and help others feel more uplifted and less alone. So, I asked myself, "How can I make the best use of my time?", "What can I do to be of the greatest service to the world right now with the innate gifts and skills that I have in order to make a real difference in peoples' lives at this time?"

After meditating on this, one day the answer came from my Guardian Angel. "Combine all your skills from Coaching and Corporate relations with your love of Spirituality and offer Angel readings for people". For many years I had been connecting with and guided by the angels, and even though I didn't discuss this with anyone, it always brought me the exact answers I needed together with a feeling of freedom and relief and belief.

I am repeatedly blown away by the messages that come through during the Angel/Oracle card readings. The angels always give the person the exact message they need to hear that moment. My clients are constantly sharing the most wonderful testimonials that are incredibly humbling, and I have been able to share these globally, online, which has led to the MADDIE SPARKLES.com brand, and website, having a much bigger platform than I ever thought possible. I am growing all the time, introducing new Oracle decks into my readings. I started with 2 decks of cards and now I have 43!

Success is feeling fulfilled when I am being of service and feeling confident in my ability to make a positive difference. Getting paid to be me feels fantastic!

Success also comes to us energetically from creating a healthy living environment, surrounded by nature and free from toxic energy. I live with my fiancé, and we have had to negotiate and navigate our living space in order for each of us to tap into being creatively productive and feeling inspired, even during the lockdown. Having a feeling of gratitude and respect for one another is a huge piece of the puzzle for feeling in flow while moving forward on the path to success.

Whenever we are starting a business or a new endeavor it will bring up our greatest fears, our saboteurs will kick in telling us why we cannot do it. But here are 5 tips for you that will hopefully inspire you to do it anyway!

1. **Share Your Passion**

What you are about to do is going to bring more peace, joy, and inspiration than you could ever imagine to every single person you share your message, product, or service with. Your message is much bigger than you. Don't make this about you; this is about being of service and sharing your unique expression with the world. Another one of my favorite quotes is by Martha Graham, the New York Dancer. She sums it up perfectly in this quote: *"There is a vitality, a life force, an energy, a quickening that is translated through you into action, and because there is only one of you in all of time, this expression is unique. And if you block it, it will never exist through any other medium and it will be lost. The world will not have it. It is not your business to determine how good it is nor how valuable nor how it compares with other expressions. It is your business to keep it yours clearly and directly, to keep the channel open. You do not even have to believe in yourself or your work. You have to keep yourself open and aware to the urges that motivate you. Keep the channel open. ... No artist is pleased. [There is] no satisfaction whatever at any time. There is only a queer divine dissatisfaction, a blessed unrest that keeps us marching and makes us more alive than the others."* (From The Life and Work of Martha Graham (1991).

2. Release Doubt

When you start to doubt yourself, know this is your ego talking, filling you with Imposter Syndrome, but it's not the truth of who you are. We all have days where we question ourselves, but this is just part of the human experience. I have taught myself and others to speak to that voice when it pops up, and say *"Hi Ego, I've been listening to you for most of my life, and while you helped keep me safe then, now you are only hindering me and preventing me from moving forward and sharing my unique gifts with the world. So, I'm going to send you on a vacation to Barbados for 2 years. Have fun. I'll catch up with you sometime in the future. In the meantime, I've got work to do!"* – it works when we separate ourselves from that destructive inner voice telling us we can't do something.

3. Commit to Self-Care

Always make time for Self Care to avoid burnout. Very often when we are in the corporate world and/or service industries - sales executives, coaches, nurses, doctors, counselors, healers, etc., we can be so focused on healing and helping others and achieving our goals, we often forget to take care of ourselves and can burn out. I really had to set boundaries for myself because I didn't want to say 'NO' to anyone, forgetting that my health and needs are just as important as anyone else's. If I don't take care of myself, I won't be any use to anyone. It reminds me of the oxygen mask on a plane analogy: fill yourself up first, so that you can help even more people and for a longer period. It is perfectly acceptable to take time to rest, relax and rejuvenate, and take naps if needed without feeling guilty.

4. Believe It BEFORE You See It

Often when we are starting something new and very close to our heart, we can think, "Is this possible?" I asked myself, *"Can I make a living doing something I truly love?"* The answer, of course, is YES! We all come here with our own gifts to share, and while there may be many others doing the same thing, we are all offering it in our unique way. Every time I have had a goal no matter how big or small, it has been the intention and the power of visualization that has brought it into fruition. By creating a vision board and repeating affirmations daily, it's not a matter of 'IF', it's a matter of 'WHEN', and it's usually not on my timing, it's on the Universe's timing, and all I need to do is learn to trust that timing and get out of my own way. Before long the thing you have been visualizing will manifest. I used this technique while I was waiting for my Green Card. I created a digital vision board on my iPhone with words, pictures, and music. Eventually, all I needed to hear was that piece of music, and in my mind, my vision was already a reality. I also had a vision for years that I would be running my Living Magically retreats globally, and this year, I heard from the owner of La Belle Sabbioneta, Jo Wiehler, who offered me the opportunity to run my retreat in Italy for 5 weeks! Another huge WIN!

5. Celebrate Your Wins

Speaking of WINS, when your projects begin building momentum and you feel extremely proud of yourself, this is great news! Don't keep quiet about it. Celebrate yourself and let everyone know. This is a wonderful way to model leadership if you do this humbly and gratefully. I was always brought up not to toot my own horn, and when I finally published my Inspirational Poetry Book, my programming was telling me to stay quiet and not 'boast' about it. I decided to ignore that untruth, and I posted a video on Facebook sharing about how proud I was that I had reached this milestone. I did feel vulnerable but also liberated and immensely happy, especially when all the supportive comments started rolling in.

It has also permitted others to do the same. When you hear of great news and success about another person, it is a sign for you, telling you that you can do it too! Remember 'celebrating' yourself and 'boasting' are two completely different things.

Success is combining mind/body/soul. I have a plethora of experience with mental wellness, having suffered from chronic anxiety, debilitating panic attacks, and severe depression which led to suicidal thoughts in my mid 20's. A decade later I discovered I had Ovarian Cancer in my mid 30's, and more recently I was diagnosed with MS (multiple sclerosis) in my mid 40's. As a result of 3 decades of health challenges, I am deeply committed to my morning prayers and meditation and feel so blessed to have the health that I do have.

Success is having a positive outlook no matter what cards you have been dealt. It is about bringing good to everyone who crosses your path. Being my authentic self and doing the things I love to do, allows me to walk the talk, share the love, and be of service. Sharing love, light and joy, and hope, this is what I am here to do in the world.

It's about releasing all your fears, stepping into your full power and, living your most magical life by allowing yourself to feel divinely guided and appreciate the full abundance and flow of the universe!

What are you here to do in the world? If you feel inspired to do the things you truly love and you follow those urges with even a little bit of faith, you will find that success comes your way.

I can't think of a better, healthier, and more successful way to live life. Can you?

Amelia Johnson

Shy Gentle Spirit ... becomes ...
Care Giving Leader and Warrior
By Amelia C. Johnson

My name is Amelia C. Johnson, I was born in Angeles City in the Philippines. It is funny how I ended up in the "City of Angels" again but in Los Angeles, California. My hard working and loving parents are Lucina Cunanan and Victorino Cunanan. I have seven siblings four girls and three boys; I am third to the youngest.

I don't remember much of my childhood playing or having friends while in the Philippines like most children here in America. My memories are those of mostly working to help support my family at a very young age. Our family and my siblings never had time for fun or friends---just long hours of hard work. I still have some fond memories of working and helping out my mom at the Karinderyá, which is what we call a food court in the United States.

Soon after, my family began falling on hard times we lost our home; we were in great need of help. I remember my grandmother Ursula opening her home to my family, so that we would have a place to live, and we could all be together while my parents were getting back on their feet. We lived in a small single room for quite some time.

At the age of twelve, I started working with my aunt in a marketplace selling produce like vegetables. It was a great learning experience for me. I helped wherever I could and even worked harder helping my aunt's business to become a success. Later, I decided I was going to pursue a business of my own and have my own table at the market and help my family myself. I became the breadwinner for the family with only determination and an eighth-grade education. Every day I would make sure that I brought home enough food to put on the table for my family.

Unfortunately, our family was divided in order to survive, so we became distant and weren't able to see each other as often because of the long hours of work we had to put in every day. The struggle took its' toll on my parents and me.

My education was limited, but I do remember that I enjoyed math, which I excelled in, and it was a great asset for me in the business. When asked about memories of fun things or happy times growing up, I can only remember the struggles of hard work and very hard life for me and my family. My parents never really had time to play with the children because there was always work that needed to be completed to survive

At the age of sixteen I decided I needed a change of pace, and I went to work at a textile store. It was a great learning experience I learned to speak English. I developed a love for fashion; it was a self-awakening experience.

At the age of twenty-one, I met my future husband who was in the United States Air Force and stationed at Clark Air force base in the Philippines at the time. After two months of courtship, we decided to get married. In 1976, the United States Air Force transferred and stationed my husband to England Air Force Base, Louisiana, United States. It was a big adjustment for me to be in another country and for me to live in this new life and new role as a wife in America.

I soon found out what "military life" was about, but I adjusted well. While stationed there, I gave birth to my firstborn son. We then moved to Beale Air Force Base, California, and two years later I gave birth to my daughter.

In 1983, we were stationed back to Clark Air force base in the Philippines, which was good for me because it allowed me to see and spend time with my family again. I thank my mom for her beautiful smile, her sweetness, and gentle spirit. My mom was also very personable. After all the hardships and suffering my mom went through throughout her life, my mom's story does have a happy ending. She ended up starting her own business with only one chicken and ended up turning that business into a multi-million-dollar business in the Philippines called "Aling-Lucing-Sisig" The Sisig Queen, you may have heard of this already. It turns out that a famous traveling Master Chef, the late Anthony Bourdain, heard about the Famous "Aling Lucing Sisig" and visited her thriving restaurant and ended up filming a cooking episode with her and promoted her chain of restaurants around the world.

"Anthony Michael Bourdain was an American chef, book author, journalist, and travel documentarian who starred in programs focusing on the exploration of international culture, cuisine, and the human condition.") You can view "The Best Sisig" at https://www.youtube.com/watch?v=h57Pj_1ZDfl

A lot of famous stars came to visit; she was on talk show appearances and a lot of television shows. The big highlight was when President Rodrigo Duterte of the Philippines came to visit with all his officials and other former Presidents has visited as well.

The business has been handed down to her grandchildren and future generations and has franchising opportunities to other entrepreneurs.

It was good to see that things were getting better for them. While stationed at Clark Air force base, I was able to volunteer at the hospital as a Red Cross Volunteer in the hospital pharmacy.

In 1986 we ended up being stationed back to the United States to Edwards Air Force Base, California. I began working as a cashier at the Dining Facility and was soon promoted to a supervisor position. During this time a new contracted company was taking over to run the dining facility. It was a stressful time not knowing if any of us still had a job. I was informed later that there was a position open in the office as a receptionist, and one of the managers stated it might be offered to me, but not confirmed, when the new company stepped in. I just took my belongings and moved myself and my work to the office.

While reminiscing about my past work history and work ethic, I really have to say that I owe a lot to Mr. Willie Jones who is the Vice President of the Operation of KASS Management; he saw the great potential in me as I worked my way up the ranks with integrity and skill. Mr. Jones became my mentor, and throughout my career he always admired my attitude and work ethic. He instilled confidence in me and to continue to keep moving forward in business and in life; and to never allow others to bring me down. It brings tears to my eyes today remembering all that Mr. Jones has done for me and mentoring me in the business and I owe everything to him for who I am today.

While working as Office Manager and Administrative Assistant, I learned to do just about everything in the office. Looking back, I remember this is where I learned to do payroll and then became an accountant. As Office Manager I managed and supervised the entire operation and documentation in the office while answering to the government. I was responsible for the payroll and all other office duties, all self-taught with Mr. Jones's guidance. I owe a lot to him. He accepted me for who I am and taught me many more life skills to take with me throughout my life and especially in business. While still employed, those skills allowed me to open my own business which was a Clothing Boutique in Lancaster, California.

After the military contract ended with Mr. Jones eight years later, I decided to return to school. I decided to venture into the medical field. I studied hard to become a Certified Nursing

Assistant/Home Help Care, which I enjoyed because I love to help and take care of people. While working in Home Help Care, I was offered a very good paying job as an assistant to a celebrity in Los Angeles. My employer was the first wife of the famous late Tom Petty (American Singer/Songwriter, Record Producer, Actor and Lead Vocalist and Guitarist of the band "Tom Petty and the Heartbreakers). My job was very exciting, and I really enjoyed working with her because I got to learn so much about the music business.

In 2015, I was asked to participate in the Miss Asia USA Pageant. It was an honor and truly a life changing experience. I was overjoyed when they announced my name as the

winner of "Mrs. Congeniality 2015" and I am so thankful to have won the title and well-deserved awards since then. In 2019 I received the title of Miss Noble Global Model by SeemsAfrica.

If I were to describe myself, you would see an experienced, hard-working, and extremely motivated. I am skilled in many diversified business positions. I work extremely well with others without prejudice. Currently, I have added a new set of work skills which many times amazes me. I am blessed with a magnetic yet humble personality that has opened doors for me in many fashion-designing events and modeling. You may find me on center stage or working behind the scenes in many highly acclaimed events in Los Angeles. Yet, my humbleness and sincerity remain intact.

As I review my life, I would like to send a message to everyone; that is to "NEVER GIVE UP" on any of your dreams and always continue to keep being strong and have faith and to always keep doing your best. Do what you love to do to succeed in life. You never know how your future is going to be or how your trials may turn into great blessings while you are here on earth.

I hope my story has inspired you and has helped you to see that we are all human and you never know what any of us has gone through to become who we are today.

What I foresee and wish for my future is simply this:

"I wish to be happy and healthy and to continue to be blessed. Because, after all, only God knows what is in store for me and only God's help has gotten me this far."

Special Thank You!!

I would like to give a special thank you to Dr. Carl D. Wilson, Jr. for allowing me to be part of this amazing journey. It's been an honor working with him and allowing me to be a co-author of this book along with the phenomenal women I have been working with

Dr. Rosalind Willis

"My Health Is My Wealth"
OVERCOMING THE FEAR OF DEATH IN THE FACE OF A STROKE
By Rosalind Willis

Dr. Rosalind Willis has been given the title "Woman of Many Hats" since she could remember. She has been given the honor of wearing personal hats that God created her for such as: child of God, wife, mother, sister, daughter, daddy's girl, friend, Nana, cousin, aunt, niece, mother n law, daughter of God these are her natural and spiritual hats. Dr. Willis has also been given spiritual and natural hats for ministry and the world, such as Dr., Evangelist, Elder, Pastor, Teacher, Minister, Trainer, Mentor, Certified Master Life Coach, Educator, Chaplain, Coordinator, Phlebotomist, Director, Communicator, Counselor, Partner, Entrepreneur, Writer, Author, Singer, Instructor, Presenter, Public Speaker, Prayer Warrior, Intercessor, Spiritual Midwife, Spiritual Mother, Event Planner, Wedding Planner, CEO, Travel Agent, Account Manager, Manager, Supervisor, Marketing Manager, Recruiter, Artist Manger, Founder, Business Lady, Customer Service Representative.

Born July eleventh, nineteen seventy-two, Rosalind was called from her mother's womb to be an Evangelist. Rosalind accepted her call into ministry in 1992 and was Ordained in 1995 as an Evangelist. Rosalind was Ordained as a Pastor in 2000 able to license and Ordain ministers. Dr. Rosalind Willis is an Evangelist with a passion to serve and reach the lost at any cost. She is the founder of Birthing Process Ministries International, Prophetic Wedding Planning, BPMI Leadership & Life Coaching Institute, Sister I Am Here, and Bpmi Ladies Clubs Global and is the CEO of Coach Roz Fashions LLC, Evolution Sisterhood Travel, and Co-founder of a publishing company launched January 2020 "T&R Birthing Books Publishing LLC" with her partner in life and business Pastor Tommy Willis {Self}. Rosalind has obtained her Bachelor's in Business Management, Master's in Ministry Education, and Doctorate in Addiction Counseling with an emphasis in Marriage Counseling from United Graduate College and Seminary International U.A.C.C.C.I. Rosalind is a Certified Chaplain, a published author. Rosalind has a passion to teach leaders how to walk in what God has called them to do. Rosalind is called to be a Spiritual Midwife assisting individuals to birth what God has placed inside the womb of the spirit to manifest it in the earth realm. Rosalind is married to her first love Pastor Tommy Willis and is the mother of 6---three girls and three boys and grandmother of 12 jewels and one on the way that she simply adores. Rosalind has a passion for women that are broken and do not know who they are; she loves to reach out to them. Rosalind is in her 7th year of hosting her women's community outreach called Bpmi ladies clubs global. It is a ladies' tea that she hosts in the community for women of all walks of life. This tea is usually held at a hotel, library, or event center somewhere other than a church because that was the blueprint given to her.

"My Health Is My Wealth"

The answer to the question what is success to me? I would say now it is not in how much money I have because you can be a millionaire and have bad health which would not allow you to enjoy the money. I understand now at the age of 49 that my health truly is my wealth. Here is my story:

OVERCOMING THE FEAR OF DEATH IN THE FACE OF A STROKE

Have you ever been so afraid that it made you feel paralyzed? Have you ever gone to sleep and felt as though you could not breathe? Have you ever lain in the bed feeling each beat of your heart scared that it was going to stop? Have you ever stayed up for days afraid to go to sleep because you feared you would not wake up? This, Loves, is the spirit of fear and the fear of death. I know because I battled it for years. The thing is I did not realize it was a fear because I had it for so long. I remember the day it was introduced to me when I was only ten years old. My great-grandmother was passing away from cancer and I remember at her funeral looking in the casket at what was supposed to be her. I remember having nightmares for months and became scared to go to sleep. The deception of this fear is the older you get the more you will not be afraid of dying. Yes, I was a minister then and living the life I know would reassure me a place in heaven. Yet still that fear of death was attached to me. Isn't it something how we can give everyone the motivation and inspiration to do what we really need to do ourselves? Everyone that I prayed for that was on his/her death bed I saw God heal him/her and give him/her more time. Yet still my own fear of death lingered near me until the day, that would change my life forever...

September 16, 2014 was the best day and the worse day of my life because it was a day that God showed me that my labor was not in vain. I was shopping with my sister when all of a sudden, I had a massive headache. I had migraines off and on but this one was different. I remember a throbbing pain in my head, and my eyes began to get a little blurry; however, I did not know just how bad it was. My sister drove me home, and by the time I got home I did not have energy to get out of my vehicle. My sister had my oldest Terrance to come out to the car and help me into the house. The next thing I remember waking up to him carrying me in his arms like a baby. Then I went out again. When I came to, the EMS was picking me up off the floor. They took me out on a stretcher, and I could hear my Son Terrance praying fervently. I could see him looking in the sky and praying while I was in the back of the ambulance. The EMS began to ask me questions, and I could not talk only babble was coming out my mouth. I could feel my right side numbing and tingling. The fear of dying flooded me. All I could think about is how many people God had used me to pray for that was healed from a stroke. I cried and prayed in my mind, and I could hear the Holy Spirit say to me, "This is for My Glory". Suddenly, I felt warmth of love consume me and I had total peace. Then we got to the hospital, my daughter was at work, and they rushed me in and began to work on me. I heard them call stroke code, and my blood pressure was unnaturally high. I heard the doctor say, "I am surprised she is still with us." His statement made my heart race and once again fear gripped me. My daughter Takisha walked to the side of my bed and immediately begins to pray. The warmth of love covered me again just as it did before, and peace was all over me. They rushed me back to do a Cat-Scan and said they saw a blood clot on my brain. I remember on my way back to the room I began to pray for a miracle in my mind and spirit because I could not talk. I could feel my body tingling and warm at that time. We returned to the room where my daughter was, and they told her they had a small window of time to try and save my life by giving me a medicine called a TPA clot buster. They said it is not a guarantee; however, it could bust up the clots and reverse the effects of the stroke. My daughter told them to give it to me, and they did. The medicine worked immediately, and I was able to feel my right side again and talk again. The first thing I said was "thank you, Jesus". The doctors and nurses were in shock and amazement. God truly got the Glory that day and has continued, too. I was in ICU for 7 days. While in ICU God gave me "Blueprints from Heaven", he spoke to me to bring the women together by hosting a ladies' tea. He gave me step by step instructions on what to do. He said women are hurting, and some will not go to church because they have been hurt in the church so host it in a place in the community. He gave me the entire outline. By the time I went home, it was complete. God began to reveal to me my spiritual territory and what He wanted me to do with it. I began to see the children I had birthed, prayed, fasted, and lived the life in front of pray for me the way they had witnessed me pray for others. For that reason, it was the best day of my and the worst day of my life. My husband was working out of town at the time and had to rush home to be by my side. I am blessed not to have any weakness or crippling from the stroke. My memory is not as good as it used to be, but other than that I am good. I have been hosting these teas now for almost 6 years, and I have seen hundreds of women delivered, birthed out, and set free. Glory to God! I believe God is going to take this vision all over the world.

To embrace your purpose and have the passion to do what God has called you to do, you must know who you are. When you know your value, everything else has to accommodate that revelation. I was married before to a man that did not know my worth and did not respect my value. The problem was not him; it was me. I did not know who I was or my worth, so I allowed him and others to mistreat me and devalue me. When I understood who I was and whose I was, I embraced my value. Then I was able to receive my husband of promise and someone that knew my value and honored me as I do him. God has called everyone for a purpose, and when we trust him, no matter what we go through He always delivers us. The fear of death was something that was with me from childhood when my great-grandmother passed away of cancer; that spirit was assigned to me at ten years old. I went through a lot of close call situations from asthma attacks to black outs that made it even worse. God delivered me from the spirit of fear, and I overcame the fear of death that day. Now, I walk in victory over fear because of Jesus. I still have some memory loss in areas and some weakness at times, but overall, you cannot look at me and see that I ever experienced a stroke. I give God all the Glory for that. The enemy want to stop us from producing what God has placed within us before the foundation of this world. You, too, can overcome anything that the enemy tries to do in your life. God has blessed me to write books in which one that I wrote with my husband and best friend. God has birthed out ministries and businesses, and I get the honor of making a difference in the lives of others every day. I do not allow the enemy to produce negativity in my life. It is time for you, "yes, YOU", to walk in your divine destiny and overcome every fear the enemy has tried to place in your life. Take back everything the enemy stole from you in Jesus Name!

I believe all the trials that I have been through in my life that were designed to destroy me and did not is what makes me an Overcomer. People have died because of the very same things that I have been through. The fact that no matter what comes my way I keep going. I believe that makes me an Overcomer. Not only do I overcome but I testify the goodness of God and give all Glory back to Him. As the Word of God says, "We overcome by the blood of the lamb and the words of our testimony."

Who am I? I am a woman of passion for people I have been hurt by many because I trust and try to find the good in everyone even when they are not good for me. I am a loyal friend and family member that loves hard. You can tell me anything, and I will not share it with anyone ever. I have the gift of Agape love for people and long suffering.

My advice to anyone that might be going through a difficult situation that you cannot see your way through, I say seek God with your entire heart and trust him. God will not lead your wrong; I am a witness. Ask God to help you through it. Make sure you have a good support system, and if you do not, find a mirror and speak life into yourself until you believe what you are saying. You can make it through this. Remember a time in the past that you thought you would not make it through, but you did. You are a warrior; you're beautiful. You have purpose and destiny, and you to are an Overcomer.

It has been so many times that I thought I would not make it like when my ex-husband cheated on me with a girl that I had been babysitting for. I was so broken and hurt; he would go on to have countless affairs during our marriage and ultimately bring a beautiful gift home that I still raise as my own to this very day. I remember feeling so rejected and broken all the while I was still preaching and praying for others and trusting God that he would deliver me from the bondage of that relationship because I did not know my value nor my worth. I stayed faithful to God, and He delivered me out of that bondage and blessed me with a marriage of promise. My husband whom I call "Self" because we are One. He is a good man that I know God created me for. I am a witness that if you trust God even when you cannot trace Him, He will deliver you.

The way that I strive to encourage the youth and future generation is leading by example. My life is the loudest book that people read. I am raising teenage girls, and I teach them to love hard. I pour into them and their friends. I speak to students every chance that I get. I started a talk show for my girls a few years ago called, "Out of the Mouth of Babes" where they invited their peers and interviewed them on the show. They would talk about any topics that they wanted to discuss from molestation to basketball. I have also taught my girls and their friends how to pray for their fellow classmates. I encourage them to read and expand their vocabulary. I teach them that every person they meet is important, and they can make a difference in the lives of others if they take the time to care. I have been blessed that my daughters are intelligent, respectful, and beautiful inside and out. They are both leaders, and I give God all the Glory for that as well. '

Three words that describe me are love, integrity, and loyalty. The reason is that I love to love people, and I live by integrity doing the right thing when no one is looking because God sees and knows all. I am loyal because if you do one thing for me, I am so grateful that I will always honor you. And I am loyal to the people I love and even people I do not know. I believe it is a gift.

In five years, I see myself encouraging the masses all over the world. I see myself in a place financially to bless thousands of people with houses and cars. I see our publishing company publishing over thousands of books and authored hundreds. I see myself debt free and financially, physically, spiritually healthy, and wealthy.

If there is anyone out there that is dealing with a cheating spouse, nervous breakdown, Crohn's disease, child out of wedlock, homelessness, rape, molestation, rejection, death of a father, divorce, betrayal, or any of the things that I have been through I want to tell you to hold on; you can make it. Take your two fingers and put them on your pulse and feel that beating? That is purpose beating; remember as long as you've got a pulse, you've got a purpose. No one has the fingerprints that you have. You are unique, and you have jewels inside of you that the world is waiting for. Do not let the things you are going through mute you and take your voice. You are valuable, and you are worth love. You are someone special, and if no one has told you this week, month, or year, I love you. Stay focused on Jesus, and everything else will come out clearly.

Dr. Rosalind Willis
(Coach Roz)
Instagram:
Trbirthingbookspublishing.site
Rosalindwillis77@gmail.com

Anna Smulowitz-Schutz

Anna Smulowitz, Playwright and Second-Generation Holocaust Survivor

By Anna Smulowitz Schutz

Anna Smulowitz Schutz was born in 1947 in a displaced person's camp in Plattling, Germany. Her parents, Sam and Helen Smulowitz, survivors of the Holocaust, met in Buchenwald Concertation Camp in Weimar, Germany. Her father survived by working in the kitchen, and her mom was for a time secretary to the notorious Adolf Eichmann. A year after the war while searching for surviving family, they accidently met on a double decker bus in Munich. They reunited and married a week later. A few years later with baby Anna in tow, they immigrated to America. They were sent to Louisville, Kentucky, where Sam worked as a Kosher butcher. Growing up in the South as Jewish immigrants, Anna and her parents experienced racism and anti-Semitism throughout the 1950's and 60's. On her way to the school bus stop with a friend they saw a sign at the Country Club front gate. It read "No Blacks, No Jews, No dogs". Here friend Margie said, "Wonder what they got against dogs!" Anna's mother often told stories of similar signs hung on Jewish businesses in Germany.

Her mother as age thirteen also had a Jewish Star emblem sewn on all her clothing. That sign was her first racist experience in America but not her last. In fact, the hateful warning sign, and the prejudice it represented made a lasting impression on Anna. Eventually she saw the parallel between her parents as victims of hate in German concentration camp and African Americans as victims of hate right in her own back yard.

One day at dinner when Anna was eight years old, she finally asked her parents why they had blue numbers tattooed on their arms. A few years later Sam and Helen shared their stories and how it came to be that most of their family members were murdered at the Auschwitz Camp in Poland. Afterwards, Anna vowed never to forget her people, the extended family whom she had never met. To honor and remember them and have the world know who they were, Anna wrote her first play, Terezin, Children of the Holocaust. Her award-winning play will celebrate its 50th Anniversary in May 2021. It opened in Cincinnati's Regional Theatre, the "Playhouse in the Park" in May 1971. For 35 years the play has toured the U.S. and Europe, including performances at Terezin Camp, Prague, and Auschwitz as well as Germany and Cuba. In 1984, Terezin won the American Children's Television Award" for an early production televised by CBS. Recently, Terezin premiered as a 'film which can be viewed at terezin.org.

Anna has earned a B.A. and M.A. in Theatre Arts and has also taught acting at the University of Maryland. In 1980 she continued her education by earning and M.Ed. at Lesley University, majoring in Drama as Therapy. In 1986 she earned a third Master's degree from Brandeis University. In 1979 Anna moved to Newburyport, Massachusetts, with her young son Aaron Clopton and established the Newburyport Children's Theater. It is celebrating its 41st year and is today run by her students and is known as "Theatre in the Open" at Maudesly Park. Anna went on to form her own production company and theatre training school. (See Smulowitzproductions.com) For 50 years hundreds of students have studied acting and directing with Anna. As a result, many have performed in film and television and in leading roles on Broadway. Others have become notable directors, playwrights, and theatre educators. Anna married the love of her life, an MIT engineer, Alan Schutz, in 1986, and together they raised five children Chris, Jeremy, David, and Shayleen and Anna's son, Aaron. Theatre and the play Terezin quickly became a family affair with each participating in his/her own way. Alan, Shayleen, and Aaron traveled, worked. and /or acted in the production at several destinations: Terezin Camp, Prague, Germany, and Poland; David and Jeremy built a few of the brilliant sets. Chris watched enough performances to give constructive criticism. Anna's former husband and theatre artist, Marc Clopton, directed the 2011 five-star review version of Terezin presented for the Fringe Festival in Scotland.

In 1997 Anna won the Newburyport Mayors Arts Award and the 2008 Anti-Defamation League's Leadership Award for her life-time resistance to the rise of Anti-Semitism as well as her social justice work with global racism. In 1994, the Timberland Corporation named Anna a "Model Person' for her work in a national ad campaign entitled "Timberland Gives Racism the Boot". At the age of 55, Anna decided to follow a different path toward hospital ministry. She attended the Chaplaincy Institute of Maine. In 2005 she was ordained an Interfaith Minister and is now a clinical chaplain at Brooksby Village in Peabody, Massachusetts.

Anna Smulowitz Schutz
Chaplain Braeburn Gardens
Pastoral Ministries
100 Brooksby Village Drive
Peabody, MA 01960
www.EricksonLiving.com

Michelle DeLizio-Podlesni

Transform Your Career and Go from Burnout to Bliss

By Michelle DeLizio Podlesni

President of National Nurses in Business Association (NNBA)
UNconventional Nurse® Going from Burnout to Bliss! Founder & Author
Bloom Service Group, LLC. CEO & President

Michelle DeLizio Podlesni, RN (UNconventional Nurse®: Going from Burnout to Bliss!), is President of the National Nurses in Business Association and CEO of Bloom Service Group, LLC. She is an accomplished businesswoman, US Navy veteran, and nurse with over 30 years' experience ranging from clinical care, case management, and healthcare information technology to nationally known speaker, bestselling author, and serial nurse entrepreneur. She has a proven track record of leadership success in executive management of start-ups and established multi-million-dollar SaaS (software as a service) companies serving Fortune 500 clients.

With real world experience from the bedside to the boardroom and beyond, Michelle's true passion for mentoring and helping others succeed in business has made her a sought-after business coach, speaker, and business advisor. Michelle is a widely recognized and respected authority in business and speaks nationally on the empowerment of nurses through entrepreneurship.

Established in 1985, the National Nurses in Business Association is dedicated to advancing and expanding nurse's role in business. The NNBA provides nurses with business education, strategies, best practices along with an extensive network of colleagues, and resources helping nurses navigate the journey to entrepreneurial success. The NNBA has assisted thousands of nurses to launch, build, and manage their own business. NNBA's Annual Educational Conference on Nurse Entrepreneurship & Career Alternatives is each Fall. www.NursesBusiness.com

Transform Your Career and Go from Burnout to Bliss!

Of the more than 3 million nurses in this country, over a third are dissatisfied with their jobs and will be taking steps to change their work. Burnout is the number one reason why nurses are looking to make these changes. I've been there and went on to leverage my nursing knowledge to experience great financial success and fulfillment in business and entrepreneurship. I'm still a nurse, but an unconventional nurse, and still driven by my passion to help people and make a difference each day.

Entrepreneurship benefits the nursing professional because they share many similar characteristics. Nurses make such a difference in people's lives, and I felt compelled to do something to help nurses make a difference in their own lives. I wrote Unconventional Nurse: Going from Burnout to Bliss! to help nurses become more business savvy and see the potential in entrepreneurship. I share 10 steps covering the mindset, strategies, and skills I have learned over the past three decades that gave me confidence, competitive advantage, and marketability for unlimited opportunities.

10 Steps to Transform Your Career and Take Charge of Your Life:

1. Develop an Entrepreneur's Mindset
2. Identify Your Passion and Purpose
3. Have Insatiable Curiosity
4. Manage Your Time, Manage Your Life
5. Improve Your Communication Skills
6. Understand Influence and the Art of Persuasion
7. Develop Confident Decision Making
8. Get Comfortable Being Uncomfortable
9. Cultivate and Nurture Relationships
10. You Need to Lead to Succeed

I wrote UNconventional Nurse ® for nurses because I could

see that nurses were under-served, devalued, and overworked. It hurt me to see nurses in a profession I loved not being happy in their jobs. The level of burnout was rising to 35%, and this is well before COVID-19. I wanted to help in the best way I was able and that was to share with nurses the business strategies, skillsets, and examples that I knew could change the trajectory of their careers and their life. Today, as the president of the National Nurses in Business Association, it is such a privilege to assist nurses that are in different stages of business. Every day I am inspired by the innovative ways nurses use their education and experience in creating rewarding, thriving, and profitable businesses.

I was raised in a small town in Western Pennsylvania known for steel, football, and food. If someone would have told me when I was nursing at our local hospital that I would be the president of a major multi-million-dollar software company in Newport Beach, California; I would have never believed them. But that is exactly what happened and led to so much more. I encourage you to push through the limits of your expectations and live a life greater than you have ever imagined. You can go from burnout to bliss!

Best piece of advice for the younger generation that will help you blaze toward success:

Cultivate and nurture support systems. Entrepreneurship can be lonely; you will need to surround yourself with people who believe in your dreams and support them. From a professional standpoint, there are many organizations that can support and encourage you. Many nurses attribute their membership in the National Nurses in Business Association, NNBA as being pivotal to their success as an entrepreneur. Seeing concrete examples of nurses that have made the transition to business and are resources available to ask questions. Members have made lifelong friends and have worked on many collaborative projects. There are supportive organizations that are specific specialties within nursing and outside nursing. For example, I used to be a member of the American Board of Quality Assurance and Utilization Review, and I've been a member of various Chamber of Commerce's and local area business networking groups---all invaluable to providing support and resources.

I've grown several successful corporations and businesses. My nursing education and experience set the foundation for me achieving success beyond what I ever dreamed was possible. Did I make mistakes? Too many to count, and every day I am learning. But this I know: Nurses make great business owners. My best piece of advice is to cultivate and nurture your support systems. Relationships are everything, and much study on our well-being supports this. Having solid personal and professional communities will help you get on the right track; it will open doors and provide resources. You can achieve all the other lessons in business *just by getting started in business,* however, personal, and professional support is what will sustain you. Then you will have a great cheering section!

Desziree Richardson

I Took My Power Back and Aligned It with My Destiny
By Desziree Richardson

My life to date has been punctuated by aha moments, despite moments of self-doubts, obstacles, dark clouds, and poor judgment. I believe the time I have today would not be feasible to share it all. What I am about to share with you today is only the tip of an iceberg grounded in an ocean of lived experiences. The streams of memory flowing through my head provide me with a splendid vista to share with the manifestation of these instances.

I am Desziree Richardson, and I come from humble origins---born and raised on the tiny island of Anguilla in the British Caribbean and now living in the UK. After taking counsel with my universal inner voice, the law of attraction drove me to pursue my dreams as God controls my destiny.

As the fourth child in a large family, I was used to seeing my mother struggle to guarantee a life for her children. But, despite her best efforts, it became unclear that some girls were unrecognized because they did not come from a family in the right tax bracket; that girl was me. Despite the many praises for my many revolving talents and abilities, they were unfortunately deemed insufficient in the wrong circles, which left me feeling unworthy. Even though I was living without life comforts, my experience as a child was cheerful and playful. However, these youthful experiences have shaped me into the person that I am today. They have grounded me and opened my eyes to the various realities of life and life as a woman.

My life experiences have propelled me to make a difference globally, which I envisioned at a tender age.

My work is to reach a broader audience to impact the lives of every human existence, to create a positive change in the minds of readers, listeners, and viewers, to help change the world through changing lives, and to empower the world to become kinder and to share love towards humanity through my projects. I feel a genuine desire and devotion to the well-being and welfare of my fellow human beings. Furthermore, I enjoy being a service to others and believe it is my sole purpose in sharing my story and wisdom to help empower positive changes in the lives of many people around the world.

I use my experiences and my voice as a vehicle and an instrument for change and to empower, heal, motivate, and help transform lives into a more fulfilling life of love, kindness, peace, abundance, and acceptance through my accolade of creative projects, purposely design for women empowerment passion and soul purpose. My platforms bring a powerful magnetic energy and a unique array of women advancement projects to celebrate, motivate, and empower women worldwide. Our network of leaders teaches and supports women on how to empower themselves from within and find their voices and become leaders and decision-makers through the stories we share and the work we do, geared towards promoting the values of excellence, generosity, and pride in the actions of women as well as celebrating their achievements.

My mission is to help change lives and to influence others positively through my empowering projects. I believe women are the guiding lights in our rational world. Throughout the universe, women are the pillars of our hospitals, schools, and care infrastructure and in our homes. They are also the managers in our offices, the dreamers in our creative world, leaders in our communities, and the beating hearts of our humanitarian sectors. In all these spheres, women's light is central and undiminished. They are fixers, care givers, teachers, leaders, and peacemakers.

Through empowering platforms, such as the Women of Heart Awards, I support women and appreciate men who lift us. In addition, the Women of Heart Awards is a great forum to forge connections between like-minded women. I believe the world we live in could become more beautiful if everyone thought positively and shared positive energies wherever they go. I use these platforms to motivate them to believe in the power of choice. Therefore, they can choose what they allow to manifest in their lives; opportunities could open for them with the right choices. However, as humans, we should all gather our good thoughts and deeds by accepting and welcoming different cultures and religions in the workplace, society, and social norms. As a leader and visionary my projects sustain, support as well as implement diversity, and inclusion. The Face of Woha, Women of Heart Awards, and Women of Heart Foundation represent a sense of belonging and contribute to embracing these factors.

I specialize in women's empowerment as a thought leader, transformational and motivational speaker, and fashionista. I use my voice as a powerful magnetic vehicle to convey positivity and empowerment to help change lives. I do this so that women can feel empowered, seen at their best, brightest, and boldest through the Women of Heart Foundation, Face of Woha, and Women of Heart Awards, and uplift and influence others positively through my fashion brands.

As a thought leader, transformational motivational speaker, International best-selling author, model, humanitarian, and entrepreneur, my authentic presence and sincere transparency have showcased my unique talents as a speaker, author, media personality, broadcaster, and witty reporter. I am honest and personable and a consummate professional. My magnetic voice has made me famous with my listening audience as one-part smooth, two parts delightful, and a large portion of entertaining and joyful communication. Alongside my established media and celebrity career, I am dedicated to helping people in need and have a real passion for empowering women, volunteering, and philanthropy.

As a previous Project Leader at the University of West London, I actively lead and organize projects, volunteers, and events in the community, such as planting trees in the Gunnersbury Park and creating outdoor community projects that benefit the community and environment. I have also volunteered my time teaching in Asia and completed projects to give back, such as the Sanitary Napkins campaign for young girls and Women of Heart Foundation Golden Awards in Kenya and projects in Uganda, Liberia, and Nigeria ground. I have also helped with Fundraising for the Have a Heart Appeal, Help a London Child, The Classic Foundation, and campaigning for the Hunger Summit and IF Enough Food for Everyone and UNICEF. In addition, I have contributed to many funds and awareness-raising campaigns, including live auction bids with other celebrities and volunteering as a UNICEF Children's Champion.

Since moving to the UK, I have helped and inspired others; I have received awards and recognition for my work, including the Award-Winning World Women Visionary Leader Award, AAA, Humanitarian Award, the England Gold Award, Red Blazer of Excellence and Achievement. She Rocks Women Empowerment Lifetime Achievement Award, WAW Hall of Fame Honorary Award, Innovative Global Women Empowerment Leadership Award, Woman of Excellence Humanitarian and Leadership Honorary, Eippy Awards International Best-Selling Author Awards, Leadership Mind Ambassador, Blue Titanic Necklace Award, and Entrepreneur Crown Award reflecting my passion, leadership, dedication to various causes, and many other prestigious awards, such a foster parent and. In addition, I am the Women of Heart Foundation founder, which raises funds to celebrate, support, promote, empower, and educate women globally.

Women of Heart Awards launched in 2020---celebrates and honors fifty global iconic and unforgettable women who make a difference in the world. The Face of WOHA is a platform designed to connect, support, and promote women to become leaders and instrumental in making the world a better place and securing diverse women for a better cause.

Writing high-quality fiction and nonfiction, I have swiftly become an international bestselling author with a dedicated fan base and successfully moved into the world of international publishing. I aim to connect diversity for a better cause, create awareness, and invite women worldwide to showcase a healthy, balanced world and share messages that will help change the world positively while showcasing beauty in diverse women as a visual component.

I believe the world we live in could become more beautiful if everyone thought positively and shared positive energies wherever they go. I use these platforms to motivate them to believe in the power of choice. As a leader and visionary my projects sustain, support, as well as implement diversity, and inclusion. The Face of Woha, Women of Heart Awards, and Women of Heart Foundation represent a sense of belonging and contribute to embracing these factors.

In 2018, after going through adversity, I took my power back and relaunched and created projects to help others overcome the many barriers and to help change their mindset to know that they are worthy of it all.

The Women of Heart Awards is a significant new event cut from the philosophical fabric as a Women's Empower Movement. The Women of Heart Awards is dedicating to highlighting and rewarding courageous and inspiring civic-minded women--- women like you.

As an essential award celebrating the innumerable deeds of our universal sisterhood, the Women of Hearts Award holds to a humanist tenant of the immutable right of equality and dignity for all human beings. Baked into its credo is the immovable belief of human goodness as often expressed in the countless civic-minded deeds of countless women.

A celebratory bonanza of entertainment and inspiration as part of our yearly black-tie democratized space, diverse everyday women are celebrated for their exceptional work. Women of Heart Awards is also a great forum to forge connections between like-minded women. Our network of leaders teaches and support women on how to empower themselves from within and find their voice and become leaders and decision-makers through the stories we share and the work we do, geared towards promoting the values of excellence, generosity, and pride in the actions of women. as well as celebrating their achievements. Throughout the world, women are the pillars of our hospitals, schools, and care infrastructure. They are also the managers in our offices, the dreamers in our creative world, and the beating hearts of our humanitarian sectors. Women's light is central and undiminished in all these spheres, and WOHA aims to highlight and celebrate those women who go the extra mile every day of their lives. "I have always dreamt of this night."

FACE OF WOHA, in front of Women of Heart Awards, is designed with a message to bring leaders and aspiring leaders from around the globe on one stage to inspire, educate, empower, and positively influence the world while supporting women and adolescents' children. In addition, the Face of Woha gives back to the Women of Heart Foundation to support their education and well-being in remote areas through its causes.

Our enterprise openly invites women to participate and be crowned The Face of The Women of Heart Awards. Contestants are selected for their rhetoric abilities and not their beautiful qualities. We provide a first-class service designed to imbue them with the confidence and necessary leadership qualities to compete for those lacking the loquacious characteristics we hope will keep them in good stead throughout the life.

The front of Women of Heart Awards, a platform created and designed to connect, support, promote, unites diverse women and women leaders and young girls for a better cause globally and supports unity among diversity, is continuous.

A public speaking onstage forum is for diverse women of the universe from various backgrounds age eighteen and upwards worldwide who are ready to share their message. We invite young girls ages fifteen to seventeen to join as strong faces to showcase the beauty in diversity through a photo contest. However, we believe in empowering the new generation to showcase diversity through visual components. The winner then joins the group photo of selected diversity awareness leading women winners each year.

The platform provides an opportunity for face models and women speaker's inexperience and experience. Our aims are to uplift and support women and young girls, creating opportunities to help change the world through speech and showcase the beauty in diversity as a visual component among young women and women coming concurrently.

When we face challenges, there is always a way to help us overcome adversity—search for empowering books, speeches, daily inspirational quotes. Words of encouragement, empowerment, inspiration, and wisdom will help us find the best answers to our questions. Unfortunately, many people with inadequate living conditions cannot access primary data, so word of mouth from community leaders and prayers to help raise their energy is crucial to their emotional well-being.

If there is a story, a vision that you are connecting to and you hope it will make a difference, please get involved with organizations, such as volunteering in your communities; this has helped me learn transferable skills for business and career job prospects, and I am sure you will adopt different skills to help you expand. I had the opportunity to meet amazing people along the journey involved in community development and humanitarian work. I encourage you to show a substantial amount of Interest to learn the necessary skills to elevate you and propelled and prepared you to be in the right direction to receive unexpected opportunities.

Furthermore, writing a book to share your story and share your expertise and experiences will also open doors for your message to be share and listen to by millions. Therefore, you will need to have a positive and creative mindset for wisdom and understanding, strength, determination to Initiate the legacy you will leave in the world as you help others by showing them compassion and teaching them how to be kind, grateful, humble, and caring. Furthermore, to lead, you will have to be empowered with these crucial elements of everyday living, such as self-determination, self-love, self-esteem, self-confidence, self-reliance, self-care, and self-love.

You are here for a reason, and for whatever reason, that is destiny to you from birth. Once you find your true calling and purpose, it allows you to know that you will take full responsibility for your actions with great intentions for yourself and society. Suppose you do this one thing. However, if you are wondering about the one thing I am speaking, it is called love, and it is free; put it in everything you do. If we all do, the world will heal. It would help if you were always prepared to start making the changes you need to create and surround yourself with ambitious people. Then, it is possible. How you live your life will become more important to you.

I encourage you to start believing that it is possible to achieve and that you genuinely deserve what your heart desires. However, during each step you take on your journey to get there, remain grateful and humble. I inspire women to become innovative by creating ideas that will help them succeed by doing what they love and enjoy. I will encourage them to have good intentions for the world and mankind and everyone close in all their endeavors.

Furthermore, I encourage other women to positively make a difference in the world. I will use my platforms to motivate them to believe in the power of choice. Therefore, they can choose what they allow to manifest in their lives; opportunities could open for them with the right choices. Moreover, remember to thank everyone who played an essential role in helping you reach your full potential. When you are at the top, please help others; the most vital is to give back. You were created in the world to love and be kind.

I wish everyone to be inclusive and happy and live in a world where diversity, peacefulness, and cosmic love's energy can be radiated and felt through every human existence.

With love and gratitude,

Desziree Richardson

Michele Lee Malo

I'm Not a Runner but I Play One on Facebook
BY: Michele Lee Malo

"The #1 reason people fail in life is because they listen to their friends, family and neighbors."

-Napoleon Hill

So, in the interest of full disclosure, total honesty, shooting from the hip and telling it straight, I'm going to start this by telling you the past few years have not been the greatest. Oh, wait no news flash here; just this past year has been epic for everyone, ugh. But that's not to say some good stuff hasn't come out of such a rough few year—adversity often brings about good stuff (to use the technical terminology). But it just seemed that these past few years were full of loss and struggle. That's right; the struggle bus pulled up to my door and dumped a whole lot of crap on my doorstep---relatives and friends passing away, my marriage ending, health issues, rebranding my business, a pandemic.

But that's not the point. The point is that to the rest of the world (those people out of my inner circle), it appeared that everything was coming up roses for me. To those who were viewing my life from the front row on Facebook, Instagram, and Twitter, it appeared that I had it all together, that life was treating me well. I was traveling all over the country, meeting celebrities and yes, even running a marathon and doing all with ease. Nothing could have been further from the truth. I was struggling and struggling hard—it just didn't come across that way on social media.

It's only natural to compare ourselves with others and what others choose to post to their accounts. But trust me, there is nothing that will chase you into an evening with wine and Ben and Jerry's quicker than Facebook comparison shopping.

But the truth is we love to post the good stuff, the sparkly goodness of our life. That's what people see. But it's not the whole real truth. The lessons you will soon read about all come from my mistakes and research and how to course correct.

As I said, these last few years were tough ones---not to mention all the other more minor struggles that crop up from time to time like car trouble and lost credit cards, but I didn't choose to post any of that on my social media. Nope. Social Media allows us to edit our lives to show only the good. On Facebook you saw me all dressed up and snapping pictures with celebrities, speaking at pre-Oscar City Gala, and hey, I met Richard Dreyfus. "I think we need a bigger boat." That is the stuff I posted. That was the sparkly goodness I chose to showcase.

What I didn't post were the negative things, the things that were weighing me down, the things that were causing the tears and hiccups and yes, even some late nights with a pint of Chunky Monkey, making me a chunky monkey.

I titled this I'm not a Runner but I Play One on Facebook to illustrate this point. Yes, I like to run (Like is a bit of a strong word) but I do enjoy race day; the running community is so strong and supportive. There is nothing like crossing the start line and a well-deserved beer waiting for you at the finish. I post pictures of me crossing the finish line and cheering, holding up my finishers medal with pride. What you don't know is that I probably finished at the back of the pack. Running is not always glamour shots. There is vomit, people swearing, and pain, but we edit that out and get to the good stuff.

People sometimes ask me to participate in marathons or run together after seeing my FB feed, and I have to tell them, "Hey, that's cool, but you have to understand, I'm not really a runner. I just play one on Facebook." Then we all have a good laugh, but it's the truth. You know what, I'm OK with that. Now that I've learned to overcome the perfectionism trap, it's more important to get in the race, cross that start line, and finish what I started. You see there are many things that happen between the start and finish, and it's that journey that we learn from and get better---just like life, your birth, a dash, and death, but the dash is where all the fun is at. There's so much comradery and support on race day as well as in life.

Running or even sometimes walking at the back of the pack gives me an opportunity to talk to other people who are fighting the good fight.

Social Media is a great place to hide the truth. It's a lot of smoke and mirrors and calculated to get the best response or the most likes or shares or comments. That's why it's easy to compare your life and/or your business with others.

> *"Be a person that others will look for your posts daily because they know you will encourage them.*
> *Be the positive one and help others to have a great day and you will find that not only they like you, but you will like you too."*
>
> — *John Patrick Hickey, Oops! Did I Really Post That*

But it's a balance. It's a great way to learn one of your long-lost friends got engaged or your family is planning a reunion, and you weren't invited. Social media is a great place to raise awareness for a favorite charity. You can reach so many people quickly. I for one would rather discuss the I Am Enough Movement tm 501c3 than show you an image of the salmon I ate last night. But it depends on the story you are telling. Maybe you are a food critic or work in the industry; then it does make sense to show that beautiful salmon. You want your social media to reflect who you are and what you are doing and your message in the best, most positive light. You do not want to give anyone the slightest reason not to do business or hire you.

I work with many clients who are in prestigious life positions. They entertain, they travel, they speak, and they write and run businesses, but all the public sees are the triumphs. Dr. James Dentley, owner of Inspired to Speak University, and his fellow coaches call these optics. You need positive optics, so others can see what they will get when they work or hire you.

One of my clients was on The Voice. When you see her on any social media, she looks great, well put together, and successful. She is amazing and fierce, but what you didn't see were the mornings when she couldn't get out of bed and when she was exhausted from trying to get a gig and worried about putting her two beautiful kids into college. Most people don't have the opportunity to peak under the tent and see the pain and anguish and struggles that even the most successful people endure to get to where they are today. You just see the tip of the iceberg above the water, and none of the foundation that lies underneath.

Don't Share Everything

Conversely there are some people who think nothing of sharing all the gory details of their life---all the pain and struggle. They complain and whine, share political views, and rant on social media.

My advice? Don't do that. Remember, you are building a brand— you are showcasing your product; you are a role model for other parents or colleagues. If you're in business, you want people to have confidence in you and your product. If they see you whining and complaining on social media, they will lose confidence and stop believing in you. Don't be a negative Nellie or a Karen. Be a positive thought leader.

A big no is when a person sends out that little Facebook warning RANT COMING. Ugh. Your social media account is there to highlight your business or product, to tell a story of how you can help take away someone's pain point. It makes you look like someone you are not or someone you don't want to be, especially when you've had a chance to cool down, and that particular little meltdown is no longer quite as important as it was two days ago. Be selective and aim for the good stuff. Don't weigh yourself or others down with negativity.

Now that being said, life and success are about the journey, and all journeys have times of struggle. It's important that your clients or the public or friends see some of the struggles. It's authentic and part of the story. It just needs to be balanced; if you can show how, you overcame that struggle, then you have provided a great ending to the story.

A Little Laughter Goes a Long Way

Of course, a little humor goes a long way. Self-deprecation is a mighty tool. The ability to be critical of yourself and do it with humor is social media gold. People love to laugh not at you but with you. Why? Because you are relatable.

Not Good Enough

There it is again. That old bugaboo—perfectionism. It can even show up in social media. That feeling of "I'm not good enough" will rear its ugly head at every turn if you don't look out and if you don't take a moment and understand you are the good stuff. There's more than meets the eye. So, relax. You are good enough. My friend Megan R. Fenyoe started the I Am Enough Movement tm, whose mission is to empower individuals to rewrite their story and shift their mindset to embrace their bravery and boldness and never apology for who they are because they finally believe they are enough. It's powerful, and I encourage you to check it out. Social Media is not about being perfect. It's about showing the good stuff tempered with a little of the bad and also the humorous. Balance is key. You are enough!

Message and Method

Social media is a wonderful place to connect and reach out to people with your message. That should be the focus of your posts. That's not to say you should never post anything personal, but too many images of you holding a margarita in your hand at a party can have some negative results. People will react to those pictures. So be wary. Post the good stuff. The stuff you want people to remember about you and your business. Be the person they get to know, like, and trust.

There should be nothing on your social media that could weigh you down or damage your career. Take a good look at your pages and delete what shouldn't be there. You are branding yourself. Most of your clients or customers will only know what you allow them to see. So be diligent.

Personal Branding

The notion of personal branding is a relatively new one. It is an important one any businessperson should embrace. You are not only representing your business and products you are also representing yourself. People will react to you, and that will reflect on your business.

After all my years in business, I learned something very important. People buy people not products. Earlier in my career when I would meet a potential client or partner at a networking event, I would launch into a very robotic elevator pitch about me and my company. "Hi, my name is Michele Malo. I'm the brand manager for---blah blah blah." The thing is that doesn't tell anybody anything of any substance. You are not your business card, your title, a parent, or a spouse. What makes you unique? How can you add value to the person you are connecting with?

It might have something to do with social media, but people have come to expect something more from you. They want to know you---not your professional role. They want to see pictures of your family or your dog. They want to know you. So now when I am introduced to someone at a professional networking event I say, "Hi, my name is Michele, The Change CEO, and I spark change in corporate go-getters guiding them to their next destination in life." It's provocative. People will ask questions. We are hard wired for story, and people want to hear your story. What is your headline? This is what people relate to and want to read or listen on. Those connections and what those connections say when you are not in the room is your personal brand.

Even if you aren't quite there yet, but you have plans to begin a new venture, now is the time to secure your domain name and email. You don't want your college email like iamtheman@gmail.com or gigglesnort@yahoo.com (yes, Gigglesnort was my nickname in college) representing you professionally. I know if I am a hiring manager or a potential client, I would have my doubts. In addition, invest in having an email that is your name or business. If you still have a Gmail or yahoo account that shows you don't think enough of your business to invest. Lock it down so no one else can claim it. Invest in professional head shots and maybe some pictures of you at work, speaking, involved with clients and personnel. Put yourself in a position of power. People are visual. Own your story.

A Two-Way Street

Social media is an information highway. It's an excellent way for you and your business to get recognition, but don't forget to return the kindness. Show your support for others and their charities and businesses. Make it a habit; always travel down this two-way street.

As an example, Blessons has provided scholarships to women over the age of 25 who for whatever reason have had their plans derailed. It is their goal to give women a second chance through education. I donate my time, and I always try to share and solicit donations through my contacts on social media. Their Founder, Khit Masoud, has a special place in my heart as she has fought many battles from leaving her family at 16 to escape and arrange marriage to several bouts with cancer. This is the true power of social media, the power to make a difference.

Find ways to take the spotlight off you and put it on others. Trust me—the dividends are amazing.

Decisions You Can Make

Decide to cut back on social media.

Social media weighs you down because you naturally start to compare yourself with what you see often forgetting that the truth is hidden. Plus, all the negativity in the world right now can really affected your mindset and focus. Turn your focus on things you can change instead of all the things that you cannot.

Decide to revamp the way you use social media.

If your primary goal is to further your business or sell your product, then be judicious and thoughtful about your posts even if you just use it as a personal connection tool. We live in a reactionary society. Before you post, ask yourself: How will people react to this? If your post receives comments and some of those comments are negative—decide not to defend yourself but be open to a new perspective and an open conversation. You will not change anyone's mind about anything through arguing. Just walk away.

Decide to use social media in order to

Communicate. Educate. Lead. Serve. Love.

Donna Sparaco Meador

Your path will unfold in front of you. Just Walk It

By Donna Sparaco Meador

Donna is an International Best-Selling Author and Women's Empowerment Coach, specializing in women dating "again" bringing forth resources that guide entrepreneurs and individuals alike through the dilemmas of life. After the loss of her husband in 2016, her message of self-caring via her vlog "Daily Dose A Donna" took the media by storm. Her unique message of intent and readjusting to life after loss offers strategic yet simple and effective tools providing inspirations, clarity, and purpose for those looking to flourish.

In 2020 Donna and her husband Jeff won the Forbes Riley Excel "Power Couple of Excellence" Award and can be found starring in "The Meador Affect" which they have since co-created.

Donna's love of Small Business has been passed down through the generations, and she herself has been an entrepreneur for the last 12 years. Additionally, her love of writing can be found in the many articles and books she has co-authored as well as privately publishing her first book DATING: It's Not Personal in 2014 with another on the way.

On an emotional level, Donna has always been intrigued as to what made her tick. She has spent her entire life peeling the layers of that emotional onion, so she could focus on walking the path she was meant to walk. "If you want to achieve anything, it's a whole lot easier if you clear the path first." As an Empowerment Coach, today Donna offers Dating Workshops to help women understand their self-worth as they walk into the unknown world of dating again, as well as bringing awareness about affordable legal access. "As a widow who got denied a claim and then received over $13,000 because this service wrote a letter on my behalf, well, this is just too good a benefit to keep secret."

Donna has been a LegalShield Associate for ten years now, has won numerous trips, was the Top Recruiter a few years in a row, achieved the Rising Star Award in 2016, and has held a bonus level for 120+ consecutive months. Donna knew from the moment she discovered this empowering service in 2011, she would be a forever advocate.

"Your path will unfold in front of you.
Just walk it."

These were the words Mama spoke to me shortly after the passing of my husband in 2016. From that day forward I would live by them.

Thinking about it now still makes my heart swell. How did she know I would need to hear those words?

When I was younger, I didn't really understand the importance of a thought or decision and how it would play out in a day or two or even a year later. I now understand that every step taken is a precise calculation of stepping into my desired life. Each step means something and should only be taken if it feels right. Whether it was something to eat or an invitation to go somewhere, I didn't do it if it didn't feel right. Without looking for approval or validation, every step had to result in a better feeling. "Feeling" is the optimal word here. If you make decisions that don't feel right, that usually leads to regret later. It's only now that I'm older, and I like to think wiser that I understand the value in being still long enough to hear what my inner self is saying. There were times that all I could do was plop on the couch and lay there motionless.

Before I discovered this passion that was buried beneath the surface, I went out dating in my mid-life years. Talk about a rollercoaster ride. I was job-hunting and man-hunting (I mean dating) at the same time. Can you Imagine?

If you think job hunting is tough --- try dating in your 40's. Rejection is happening at every turn and taking any of it personally could only lead to disappointment.

As if that wasn't tough enough, I did it again ten years later after the passing of this wonderful man I was married to.

Interestingly, it was that very experience that revealed this deep passion within. It inspired me to write a book and put together a dating workshop for widows and other women. It inspired me to get out and speak about loss and loving again. It was that very experience that propelled me forward to walk the road I'm on now.

Looking back as I connect the dots, I can see that this path has always been in front of me. No doubt, that's true for a lot of us.

Success in life usually doesn't reveal itself until after it's been done. We usually don't see the brilliance of our decisions until we are well in front of it. In the 80's I was working for a new up and coming airline called PEOPLExpress Airlines. What made this so new wave was that it was breaking all the rules. For one, we weren't called "Flight Attendants" but rather wore the title CSM (Customer Service Manager). That was important because our flying hours weren't regulated by the FAA resulting in part to lower fares for the passengers. The goal of the airlines was to deregulate fares, so everyone could afford to fly. In the midst of this all, there was a female pilot named Lynn Rippelmeyer. Look her up. Lynn became the first woman to captain the 747 also known as the "jumbo jet" across the Atlantic Ocean while at PEOPLExpress Airlines in 1984. I didn't know Lynn was making history at the time. I'm not sure Lynn knew, but here she was making history simply because she was following her passion for flight.

Being a trail blazer often happens like that. You're so driven that you just put your blinders on and do the thing that people think you're crazy for doing. My own mother opened a health food store in 1977. That was an idea way before its time. Mainstream had no idea the value of good food and how it played a part in your health. But my mother cleared the noise around her and stayed the course. Her passion "A-1 Nutrition Store" is still in operation today 44 years later.

In 2004 I became obsessed with women who were dating "later-in-life." Why? Because I was one. It took on a life of its own as I watched way too many women undervalue themselves as they ventured out into the dating world. I had read all the books out there about dating and that really helped, but there was something missing. The need to fill the gap brought forth a desire, and just like Lynn's journey of going from flight attendant to Captain, I went from dating to a Dating Coach and the idea to write my own book was born. The idea always comes first. The follow-through is where most people stop unless, of course, it's your passion.

My dating journey the first time out lasted about three years before I met and married an "off the boat Italian" but it wasn't until 2014 after getting through the '08 crisis that I focused on publishing my book: DATING: It's Not Personal. Pietro was debonair and romantic, taking me back to the country my own grandparents immigrated from back in the early 1900's. The writing of my manuscript turned out to be the documented version of all that I experienced right up until we met and is now a love story that will reach generations to come. Am I making history? Who knows? This experience brought forth an idea that might. I'm once again obsessed with adding a "phase" to the grieving list. The list of phases that everyone talks about somehow has omitted the intimacy phase. I'm set on adding this very important emotion to the list. You might say I'm a trail blazer, but we really can't acknowledge that until it's a done deal. I fully intend to be making history, but right now I'm in the midst of it. Here's what I know. It's impossible to stop someone who will not quit mainly because he/she is following his/her passion.

It's interesting to realize that this journey didn't even begin until after the passing of my husband. I was catapulted forward creating a wake of viewers from all over the world as they watched my vlog: "Daily Dose A Donna." My message "Set Your Dial to Joy" was one of hope and self-healing, and people tuned in as I literally showed the public, in real time, how they could set "their own dial to JOY" in the midst of heartache and despair. This became my mantra and in turn I discovered it was a much-needed message. People reached out and told me how they viewed me as a ministry. Life Coaches said they loved my message of self-responsibility, and there have been those who said it was like watching a reality show. While in mourning, I was going live on social media.

When the time felt right, I slowly re-entered the world of dating, *again*.

As I walked this tender pathway, reacquainting myself with what lay ahead, people watched and waited. They were curious as to how I would navigate this unspoken phase of grieving. Dating, meeting, and falling in love with Jeffrey in 2018 seemed to give permission to those who have loved and lost...to love again.

When a girlfriend turned to me and said, "Girl, how'd you find love two times in a row?", at that moment I knew my ability to attract and recognize love was undeniable. I knew the secret.

Until now, my gift to help others over the last 20 years has mainly been through social media. As a Certified Women's Empowerment Coach, I have mentored women when they set out to re-discover themselves often in the unforeseen new world of dating. When I walked that road the first time and again as a new widow, my enlightenment became more apparent as women from everywhere reached out to me. My red twirl was like a beacon. *Daily Dose A Donna* was brand-recognizable and had a new message. *Dear Dose* A was born. My fun, no-nonsense "Dear Abby" approach is being sought after and has propelled me into creating Online Dating Workshops. This is for those who are trying to figure out where to start, how to fix their picker, how to look for love in all the right places, how to understand the best way to put a dating profile together, and how to smell a scam, to mention a few. Welcome to dating in the 21st century! Am I blazing another trail? YES, because I am following my passion.

For the record, it was my own insecurities of not feeling good enough or pretty enough that prompted me to figure out the secrets to dating, and this is the very reason why I'm here today. When your self-talk keeps you down, it not only prevents you from having success, it also means you're not having fun. You may sit there thinking well isn't that obvious, but every single thought or word that is not for you is *against* you. It whizzes by so fast you don't even realize it. I have taken many courses and have spent a lot of money and hours learning and understanding how our subconscious is actively working even when we think we're just sitting. I've been on plenty of dates, each one bringing its own pleasures as well as disappointments. While I was venturing out looking for Mr. Wonderful in the name of research, I worked out the kinks, went out on the limb and even fell off a few times. My ability to guide women in this capacity is irrefutable, and in spite of what they initially tell me, they admittedly are excited to start enjoying the dating game with their new perspective!

A date I was on over 25 years ago has only now come to fruition. Even though we weren't on the same page, we enjoyed the evening and talked about how odd it was when people took it personally if they weren't a match. Snap! Just like that, the title of my book was born even before one word was written. Understanding, implementing, and learning how to communicate your intentions makes all the difference, and the confidence you gain as that proverbial bar gets raised is priceless.

If you'll allow me to offer a bit of advice, I would say to be mindful of what you read or listen to and who you spend time with. This is as true in your personal life as it is in your professional life. I'm sure you've heard this before. What goes in must come out, whether it's what you feed your body or what you feed your mind.

So there it is--the calling that emerged out of adversity to teach single women who are interested in finding out some secrets to dating, such as 1) what three letter word can literally save you hours of anguish, 2) how to know within four dates if you're on the same page, and 3) the easiest way to increase the odds of a good connection.

I hope I've got you thinking. The goal in life is not crossing the finish line, but rather enjoying the journey - which encompasses work, enjoyment and love.

All you have to do to make that happen is follow your passion.

MeadorAffect.com

The BIO Photo credit goes to Terry Brennan @TBLSPhotobiz on FB or use https://www.facebook.com/TBLSPhotoBiz)

The Chapter Photo credit goes to: https://christinelowellphotography.com

Shawn Saxton

Success Is a Journey
By Shawn Saxton

Minister Shawn Saxton is the Founder of the Ramah Empowerment Center, Inc. She founded the organization to empower girls and women who have and are affected by trauma from Domestic Violence, Sex Trafficking, and HIV. Shawn knows that the work she does today is helping to empower the next generation to be set free from the abuse that destroys women for a lifetime if not addressed at the root.

Whenever she can help a woman out of Domestic Violence, Sex Trafficking and or a woman living with HIV and she takes control of her life, she knows that she has made a difference. (M.A.D) As she looks back over the years, she has met many women who are now thriving for themselves and making a difference in other women's lives because of the impact she left on them. She is reminded of people who wanted to just pass the HIV virus to everyone they came in contact with because of what's been done to them. Taking the time to listen and encourage and their willingness to listen when she spoke, they themselves have now become advocates. Shawn is a published author, A Tribe out of Domestic Violence and Co-Author of two other published books. She is a Public and Motivational speaker, a Domestic Violence, and HIV advocate and is waiting for certification in Sex Trafficking. By the time this book is published, Shawn Saxton will be a licensed minister with the United Pentecostal Church International. Shawn Saxton holds a Master's Business Administration (MBA) and Bachelors Science in Criminal Justice from Florida Metropolitan University. Shawn is a part of global networks to include but not limited to GEWS-The Executive Vice-President of the USA and President/ Ambassador to the state of Florida. She is connected to Female Wave of Change. She sits on the board for a Suicide Organization-Blue Moon two chapters, one in Florida and the other in the state of Georgia. For speaking, Booking, and contact: Minster Shawn Saxton MBA, BS

(860) 800-2079 or (813) 453-2646

Merriam Webster defines Success as favorable or desired outcome; also: the attainment of wealth, favor, or eminence. What does success mean to me? As I ponder this question in my mind, it brings a measure of clarity to where I am in life at this juncture. If I were speaking to my younger, inner self from where I began this life's journey until now on this journey called life, I would say that my concept of success paved the way to how I deal with the conflicts and confusion.

I can see the tenacity to succeed was birthed in me as a child, and it meant doing what seemed impossible yet with the final analysis being that I would always be true to myself and successful in all walks of my life. Success was something I desired and was willing to work towards accomplishing that goal. I think that so often we underestimate the power of the word success if we would grab a hold to not only going to school but excelling in school and going beyond what others are willing to do.

Success meant not just going to school but excelling and going beyond what your peer group didn't want to do to become successful. It meant showing them there was a better way even in the midst of doubt and disappointment. It meant moving forward to obtain not only my high school diploma but persevering to graduate from college and move forward to achieving and obtaining my Master's Degree in Business Administration.

My success meant envisioning, believing, and putting plans in motion that I would enable me to leave my neighborhood in Harlem, New York, and being able to build the culture and life that I dreamed of. These ideals were birthed in me early in my life. It was my desire to see the dreams come to reality. Because of what I saw and experienced in the neighborhood of my upbringing---a neighborhood that offered limited resources for young women of color, my biggest dream of all was to have an organization that would be geared towards empowering girls and women who were experiencing some of the same social ills that I was---a place where girls and women could go to find that if they were strong enough to dream, that dream could become a reality. I wanted to create an atmosphere that garnered hope---a place that fostered the concept that there is success waiting for them and people were in place to help them to become visionaries; that what some saw as a no-win situation, they could become winners over their adversities in life.

Doing what I saw my family and friends do and being able to do and more or something different was the success I crave for myself. I watched my mother as she offered and assisted young single moms and women reach for more than what was directly in front of them to something higher than themselves. I witnessed my mother promote and organize groups to help single mothers/women generate income. All of this was before the word entrepreneur became a household word in my community and among my peers living in homes of the people reflective of who we were as a family. This was a dream once denied becoming a reality. Success had come to my mother, but it cost her much. But to do what she felt she was called to do was a price she was willing to pay. I also saw that success was attainable but only through my personal failures and my willingness to go after what I desired as success. Success did indeed come to my mother.

However, before it made its genesis, I saw her struggle; I saw her pain and tears. One of the most vivid of all my memories was me seeing and hearing my mommy pray over her children during the late-night hours. It is my belief that nothing is more successful than having a praying mother and/or grandmother, who have prayed prayers that you are receiving the benefits of and living them out in your lives now.

Success to me means having the respect of my family, friends, and peers. Success means being able to make a marked difference in the lives of those who I would come in contact with on a daily basis.

Success means having people call you on the phone when they have no one to turn to because they value what you say, what you do, and how you do it. It means that they value the way I have chosen to live my life and feel as if my voice is one, they need to hear.

In a nutshell, I can say that I am successful because I have my basic needs met to include food, clothing, and shelter. I am not living under stress to keep up with what everyone else is doing. I can go to bed at night, rest unfettered, and not be concerned about what is going to happen with the stock market, and if it crashes, I am doomed.

Success meant that every time I encountered a failure, it was a successful moment because I would have learned from that failure an important lesson to govern the rest of my life. Early on, I knew that I had to have a network of people doing positive things and that would help to motivate me toward my own success. I made sure that I surrounded myself with people who had the ambition and the drive to make success happen. At one time in life, I considered it to be the success of the ones that I saw doing a myriad of things to look successful. But when it came right down to it, all I saw was fancy cars, shopping sprees, and taking vacations. I used to look at those things as successful. I had to reset my thinking and look at how the Lord viewed success and concluded it was walking in His ways, His precepts, and His judgments. Success had become, following after Him with my whole heart, making myself available to Him and His Kingdom, walking in his way, and living a life that is pleasing to Him. Now, I have come to a place in life whereas I reflect on success. I understand that this life the Lord has graciously given me is not my own. I was bought with a price by Him who knew me before I was formed in the belly of my mother. I'm reminded of the Lord Jesus as he spoke to me on May 19, 2004, somewhere between 3:00 and 3:30 in the wee hours of the morning. As I meditated before Him, He gave me this scripture, Jeremiah29:11: "For I know the thoughts that I think towards you, said the LORD, thoughts of peace, and not of evil, to give you an expected end. To me, this in itself spoke more to me concerning success than the day I received my MBA on Jan 15, 2005. Success to me means making a difference in the lives of others but more importantly, living a life that will cause my Lord and Savior to say to me, "Well done, my good and faithful servant!" Success is also having the discipline not to give up when everything seems as if there is nothing else that can be done to take you to the next level of where you are trying to go. This journey to success has caused me to keep going when there is no one around to push you.

You have to keep your stride when it seems like you have no energy to walk nor go a single step further in my own strength. My success journey meant giving some things up to have the success that I have now. I count it a privilege and a joy to have been able to obtain the measure of success that I am experiencing at this point in my life. As I look back over my life, I understand that I was given the opportunities that some are never given. I embraced each one of them, kept my eyes focused on the prize, and I prevailed over every obstacle, every roadblock, difficulty, set back, and disappointment.

My words to the younger generation and my word for you would be to discipline yourself while desiring and or working towards achieving success in your life. Success means different things for different people. As a follower of Jesus Christ, I would pray that the Lord would help you be obedient to Him and know the will of God for the life He has planned for you. Remember you were made according to His pattern. There was a saying few years ago:" God made me, and He don't make no junk!' Think about it; He spoke this world into existence. He created man in His image and after His likeness to be heirs and joint heirs with Him. Now this does not mean you are not going to experience difficulties and setbacks, but you have a God that knows your thoughts afar off, the number of hairs upon your head, everything about you, and He still loves you. You are going to go through the fire to receive your success but never stop moving forward. Although you will go through the fire, you will not be burned. I want you to know when you are following Jesus Christ, you can never be in the fire alone. Consider the story of the three Hebrew boys in Daniel the third chapter in the Bible. When you read the story, you find these words, "Then the king commanded, and they brought Daniel and cast him into the den of lions." Even the King of that day knew the three Hebrew boys were destined for success because we find these words coined, "Now the king spoke and said into Daniel, Thy God whom thou serve continually, he will deliver thee." Even the King saw the greatness in them. Just like the Hebrew boys, you will encounter some obstacles on your journey to your personal success. However, knowing who walks before you should be a reminder that you will make it even when you don't see it. Everybody and even nobody may understand the determination that lies within you, and just like the Hebrew boys, you will encounter some obstacles on your journey to success. There will be naysayers who will come to deter you on your journey to success. However, knowing who walks before you should be a reminder that you will make it even when you don't see your way clear. I would like to add that the story of success in the Book of Daniel is about the Jewish people and their success and how those who were not Jews were unsuccessful in their attempt to kill what the three Hebrew were called to do---their refusal to bow to any deity other than the one and only true God, especially the King. Take this story as a roadmap that you do not have to bow to the pressures of this age to fit in. You can be unique and still be successful because of whose you are... Success and failure will meet up but the difference to attain your desired results depends upon you. Success is to never stop moving forward on your journey. If you stay the course, you will meet success at the end of the road. Success could and does mean different things to different people. Popular culture says success is having a big fancy house, car, job, and other toys. Success for others may mean having all the glam; buying into this is not the success that you want. The success that you should desire and live for is having peace of mind, being able to sleep at night, and knowing that you have done your best. There is nothing more satisfying than knowing you have given it your best shot. Surround yourself with positive likeminded people and find someone that you look up to and ask them to be your mentor or accountability partner. Don't try to accomplish everything in a day. Prepare a "to do" list and work one thing at a time. Set daily, weekly, monthly, and yearly goals for yourself and keep a record as to what you have accomplished.

Homework:

Work on this section alone and then with a family, friend and or anyone. Compare how success was and is viewed as the generations have changed views and values.

Boomers, Generational X, Millennials and Generation

Space for Questions:

_____

_____

_____

Success is Discipline: Discipline yourself for success!!

Carolyn McGee

Balancing Intuition and Logic for Success
By Carolyn McGee

As a child I was curious, imaginative, and deeply connected to nature, angels, and intuition. Who I was and how I was perceived were not completely the same. I was celebrated and seen as the good math and science kid. I received attention for being an honors student and being logical. My stories of angels and talking animals were dismissed as "being fanciful."

The truth is I am both: I am highly intuitive and connected while also being a genius in logic and technology. Now, I know there is a deep synergy between the energies, and I celebrate both. It took me years of not trusting and acting upon my intuition to recognize it and have faith so I could take inspired action even when logic said not to!

Growing up, I stopped listening to my inner voice and valued the opinions and directions of society and family above what I felt to be true. I needed the validation and acknowledgement of being seen as good at something. I shut down the creative side and focused on the tech part where I was noticed.

Attending an engineering college was the next logical step, and I thrived being away from home and the expectations to fit into a mold that wasn't me. Technology is easy for me, so I got the chance to experiment being a little bit more of the rest of me. I was great at problem solving for technical stuff and relationships. I became known for giving sage advice and helping others to navigate difficult situations yet was not doing it for me.

As I started interviewing for jobs, I felt a pull that I couldn't explain to work for a big company in Boston. Two uncles worked for this company, so I had a logical explanation. I also KNEW that there was another reason that I needed to be there. Six months after I started, I met the reason.

As I started my High-Tech Manufacturing career, I started to notice that using my feelings (I didn't understand that it was intuition yet) at work helped me. I could tell when there was something off in a meeting. During negotiations, I just knew when people were holding back or not being completely honest. I knew when a design wouldn't work even if I couldn't logically articulate it. I developed a reputation for being right and saved the company lots of money, and others started to trust my feelings to evaluate what I felt deeper. This gave me confidence in trusting myself even when it didn't seem logical. I learned to start to speak my truth even when it didn't "make sense."

During this time, I met my husband-to-be at work. While my confidence at work grew, I began a deep healing journey to trusting myself in personal relationships. My (now ex) husband became one of my greatest teachers fulfilling my soul's call to work at this company, so we could meet and work through our karma. Looking back, I can see each step that brought me to meeting him, the opportunities I had to follow the intuitive guidance and learn the easy way and the choices I made from fear and conditioning that made my life difficult.

My career path took me into start-up companies that required creativity and the ability to build something from nothing. I was a corporate superstar, yet I joked with my friends that I left my personality at the door when I got home. A small voice inside me said that I needed to be a different model for my son and daughter on how a woman is treated and valued. I focused on the outer success I had at work and made the difficult choice to end the marriage. I started to follow my inner voice.

As I became more me, I shone even more at work. I was successful in the traditional manner. I continued to use my intuition and creativity to help the company grow, but I didn't feel successful as a person. Often, we can equate work success with personal success, but I feel they are quite different. If we are good at something, but it doesn't bring us joy, we are not completely successful. I started to evaluate what success meant to me. My heart and soul wanted to make a difference in people's lives. The drive to help others feel happy and have easy, joyful lives motivated me.

As I reflected on "what is success", I was downsized from my corporate job, and instead of feeling panicked, I felt empowered. I decided to channel my love of helping others and animals into a business. I created a dog walking and pet care company. While I cared for my clients and their pets, I also made myself a priority. I used my gift of development to organize and grow the business. The company quickly expanded, and I hired staff. I trained people and created repeatable processes. Manuals were generated. The company grew to the point that I needed to incorporate and hire support people. I was successful in providing employment to others and providing peace of mind to people when they could not be with their pets.

My connection with animals deepened, and I felt my own personal energy become more tangible, grounded, and present. I remembered my innate connection to animals and that I could communicate with them. I allowed this ability to help me expand the ways I could provide service to my clients. It became a fun and positive challenge to find new ways that I could support my pet clients, be of service, and be compensated. I expanded on my ability to look beyond the traditional and find creative ways to make my clients lives easier and richer. I was living my version of a successful life.

As I used my desire to help others, while also helping myself, I opened myself up to other gifts and possibilities. I learned about energy healing and added it as a service for pets. I loved the creativity and expansiveness of the pet business. Every day was an adventure into what was possible. I was providing great service, helping others, taking care of me, and being a great model for my children. This was success.

It was during this time that I rediscovered my connection to the angels. As I relearned, accepted, and trusted my gifts of divine connection, I remembered how easy it was for me to provide advice and support in the past. I realized that this was being a channel for divine love and guidance. I gained confidence in my ability to understand this divine guidance and trust the messages that I received for others and myself.

I opened my second business as an intuitive coach and teacher to help others to use their intuition to shortcut their journey to connection and inspired action, to utilize this inner knowing to make empowered choices, trust them and act on the guidance. During my journey, I documented my path so that I could provide clear direction to people struggling with recognizing their intuition. It was fun to combine my gifts and talents into a business that reflected me at every level. This was deep success to me.

I realized that the way we make decisions is universal. How we show up in one situation is how we will react or show up in every situation. If we have a hard time making decisions or getting clarity about what our next right step is, it impacts every aspect of life including our business or career. Your business or career is an extension of you. Your choices shape the direction and growth of your business. Your feeling of being successful will expand as you confidently make choices, take action, and not look back.

The way I support my clients is to give them crystal clear clarity of their soul's purpose and mission. I teach them to utilize their intuition as a tool for unparalleled success to tune into their intuitive superpowers so that they can always feel confident and aligned in making decisions. This underutilized gift takes the stress and struggle out of determining their next best step in growing their business or living a confident and fulfilled life.

Success to me is living a fulfilled life. It is utilizing all the gifts that we are born with to maximize impact in our lives and the lives of others. We each are born with a unique purpose. We are here to be the best parent, plumber, creative, leader, accountant, friend, or gardener. It does not matter what we are doing as long as we are happy and fulfilled doing it. Abundance and support will flow magnetically to a happy person who is living their purpose.

The energy of doing something from a feeling of obligation or expectation weighs us down and diminishes the sense of success. There are many people who are at the top of their class or top earners in a company who are miserable. They are living someone else's dream and not theirs. They feel lost and each day is a joyless repeat of the day before.

To truly be successful, we each must take the bold look at our dreams and follow our hearts desire. We must feel creative and know that we are making a difference in the world. Creativity can be making the better mouse trap, painting, teaching a child to tie their shoes, or finding a way to save your company money or time. There are endless ways of being creative.

A true measure of success can also be found in our friends and relationships. Do you have a support team? Are there people you can call to get feedback on an idea? Will people tell you the truth if they feel you are making a mistake? Do you have a team/friends to celebrate with?

To me success is navigating and thriving in the balance between personal and professional life. When our purpose is defined by our work, we can lose our value as an individual. It is a balance between using the divine masculine of inspiration and action with the divine feminine of creativity and being grounded.

Success is having the confidence to make a decision and follow through on it without second guessing.

The best advice I can give is "to thine own self be true." We each have an innate sense of self. What is good for you? What is not? Honor yourself enough to be true to your own energy and interests.

We all have foods that we like and dislike. We have no issues saying, "I don't like lima beans." Someone might try to get you to try it again but most likely you can easily say "no thank you." Or perhaps you just don't like the color Orange. Are you going to paint your home or room a color that doesn't resonate with you?

The same is true for relationships and careers. We have needs and wants in how we spend our time each day. Yet we can allow others to influence our choices in the biggest time investments of our lives. If we don't trust ourselves and the ability to read our own energy, our decisions are not truly ours.

I have found that my intuition is my truest guide for optimum choices. What is Intuition? Intuition is an internal guidance system. It is like a GPS that you can follow to get information to help you make decisions for your highest good. Your intuition is your body's resonance with the divine energy that is out there to help you with making choices that are beneficial.

We all have a certain level of intuition. It is like a muscle. You just must practice using it. The more you practice, the more you exercise your intuition, the stronger it becomes. The more you utilize it to make decisions and experience the beneficial results, the more you will trust yourself to step out in life and business.

Also, knowing when to balance my intuition with my technology skills and logic is key. We need this balance to move successfully and easily forward in life. One without the other can create disharmony and disrupt flow. If do not embrace all aspects of our energy, we are not thriving and as successful as we can be.

I now embrace my passion to serve and my uniqueness as a gift to myself and the world! Following intuition and balancing logic is the key to living my successful life.

Biography

Creatrix Carolyn McGee is the architect of the Sacred Haven for Empowered & Intuitive Living Community which includes North Carolina retreats, virtual gatherings, powerful workshops, private coaching, and soul-nurturing VIP weekends. She serves women ready to connect with their inner wisdom, to trust it to make empowered decisions, and then to take inspired action and discover the power of nature's cycles to create a life that lights them up. She has co-authored 10+ bestselling books and is a popular Radio & TV host, sought-after speaker, and blogger. www.CarolynMcGee.com

Dr. Imelda Yap-Ugalde

The Role Model
By Dr. Imelda Yap-Ugalde

Dr. Imelda Yap-Ugalde, FPDS, MD, MAN, RN, BSc, CPC-A
Fellow, Philippine Dermatological Society
Diplomate, Philippine Board of Dermatology
Dermatology Residency, Skin and Cancer Foundation, Inc.
Doctor of Medicine, University of Santo Tomas, Faculty of Medicine and Surgery
Master of Arts in Nursing – University of La Salette
Bachelor of Science in Nursing – University of La Salette
Bachelor of Science in Psychology – University of Santo Tomas College of Science
Certified Professional Coder – HIM Training Institute (AAPC accredited)

YAP FAMILY

Education is part of my DNA. As an educator, I grew up seeing my parents be truly generous in providing opportunities such as scholarships to help students reach their potential. They built schools from the ground up, and though I have seen them struggle at times, they role-modeled "giving back" to the communities our schools served---an act that has become part of who we are as a family. In a family of educators, one takes on various educator roles. From being a teacher, where you are the "sage on the stage" for your young children to becoming a facilitator or a "guide on the side" as your children start to mature. Our family grew up knowing that education is important in one's life. It opened opportunities and possibilities for us. We became competitive not just with each other but more to ourselves. With the watchful eye of our parents, we ensured we gave our best whether rewards were a natural forethought or not.

At a young age, we were exposed to the rudiments of running a school and dealing with teachers, school personnel, and most especially other students. My parents dreamt, designed, built, and sustained the development of a couple of schools that catered to the needs of their locations' communities. From high school up to graduate school level, these were their legacy. The schools' names were Saint Anthony College of Technology (SACT) and Dau Academy (DA), both in Mabalacat, Pampanga. My eldest brother continued this legacy and expanded the offerings introducing preschool and grade school as well as vocational and continuing education programs like piloting commercial airplanes and government-regulated drones. He retained the name SACT but updated Dau Academy into Saint Mutien Marie College.

My late father, Catalino, finished his Master of Arts in Education degree at the University of Manila while my late mother, Benita, graduated from the Centro Escolar University with a Doctor of Education degree. My eldest brother Antonio had his Master's in Business Administration degree at the Asian Institute of Management (AIM). My sister Editha finished her Master's in Public Administration at the University of Santo Tomas Graduate School. My younger brother Manuel was able to graduate from our very own graduate school with a Master's degree in Teaching and my youngest brother Robin, finished his PhD in Global Management in the USA and his post-doctoral program at Cornell University in Data Analytics.

YAP-UGALDE FAMILY

After four years of being a couple, I married my one and only boyfriend on that balmy day in January 1984 at San Agustin Church, Intramuros, Manila. My husband, Rene's, father, who was a general of the Philippine Air Force, stood smiling with pride of his son, and alongside were Rene's former beauty queen sisters, who embodied their mother's grace and elegance. Ten years into our marriage, we adopted a lovely baby girl whom we named "Marie Eula Lauren" and nicknamed her Eula. She is a true San

Beda College Alabang alumnus having studied there since she was in nursery school. Her volleyball awards spanned through her college years and graduated with a Bachelor of Arts degree in Psychology. Eula works as market research lead of the executive management staff at Filinvest Land Inc. She now has a child of her own, named "Erin Fatima," aged 4. Three years after Eula was adopted, "Renald Ian" was born. Like Eula, Ren is a true De La Salle Zobel alumnus having been in the school since he was in Junior Prep. Being a consistent honor student, he graduated with a Bachelor of Science in Business Administration degree at De La Salle College of St. Benilde. With a major in Human Resource Management, he learned the importance of having a multidisciplinary background to being relevant in the job market. With that in mind, he recently became a Certified Professional Coder (CPC-A) and now works at Omega Healthcare Philippines.

TRAVELS

Rene has been a good provider for our family. He is also a board-certified dermatologist and practices in Metro Manila. We were classmates in medical school, and he had the same residency program in dermatology. We have been fortunate to be able to travel abroad and like my educator-parents, I find myself in lively discussions with the family on these travel experiences as they are good learning opportunities for everyone. We discuss how we can be better people through what we have learned about other cultures, about their cuisine, and about the people and the environment we have interacted with.

My hope, like my parents, grandparents, and their parents before them, is for my children to be happy, content, and grateful for all the blessings, the challenges, and the successes they encounter in their lives. These are all opportunities for growth and maturity.

Whether we travel as a family or individually, I find that travelling allows us to gain immeasurable understanding of people. To date,

Asia has been a favorite destination; that may be due to proximity. I have been to North America and have seen the beauty of the land and the culture through the eyes of my siblings who live there. One of my more memorable travels was to the Holy Land and my Marian pilgrimages. I am a prayerful person, and these pilgrimages helped me feel as if I am closer to God. Like a faithful Catholic, whenever I travel to a new place, I always visit a church. Locally, my family and I have travelled extensively as far as Ilocos, Baguio, and La Union in the north and as far as Davao in the south. The Visayan islands were the most frequented and these included Cebu, Boracay, Palawan, Leyte, Bacolod, Iloilo, Dumaguete.

VOLUNTEERISM

As a doctor, helping people comes naturally to me. The satisfaction of seeing a patient improving is better than any monetary gain. Thousands of patients later and with a bit more maturity, I started volunteer work. One organization I have fond memories in as a volunteer was acting as an assistant coordinator of PREX 28 (Parish Renewal Experience), a Catholic church organization. I took on different roles here from administrative activities like scheduling of priests to physical arrangements to even building a menu. It was out of my wheelhouse, but it turned out to be a success. We also visited elderly females from an assisted living facility, and we entertained them throughout the day. Since PREX 28 is also recognized by our church, we had our share of regular church work activities especially during holidays like Lent and Christmas.

As members of "Couples for Christ", we shared our blessings to those in need. My husband and I became coordinators for "Kids for Christ," an experience that strengthened our resolve in being good role models for children around us. We have shared our learnings not only about being children of God but to be kind citizens overall. These seemed to also be the times when we can feel the presence of God. A good example of this presence was when we had a scheduled prayer meeting with the children, but the sponsor unfortunately backed out at the last minute resulting in a lack of funds for the venue and the associated meals. Pure chance, coincidence or through the grace of God, that day my husband had more than his usual number of patients, and we were able to forge on with the prayer meeting. We chose to view this as through the presence and grace of God and noted that whenever we share our talents, time, and blessings to others, God will always be there to guide us and provide for our needs.

EDUCATION

I spent my childhood in Pampanga, one of the largest provinces in the Philippines. Being studious resulted in achieving a grade school salutatorian and a high school valedictorian award. By the time I headed to college, I joined my siblings by moving to Manila. I continued to have good grades allowing me to be in top tier of my programs at St. Scholastica's College and the University of Santo Tomas (UST) where I graduated with a Bachelor of Science degree in Psychology. This educational ethic resulted in an exemption of the entrance examination for medical school at UST. This was an honor I did not take lightly, especially when I was already being welcomed by the Dean of the UST Faculty of Medicine and Surgery while other applicants were still taking the entrance exams. It pays to study well in all levels of academia.

Medical school life was a totally different world for me. I thought I studied hard in my academic years prior to this, but the rigors of medical education meant a different studying strategy. This included late night readings and onto the next morning memorizations of Anatomy, Physiology, Biochemistry, Pathology, and more difficult disciplines like Surgery, Psychiatry, Obstetrics, Pediatrics, Orthopedics, and other sub-specialties. One must have a focused end-goal to be a doctor to get through all the work required to become one.

When I started my clinical rotation, I thought I would feel like a "doctor" already but no, there was a lot more learning to be had. Theoretical subjects continued to be part of the program until the end. At UST, a medical student cannot graduate until she passes the *"revalida"* or a "viva voce." This is where you will be given a case (patient) where you analyze and give differential diagnosis so your panel of examiners can determine your critical thinking capability and your medical competency. They also test your fortitude by asking a variety of questions that may not be related to your case. Once you graduate, the work is not done yet; there is still another year of internship before taking the physician licensure examination. It was a long arduous road, but it was all worth it.

After passing the medical boards, I went on a six months' rural training. This program was part of the government's efforts to provide opportunities for new doctors to see the real social situation of its citizenry. We not only became doctors to serve those who have the means but to serve everyone---a commitment to the Hippocratic Oath that we made when we became doctors. I went on a Psychiatry residency program, but soon after, my husband and I were at a practice crossroads. With this training came a decision for us to go to the United States but soon realized that our calling was in the Philippines, so we moved back home. I decided a residency at the Skin and Cancer Foundation was a better fit for my interests. This specialty provided by the Philippine Board of Dermatology bestowed upon me a Diplomate status. Two years later, I became a Fellow of the Philippine Dermatological Society.

VOLUNTEERISM CONTINUES

Giving back meant for me to continuously find ways to show my gratitude for the blessings my family and I have received to share with others. One of the ways I have been able to do this was to become a dermatology volunteer in charity clinics like annual free skin clinic sponsored by the Philippine Dermatological Society, giving free consultation and medicines. I also had the chance to be part of the volunteer team for Typhoon Yolanda victims. With this pandemic, financial support was given to our parish for their "pantry of blessings" as well as giving clothes and other household items to tricycle and grab drivers, garbage collectors, St. Rita orphanage, Hospicio de San Jose, security guards and other street vendors and homeless individuals. Every day is an opportunity for us to share our blessings to others, no matter how small it may be.

Concurrent to my medical fellowship was another interest that I pursued. Nursing. This allowed me another avenue to give back by volunteering in nursing homes and hospitals specifically at adult medical-surgical wards. Being a doctor and nurse helped me understand the symbiotic relationship of the two professions and allowed me to understand what "care" means to my patients. As studying has been part of who I am, I continued to grow professionally even during this pandemic. What is an ancillary and necessary activity for medical practitioners/healthcare professionals? Medical coding. I am a Certified Professional Coder, recognized by AAPC (American Academy of Professional Coders).

As an Educator

This was always a role that played throughout my choices in life and career. Like generations of educators in our family, I, too, taught university classes like Oncology at Manila Doctors

College. In addition, I also trained residents in dermatology at the Skin and Cancer Foundation. Like my mother, who made lifelong learning a lifestyle, I continue to be fascinated in the various facets of the medical field - from being a dermatologist to a nurse to a medical coder.

On a personal note, at age 63, I continue to be an educator to my children and role-model to my nephews and nieces as they carry this torch of a lifelong pursuit to critical thinking, care, kindness, and academic excellence. I believe that education is not only a vital part of one's success but also a guide on one's outlook in life.

Caroline L. Velasco

New Face (Caranova)
By Caroline L. Velasco

"In times of despair and dark times, there's a beauty inside me that shines like a lotus flower that blooms in the darkest mud."

My name is Caroline L. Velasco; I was born to Nelia Martinez Llasos and Virgilio Alonzo Velasco. I have three brothers: Virgilio Jr., Alfredo Virgilio, Aristotle Vincent, and four sisters, namely, Johanna, Ma. Kristina, Ma. Theresa and Catherine. I am a fourth child, and it was during the rainy season when my mother brought me into this world on July 25, 1976, in Quezon City; it was gloomy and raining at that time. My father named me after Princess Caroline of Monaco, his favorite royal princess. When I was very young, I was a shy and quiet loner with low self-esteem because I was suffering from dyslexia. My father always lost his cool whenever he heard me reading invertedly, and as my punishment, he left me alone in my room to stand on the top of the big table the whole day along with the big blackboard to memorize all the words that he wrote on it.

I also have hearing problems and very poor eyesight. It was late when my parents discovered my condition so that whenever I entered school, I was often bullied and ended up not wanting to go to my class. I could hardly utter simple words nor communicate well with other kids because of my difficulties. I was seven years old when my father tried to enroll me again for grade one. I was one year behind for that level at that time. When my father discovered that I had reading difficulties, my brother Alfredo and my elder sister Johanna tutored me patiently until I overcame my reading and speaking problems and eventually performed well in school from section 21 to section 1 and started to compete in spelling contests, but still I was a subject of bullying because I had disabilities. I was also too frail, and my bones were too weak to play with the other kids. I never remember having friends in school or memories of playing with children other than my siblings during my childhood years. I mostly spent time reading, studying, and doing household chores since we had a big family and did not have any house help.

Our family was having financial trouble because my father's warehouse burned down, and all his inventories had not recovered. We were forced to move to Quezon City in 1984 to start a new life. My father's career started again when he became a consultant for developing the coconut and detergent industry in Technological Livelihood Resource Center (Government Owned Corporation). But in 1986, my father was relieved of his job because he joined the Edsa Revolution to end Martial Law and President Ferdinand Marco's government. I remembered that my mom bought me a yellow dress to show support for the new government. Our family suffered for years because nobody wanted to hire my father, and we had to move to a small apartment in Novaliches Quezon City. Despite our parents' financial crises, they let us continue our education. We all studied in public school until 1989. My father's first stint in building factories for Chinese Businessmen who have big names in the coconut oil industry gave my father a break, and our situation in life improved. In 1990, my father bought a house for us in Caloocan City to stop renting an apartment in Novaliches.

During my elementary years, I was always at the top of the class but never became first honor nor valedictorian even though I worked very hard to be no. 1. I started to hate my parents for not showing support and compassion towards me and relentlessly comparing my effort to my other siblings who had excelled in school. My parents were also too strict with everyone, and we never understood them, especially my father. I again seldom met his relatives; he was too secretive about his own life. Sometimes, I felt he was a stranger because we hardly knew his background, and I did not understand why he pushed us so much to do our best in everything we did. We all knew that there was no room for mistakes; my father also implanted in our young minds not to trust people around us. During our adolescent stage, my father introduced us to business and let us work for him so we could all go to school, eat regularly, and live decently. Also, during this stage, we all became rebellious to our parents. My brothers became active in activism and my eldest sister in a school publication.

I had to change my personality when I entered high school. I became too friendly and famous in the entire school. I also joined girl groups and started skipping my class and became hard-headed. I continuously disobeyed my parents throughout my high school life and always avoided them until I graduated. Despite being a problem child as a student during my high school years, I can say I had a high regard for education. I managed not to have failed grades.

My father started to open up about his family when he realized that we were all lost and did not understand how lucky we were. Despite the hardship that we encountered, we still had a parent who could guide and protect us no matter what happened. Unlike my father, he was an orphan and was sent to Boys Town, an orphanage, when his mother died of tuberculosis when he was four years old, and his father took his three siblings with him to Spain. At the age of nine, my father escaped from the orphanage and started to work as a porter in a truck managed by a junk shop. While working as a child, he continued studying until he became a jeepney driver and apprentice in a machine shop in Tondo Manila. This kind of job helped him support his college tuition fee in Mapua, a prestigious school known to produce the Philippines' best engineers. He finished Chemical Engineering while doing that kind of job.

The hardship that he experienced when at his young age and no parents to guide and support him are all his reasons why he was overprotective and very strict to us. He was also a victim of harshness and cruelty of life, and he did not want us to experience and expose ourselves to the same environment where he was raised.

Whenever I reflect as a young girl, I remember how cruel the world was to me because of my disability. Also, our family experienced isolation because my parents' ambitions to rise above the rest made us susceptible to prejudices which resorted in abuses and discrimination. Even at my father's darkest days, my mother never left him, and she never left us. She said that we could reach our goals and face all the misfortunes coming along our way because she would support and guide us.

Jan, our eldest sister, made it to the University of the Philippines. She and Diliman are also the reason behind my success. She is the only person who believed that I was not fit for the environment that we lived in, and she convinced me to enroll in that prestigious school since I had good grades. I considered myself an excellent student although most of my teachers did not appreciate my academic performance since I was only good at the written exam. My social communication was poor since I had dyslexia and other disabilities, which I managed to overcome and live a regular life. Still, discrimination existed until I entered the University of the Philippines (U.P Diliman). I took up Philippine Studies Major in Economics and English Literature in 1997. During my college years, everything was far different from my younger years. I never experienced any discrimination at this prestigious school, and I even met daughters and sons of influential people in our country. I felt respected in this school. I focused on my studies and managed to hide my disabilities though sometimes manifested in my work.

My research and development in product development started during my days in U.P Diliman and an early training from my father's chemical laboratory. My father was a Quality Control and Product Developer from the Philippines Refining Company (PRC) and a Consultant Pioneer of the Technology and Livelihood Resource Center (TLRC). During his stint at this government institution, my father eventually made a name in putting-up manufacturing plants, including the design and construction of manufacturing plants (production facilities and manufacturing processes), fabrication of facilities and equipment, chemical processes, waste management, and pollution control system and technology transfer. He built and renovated various well-known companies from oil mills, sodium silicate plants, soap manufacturing, and some food industries. His primary clients were Mindanao Coco Oil Mills (MINCOCO), Ricor Mills, Kings Oil, Jane Castor Coco Oil, Naga Sunbeam, White House Oil Mill, Youngstown Canning Corp., Heron Chemicals, Integral Chemical Corp., Silicate Industries, Bona Scientio Corp., and W.L. Foods.

My career was started as an Environmental Pollution Control officer (PCO) while still finishing my U.P Diliman thesis in 2000. At that time, my father referred me to Sylicate Industries to worked as a Pollution Control Officer (PCO) and representative of the DENR-EMB. As PCO, I drafted standardized and implemented guidelines, policies, and management plans of the manufacturing company approved by EMB-DENR to ensure environmental safety and public health. I also implemented a waste recycling process to eliminate generated waste material.

1. Wastewater Control Process (Sylicate Industries)
2. Transporting & Processing of Hazardous Waste (Silicate Industries)
3. Transport Management Plan for Waste Chemicals (Silicate Industries)

After my graduation in 2001, I worked as a Business Development

Officer at Nel's Industrial Corporation, my family-owned company. At that time, I was in charge of developing marketing plans to meet clientele' demands from the detergent industry.

In 2004 I left Nel's and worked as a Research Writer at Yuchengco Research Center for East Asia. My short stint was recognized and made me co-authored to a USAID-AED Project entitled Assessment of the Family Planning Clinics in Industry (USAID-AED Project). During this year, I felt complete independence. I was assigned to go to Cebu to meet some influential government officials who could assist us in our project.

In 2005, I married Christian Lumiwan, my classmate and a college friend in U.P Diliman and decided to move with him and leave my blossoming career to focus on my family. I stayed in the province of Tuguegarao, my husband's hometown, until our firstborn son became too sickly. I decided to return to Manila to work to help my husband with our financial needs.

With the help of Mr. Beato Griarte, a colleague of my father from TLRC, he introduced me to some private companies and other entrepreneurs who needed my expertise in developing their products in the detergent industry. One of my clients was Primemost Marketing (PMS), a Multi-Level marketing company based in Cebu City. At first, we focused on developing home care and janitorial products, and I was also in charge of sourcing the types of machinery and raw materials that we need in the factory. Later, PMS exploited my capacity to develop more products when they found out that I had a solid product development foundation. I was trained well in my father's laboratory during my younger years. I remembered well the discipline he imposed on us. I also witnessed a chemical reaction that almost burned down our house and would have killed us all if I had made a mistake in my computation and analysis of chemicals. At this time, I understood my father because everything must be calculated well. There is no room for emotions, only scientific data. During my father's laboratory training, he always told us to practice patience and tolerance because we could not afford to make a mistake.

From detergent to janitorial products, I developed more cosmetics and later food to cater to the wellness industry. During this period, I was challenged to conceptualize more products to cater to a diverse clientele. I became financially well off because I conceptualized new product developments in the market, and at the same time, I was freely sourcing out new raw materials at my account. In 2009 after four years with PMS, they announced their separation from me. At that time, I had already finished their locally fabricated semi-manual encapsulation machine for their food supplement capsules which we manufactured at my father's fabrication plant, and at the same time, I gave birth to my third son Nathan. PMS owner told me before they discontinued my services that someday "I'll be their competitor" and that they will give me more time to focus on taking care of my children.

I was devastated, and I did not work for months. I decided to shift my career because I wanted to prove that I was a loyal person. I invested some of my money in the clothing and construction business, but I lost my investment since I was not too familiar with the industry. In 2010 I decided to return to my expertise, and this time, I was all alone. I put up my own chemical trading business – Chemscents Industrial Sales. One of my services was to supply chemical raw materials from home care, car care, cosmetic, and food products. I also conceptualized the Product and Packaging Design for start-up companies that needed help in launching new products. Because of my services, I became known to some more prominent and well-known MLM company. My services for innovating new products to throw in the market had been addressed. My success was fast, and I decided to put up another company, Caranova Marketing (it means a new face in marketing), in 2014 to separate my chemical trading from my consultancy and marketing of the finished product.

In 2015, some of my products that I conceptualized for my clients won Super Brand because of my passion for innovation that led me to achieve my goals to compete with the crowded market and succeed in competitive times. Later, I extended my services from product conceptualization to packaging design. I added product formulation with product notification and registration to Food and Drugs Administration (FDA). I assisted my clients in securing their licenses from the Local Government. I have already helped many entrepreneurs establish and set-up their companies and develop their food, detergents, car care, and cosmetic products.

In November 2018, the Department of Trade and Industry (DTI) chose me to be one of the Philippine Participants in the first China International Import Expo (CIIE) at the National Exhibition and Convention Center in Shanghai, China. in line with the DTI's aim to further penetrate the vast Chinese market through country participation in trade expositions and facilitation of business-to-business linkages.

Also, I am a registered Food and Drugs Administration FDA qualified person in industry regulatory Affairs in cosmetics.

In 2019, I partnered with a charity institution **Sgian Dubh Helping Hands U.K. Philippines Inc.**, with Ben Smith, Scottish founder, and Beth Perez, to elevate malnutrition in the Philippines.

My social and political inclination started back in my college years. Our university is a highly political institution because most of our political and influential people graduated. I live with the farmers and fisherfolks in the countryside to be aware of our country's condition. I also wrote my thesis on how to increase the Philippines' literacy rate using Popular Novels because education in our country is for privileged citizens only.

I am totally committed to my partner charity. My purpose for joining this organization is to help women and children to empower themselves through education and assistance with livelihood training seminars to elevate their social, economic standards. Since 2019, we have already visited many remote places to distribute food and educational material to indigent people.

In 2020, once again, the Department of Trade and Industry (DTI) chose me to be one of the five Philippine delegates to the United States of America and Mexico to promote the Philippines and strengthen business tie-ups.

This year (2021) I am launching Amelie International Incorporated with my younger brother to focus on system technology and system development for manufacturing and trading companies, and we have also developed our e-commerce platform. I chose Amelie because it is one of my favorite movies, but it also means hard work and passion as one of the requirements to success.

My father once said if you want to eat delicious food, you must work hard for it. You can also do impossible things if you believe in yourself but do not be too optimistic because you will not be able to see the right opportunity. If you let it pass, you will never know when it comes again. Up to now, I have never forgotten my father's words; he used to utter these lines when we were young and unstable.

Rebecca Garcia

The Grand Dame of Dancesport Asia Holds Sway
By Rebecca Garcia

This woman's biggest win. RESOLUTE, Hardworking Glam girl BECKY GARCIA finds that success is chasing after happiness until it catches you.

PROSPERITY is not about a fat bank account or a string of status symbols. Life has taught me that if I stay happy, honest, and determined, I will be successful at anything. My wellspring of goodness and of pure intentions has generated blessings from many. Apart from good health, having good relationships is a gift that money cannot buy.

My work hard---play hard attitude was nurtured by my parents Melanio and Josefina Ocampo, both accomplished and socially prominent physicians. When powerful politicians visited my home city of Iriga in Camarines Sur, the mayor invariably asked my parents to host them.

My mother, the disciplinarian, was active in civic groups. She was my Poster Girl for focus. From my father, who was an extrovert and a dandy, I picked up joie de vivre. He frequently changed clothes in a single day and simply liked flaunting them. On his birthday, without fail, he hired a big band and invited the entire community over.

He pampered me, second of his six children, the most. My clothes were made by a designer in a city Naga, a full hour's drive from Iriga. If I wanted fancy shoes, such as pumps with acrylic heels, my father from his travels would buy my clothes and shoes. Sometimes he sent his personal assistant as far as the next city or even beyond that to purchase them.

I have reveled in performing for audiences since I was a child. I was born with a piano at home, and I loved playing for guests. (I continue to surprise friends with my extensive repertoire.) At age five, I recited a poem to the archbishop and got to sit on his lap as a reward. No declamation piece overwhelmed me, ever, and I always took the front row in cheer leading during school games.

In high school, my dad's sister, who was a former Mother Superior at Sta. Isabel College in Manila, suggested that I be sent there as an interna (old term for a ward in boarding school under strict nuns). My mother wanted her children to be doctors, so some of us did take up medicine. But right from the start of my pre-med at the University of Sto. Tomas, men started wooing me. My conservative mother promptly sent me back to the sheltered life at Sta. Isabel, where I would graduate with a Bachelor of Arts degree in psychology.

Pedigree and perfume

Returning to Iriga after college graduation, I did not know what I wanted to do so while I was contemplating my future like getting engaged to my boyfriend, I decided to teach English and history at the La Consolacion Academy and the University of Northeastern Philippines, which was owned by an uncle. My classes were always packed—often a hundred students at a time, quite likely on account of my pedigree, but maybe also because of the perfume that I wore. They could tell that I was on my way long before I stepped into the classroom.

After a year I returned to Manila to look for work. Enthusiasm, emotional intelligence, and people skills launched my career. Starting out as a sales representative in Tower Hotel and eventually at the Hotel Frederick in the early 1970s, I wangled the "Disney on Parade" account—75 rooms reserved for several weeks—beating established international chains to the draw. All it took was courage to meet the handlers, an attractive package, and engaged discussion.

My reputation for persuasive interaction with prospective clients spread wide and fast. I taught sales, marketing, and public relations in a hotel school based at the Hilton. In my classes, I underscored the importance of name recall, working the adage, "The sweetest sound to anyone's ears is the sound of his or her own name."

I discovered my knack for producing when I teamed up with model Jane Umali to put up the fashion show of Spanish designer Paco Rabanne at the Manila Hotel. I was soon pirated for a slot in the pre-launch team of Tradewinds Manila, which was owned by Singapore Airlines. As director for sales and marketing, I used my social network to pack the new hotel's Chinese restaurant daily. With the airline as partner, Tradewinds presented luncheon fashion shows featuring foreign designers and models.

New ventures

Espying my leadership skills and consistently pleasant effect on people, a regular hotel guest offered me the post of publisher in a new insurance business magazine that would serve an international market. Perks in the package made the offer hard to refuse— a clothing allowance that covered designer clothes and accessories and all-expense-paid trips including first-class plane seats and luxury accommodations, plus a generous expense account.

From my network, I put together a powerhouse editorial team. We attended insurance conventions and congresses around the world. For many of those gatherings, I booked hotel suites where we entertained top managers from different firms. I enjoyed preferential treatment from top executives of leading insurance companies and even was invited to dine at the dining room of the Lloyd's of London, the world's leading insurance market.

Building on ideas and infusing life into projects and tasks came naturally to me. I soon launched my own magazine—*Career Girl*, which spotlighted stunning and successful women—at the Peninsula Manila in 1980. I worked with the best editors, such as Abe Florendo and Jullie-Yap Daza, who found seasoned writers and photographers for every issue.

Career Girl ran a good course until the EDSA Revolution in 1986. I ventured into public relations via Chase Thomas with the late PR Whiz Mars Marquez and into events organizing via a company NovelVentures I co-founded with a good friend socialite Mayenne Carmona.

By then, I was well into my second marriage. My first with banker Ramon Feliciano was short-lived but gave me a wonderful sister-in-law, Lady Minda Feliciano Lonsdale, best known as former girlfriend of British actor Michael Caine and American singer Tony Bennett.

I helped organize through a generous sponsor the advance studies in Paris and Vienna under renowned plastic surgeons of my second husband, Dr. Juan Crisostomo "Cris" Garcia, who became one of Manila's top plastic surgeons. Cris died of cancer in 1996.

I had organized milestones in social history. As a publicist, I handled the visit of Cubist pioneer Pablo Picasso's daughter, Paloma, who came to Manila to launch her fragrance and famous red lipstick. The press launch at the Hotel InterContinental Manila's presidential suite was quite memorable. Paloma was so entertained by singer Julius Obregon.

In 1990, NovelVentures organized the Filipino Designers' Group gala at the Manila Hotel, an event that attracted the power elite and top media organizations. The company likewise produced the Sergio Mendes concert at the Philippine International Convention Center.

Romance chronicles

Franco-Italian Henri Muzzarelli was an intern for a water treatment plant in 1991. Enamored of the Philippines, he decided to stay. I gave him jobs to co-produce special events. (At the turn of the millennium, Henri and I produced "Carnival in Rio"— which would be touted as the "World's Biggest Party" ——---- at the Westin (now Sofitel) Philippine Plaza.)

Through his business contacts in Europe, he acquired the distribution rights to an automatic condenser cleaning system for industrial air conditioning.

In 1994, I set up Vonotec (the name is derived from *nouvelle*, French for new innovation) with myself as president and Henri as managing director. Through my network, we bagged blue chip clients. He handled the nitty-gritty. At the turn of the millennium, Vonotec had popularized motorized gondolas for high-rises. Our business peaked during the construction boom, and we had to set up an office in Cebu.

My romance with Henri was chronicled in society columns and magazines. When we parted as friends, our working relationship became even stronger.

Coincidentally, I am happy to note at this point, my work through the years has gone beyond earning a living to living a life of purpose. The following is proof of this:

Henri has always been prudent about finances. Three years ago, instead of spending on Christmas gifts for clients, Vonotec picked a beneficiary, Habitat for Humanity, an international organization that builds decent housing for families that cannot afford it. We "adopted" a community in Payatas (former garbage dump in a Quezon City barangay of same name) and offered a specific livelihood incentive on top of building houses.

Applicants underwent rigid training as rope access technicians (RATs). Wearing safety gear and clambering up industrial ropes, these skilled workers can take on cleaning and repair jobs at high altitudes. Only a few have passed the test so far, but these few see hope for a better life with the money that they have started making. We also gave the residents classes in basic grooming and good manners.

From hobby to advocacy

Yet another accomplishment for me was turning a hobby into an advocacy that changed people's lives and put the Philippines on the dancesport map.

During a 1989 holiday in Paris when we partied like crazy, I ran into the sensuous Lambada partner dance trend. The female wore a short, flirty skirt, swizzled her hips, shimmied her shoulders, and leapt to wrap her legs around the man's waist. With characteristic determination, I mastered the moves and variations and introduced the dance in the Philippines. People were shocked by all that sexiness and the occasional flash of the thong. Yet, I received invitations to perform in top discos, TV shows, special events and provincial tours. Thus, I earned the title "Lambada Queen."

My popularity as a dancer rocketed in the '90s. The late media baron Eugenio Lopez, Jr. invited me to write a society column for the prestigious Manila Chronicle. I had television shows—*Dance with Becky* on Channels 5 and 9 and *Dance Upon a Time* in RJTV—that generated high ratings and attracted many advertisers. Fans flocked after a two-hour radio show (in Angel Radio in Makati) that I hosted and pleaded with me to demonstrate some steps at the lobby.

At that time, ballroom dancing was the craze among well-heeled women who hired partners called dance instructors, or DIs. Seeing the country's immense interest in the genre, a foreign dancesport proponent in Thailand remarked that the Philippines could perhaps aim for bigger prospects by bringing in foreign teachers. I researched the Paul Bishop Academy of Dance in Hong Kong where celebrities learned the Latin and standard ballroom dance. Soon enough, I met the Englishman Paul, also a dancesport advocate and invited him to my TV show and dance workshops. He, too, saw the vast potential of Filipino talents and recommended that the new performance art be professionalized in the country. He travelled with me all over the Philippines to organize dance workshops and propagate the sport.

Golden harvest

In 1996, I founded and became President of the DanceSport Council of the Philippines (DSCP), which governed professional dancers and competitions. Dancesport was still in its infancy in the Philippines; still, I was named vice-president of the Asian DanceSport Federation. The council is a member of the WorldDance Sport Federation (formerly International DanceSport Federation), the international governing body of dancesport and wheelchair dancesport. Since WDSF is recognized by the International Olympic Committee, DSCP is a member of the Philippine Olympic Committee.

With the help of the Philippine Sports Commission, DSCP imported foreign dance coaches who taught the professional syllabus and sent dancers for overseas training. PSC supported my trips to the provinces, which I scoured for talents and where I set up local chapters and organized workshops. In the past 25 years, our dancers, including the disabled, have brought home a robust harvest of medals. In the 2019 Southeast Asian Games, that was no fewer than 10 golds and one silver, one of the first events that brought medals to the Philippines. I was not called the Grand Dame of Dancesport Asia for nothing.

During Cebu Mayor Tomas Osmeña's term (2016-2019), the local chapter trained over a thousand underprivileged children from the mountains and street kids. The classes were seen to have kept them out of trouble. I have heard many stories of lives transformed through the efforts of DSCP.

The ballroom dance craze may have fizzled, but dancesport is thriving. I have proven for a fact that when the dancers see that the leadership is strong, this sense of stability trickles down to the whole community. Our dancers have been teaching online for a while now; some have even started small businesses. Meanwhile, we have jumpstarted virtual competitions just to keep dancing alive.

Life in quarantine

Life for me in the world's longest quarantine has been made fulfilling by my husband Dr. George Sarakinis, a polymath of Greek-German descent— political and economic advisor, physician, television personality, musician, chef, and most important, a true gentleman of the old school. Just when I started thinking that chivalry was dead, he proved me wrong with his attentiveness, not just towards me but towards all our friends.

In the early thoughts, Mars Marquez, my colleague at Chase Thomas, acquired an account from Germany—delegates from Fraport, the transport and airport operator, with a government team. The group was asked to look into legal disputes between Fraport and a local consortium in the construction of NAIA 3. George was among the German state representatives. Mars died in 2004 before they arrived, so I had to take over the account. This is where I met with George every day.

After a short while, a common friend set us up on a theater date. I did not think much of it, but George was apparently besotted. Back in Frankfurt, he told his mother about "this Filipina" that he could not forget. She advised him to go back and get me. Otherwise, you will lose her to others.

Sweet perfection

By George's observation, we are a perfect fit, being risk-takers, and equally multi-faceted. We got married in 2005 and honeymooned in Frankfurt, where I experienced my first full-on wintry weather. We lived in Amsterdam and Rotterdam at the start of our new life together. Because I have always adapted easily to any environment, I quickly made new friends and even volunteered in a soup kitchen run by nuns.

Eventually, we came back to the Philippines, where our hearts and true friends were. George and I set up small businesses, among them exporting tuna from General Santos City to the Netherlands.

I count myself lucky to have worked with people who shared the same ethical principles. My values and determination in pursuit of my goals helped me handle the huge amounts of stress that came with being a leader. My secret is to not hold on to negative thoughts and feelings, so that I can always see things objectively. This clarity of mind enables me to make the right decisions.

Throughout this long lockdown, George has kept my spirits high with his home cooking (international cuisine!) and entertaining (parlor games). We have bonded with my helper and her family, and we all pray together every day. It feels very good to be constantly assured that I do not need much to be happy.

Elma Kamari Bidkorpeh

Story of My Life
By Elma Kamari Bidkorpeh

My heart, mind, and soul make a "Story of My Life" special, unique, and beautiful. Life is a journey. It is my mission. Every step of this journey, I will have a sincere feeling that I care. It is all about what I treasure and what I am about to share.

I, Elma Rosario Fonacier, was born the fourth child among seven children in Ilocos Sur, Philippines. My parents led quite the ordinary life with my mother, Aurelia Farinas Rosario Fonacier, being a devoted grade one teacher and my father, Mariano Ulanimo Fonacier Sr., being a Philippine Constabulary (PC) officer. My father is one of the heirs of the Fonacier Mining property.

From an early age, everyone had a special place in his/her heart for me. I was the little Elma a ballet dancer, performing at school events, and the petite Elma, a volleyball player. My charisma was truly irresistible, but people in my life had no way of knowing I would eventually become a scientist, philanthropist, model, and a pageant crowned Ms. Image International and Asia-USA 2nd Runner-up and Global Ambassador. Magsingal was my birthplace, but I did not stay there for too long. I moved to Vigan, Ilocos Sur, for high school and became a star volleyball player, competing in Northern Luzon Athletic Association (NLAA).

After high school graduation I moved to Manila and lived in Quezon City and Novaliches. Despite my love for arts, fashion, music, and sports, I applied and was accepted at the University of Santo Tomas (UST), Faculty of Pharmacy instead of the Faculty of Fine Arts, to follow my eldest sibling who graduated from UST Faculty of Pharmacy and my third sister who was studying at the time at the School of Medicine, Centro Escolar University. I became popular at the university being a star volleyball player, a spiker, and a server. The Pharmacy Volleyball Team won championship trophies year after year. During my time in college, I decided to take the internship in Medical Technology. It soon became clear that my passions lay elsewhere, and my interest in sports, fine arts, fashion, and music came in handy in other lanes of life and enriched me in many ways as I would eventually come to find out. Soon after graduation I wanted to enlist in the Philippine Airforce and serve the country. I served as a Medical Technologist in the Airforce until I was given clearance and migrated to the United States of America (USA) in 1975.

I did not wait long to pursue my American dream and immediately landed my first job at Automated Laboratory. Though I was a Medical Technologist in the Philippines, here in the United States I had to take and pass the California State board exam to be considered a Medical and Clinical Laboratory Scientist (CLS). I landed a job as a clinical laboratory technician while reviewing for the board examination. Thereafter passing the board exam in 1977, I was promoted to an Immunology CLS and Supervisor when the lab was bought out by another company, the Central Diagnostic Lab, MetWest, MetPath and became the Quest Diagnostics Incorporated Chemistry Supervisor. At times I assumed the responsibility of a Lab Manager and was involved in Six Sigma Black Belt and 6S projects.

I continued to develop my CLS/MLS career when I was hired at Southern California Permanente Medical Group (SCPMG) Regional Reference Laboratories as a Chemist and eventually the Assistant Lab Director until 2009. I accepted a challenging Supervisory position at Saint Vincent Medical Center in 2011 and received an off-cycle salary three (3) months after hire date. I was involved in the laboratory design and selection of lab equipment, Lab Information System Sunquest update, Electronic Medical Record, and Hospital Information System ARCIS implementation.

You might be wondering what else my responsibilities are as a Clinical and Medical Lab Scientist in Management. I was involved in the alpha site and beta site testing and validation of new clinical/medical instruments and reagents. I was instrumental in the planning, designing, and building the new state-of-the-art SCPMG laboratory. Moving the lab to the new location without interruption was very rewarding.

Being a committee member of the SCPMG Regional Endocrinology and Regional Diabetes Management, I have researched, validated, and published evidence for the use of non-fasting samples for lipid profiles. In patients with diabetes, they are safer with much less likelihood of hypoglycemic episodes induced by fasting itself because of test requirement. One of the most notable shifts in scientific thought and clinical practice has been the acceptance of the utilization of non-fasting specimens for lipid testing and routine screening of cardiovascular disease risks.

Relevant Experience and Key Responsibilities:

- Directs and manages the operations of a multi-disciplinary department which includes all personnel activities, technical oversight, general workflow, and the budget

- Develops and uses quality indicators for process improvements and the monitoring of the laboratory quality

- Recruits, hires, trains, and ensures competency of staff

- Controls costs by monitoring personnel utilization, material usage rates, analyzing fluctuations in types and volumes of tests, and implementing corrective action

- Prepares instrument and method validation proposals and evaluates new instruments, new tests, and procedures

- Oversees and coordinates startup, implementation, and

maintenance activities resulting from new services or transfer of services

- Participates in department, inter-department, and inter-facility and inter-regional projects which help the organization achieve the goal of providing quality service and client support in a cost-effective manner

- Serves as primary liaison to Laboratory Management System for ongoing and new issues

- Consults with physicians, nurses, and other healthcare providers on the technical aspects of methodologies used, appropriateness of test utilization, and interpretation of patient results

- Ensures creation of work groups to resolve problems, address issues, and/or champion the goals of the organization and the department

- Effectively creates and facilitates collaboration and cooperation among diverse groups, people, departments, and professional disciplines

- Justifies the internalization of new tests and/or conversion to new instruments/methods and maintenance contract terms and agreements

- Continuously monitors to ensure that the day-to-day operations of the department are effectively directed and controlled, displaying knowledge of procedural details and optimal workflow patterns, staffing needs [by ensuring coverage at all benches, reassigning/relocating staff as needed], pulse of the department, and the staff's engagement with our mission of quality member service

- Manages and oversees departmental quality assurance and College of American Pathologists (CAP) readiness programs

- Performs preventative maintenance and troubleshoots instruments as needed.
- Performs high volume testing and reports patient information and results.
- Facilitates the ongoing learning, well-being, professional satisfaction, and development of supervisors and staff, and provides work assignments that stretch employees' capabilities.
- Celebrates achieved results through rewards, recognition, and public communication.

Noteworthy Accomplishments:

1. Executive Management Scholarship Program, Mendoza College of Business, University of Notre Dame, South Bend, Indiana, UCLA Executive Education Program, UCLA Anderson School of Management Working Mother Media's 3rd Annual Los Angeles Multicultural Town Hall Theme "Trust a Business and Cultural Imperative"

2. Licensed Clinical and Medical Laboratory Scientist, Certified American Society for Clinical Pathology (ASCP), Retired Assistant Director of Southern California Permanente Medical Group (SCPMG) Lab Services, Adjunct Faculty of California State University of Dominguez Hills (CSUDH), Medical Technology Board Reviewer, College of American Pathologists (CAP) Inspection Team Member

3. President of the Philippine Association of Medical Technologists (PAMET)-USA, Inc. Southern California (SoCal) Chapter 2017-2019, National PAMET-USA, Inc. 1st Vice President 2018-2020, Board of Director and Legislative Chair 2020-2022, Assistant Financial Officer of the SoCal Philippine Independence Coordinating Council (PICCSC),

American Association of Clinical Chemistry (AACC) SoCal Section Education Board Member

4. Clinical and Laboratory Standards Institute (CLSI) active member since 2001, Subcommittee Member and Advisor on the development and completion of standards that can be adopted by laboratories, clinicians, regulatory agencies, and industry to improve public health globally, Subcommittee Chair of the Clinical Laboratory Technology Advisory Committee (CLTAC), California Department of Public Health, to enhance the CA State's efforts response to COVID-19

5. Honored and crowned 2nd Runner-Up Ms. Asia USA 2006 and Global Ambassador 2014-2015, Ms. Image International 2016-2017, featured as one of the Inspiring Women in the song "ELHAM" (Inspiration), 2019 Judge #2 Continental Miss Philippines America, the official representative for Miss World, modeled and walked the runway, appeared at several "Red Carpet" for charity events, 2019 Fashion show fundraiser to benefit underprivileged Filipino Youth, Philippine International Aid "Giving Hope to the Children"

6. Served with commitment and distinction, joined PAMET Inc. and Safeguard Advocacy on the Prevention of COVID-19 Infection through Proper Handwashing

Recognitions and Awards:

- CLSI Appreciation for commitment to supporting standards and guidelines that directly impact the delivery of quality patient care around the globe, acknowledgment from CLSI and its Board of Directors for an outstanding volunteer service during the development and successful completion of C-54A, Verification of Comparability of Patient Results Within One Health Care System; Approved Guideline and the C49-A, Analysis of Body Fluids in Clinical Chemistry; Approved Guideline

- Recognized by the SCPMG Medical Director and Chairman of the Board and the President of the Kaiser Foundation Health Plan and Hospitals, SoCal Region as an "Everyday Hero" for going above and beyond to deliver excellent service, and makes a difference to Kaiser Permanente (KP) members and the communities we serve

- Honored and appreciated for professional commitment and as a member of the Planning Subcommittee and contribution to the success of the KP Annual Diabetes Symposium

- Certificate of Appreciation from KP Regional Laboratory for the presentation to the KP Work Preparation Program

- Lapel Pin recipient for helping KP achieve an unprecedented three Blue Ribbon Awards from the Pacific Business Group on Health, the pin symbolizes our shared commitment to achieving high standards for quality, value, and consistent delivery of a great care experience to every member

- Recipient of a heartfelt reward from the Care Management Institute Executive Director for the wonderful work in taking care of KP members with diabetes, which contributed to receiving the National Exemplary Practice Program Award from the American Association of Health Plan and the Employers Managed Health Association Care whose goals are to encourage the rapid adoption or adaptation of innovative ideas and approaches to chronic care delivery throughout the managed care industry

 - KP Health and Safety Team letter of recognition for the participation and success of the Annual Health and Safety Fair

 - KP Community Relation Manager SoCal Kaiser Foundation

Health Plan and Hospitals and the American Diabetes Association, certificate of recognition for the support as Team Captain for the KP/ADA "America's Walk for Diabetes" to raise funds for leading-edge research on the prevention, cure, and treatment of diabetes

- KP People Pulse Survey High Scores Recognition in 2007 and 2008 for the employees' and supervisors' level of engagement, commitment, involvement, and attitudes on critical items related to work life and customer satisfaction

- KP SoCal Region Variable Pay and Performance Recognition Program 2009 Individual Award

- AACC Advances in Clinical Chemistry, Education and New Technology; Clinical Chemists Recognition Award for participation in the ACCENT program and demonstration of professional development through continuing education in clinical chemistry

- Certificate of Appreciation for significant contribution to AACC's growth and success, through worldwide leadership and dedication that AACC continues to be the premier organization for Clinical Laboratory Scientists

- Los Angeles Maharlika Lions Club, Citizen of the Year Awardee for Community Service and Healthcare Education

- Certificate of Appreciation from the Consul General in recognition and gratitude for the assistance and services during the Filipino Community event with the H.E. Benigno Simeon Aquino III, President of the Philippines

- PAMET-USA, Inc. National President 2018-2020 certificate of appreciation and grateful recognition for the dedication and efforts to ensure the vitality of PAMET-USA, Inc. SoCal Chapter, and support to its members, and for outstanding service to the medical laboratory profession and to the patients and communities we serve

- President of the Philippines, Rodrigo Duterte commendation to the PAMET-USA, Inc. SoCal Chapter for successfully uniting Filipino American Medical Technologists in the United States towards enhancing their competencies and advancing the field of clinical laboratory science and for the unwavering commitment to this undertaking which led to the success of the community programs, including medical missions and healthcare outreach activities

- Northern Philippines Academy, Centro Norte, Gattaran, Cagayan Certificate of Appreciation from the School Chaplain and School Director for conducting a Health Education and Nutrition 2-day Seminar through the Cagayanos of Luzon Incorporated

- Philippine Children's Charities, Incorporated (PCCI) Executive Officers and Board of Directors, 2019 Outstanding Filipino American in the USA, Medical in All Fields category for outstanding contribution, leadership and humanitarian endeavor and support for the 2019 Medical/Surgical/Feeding Wellness Program Missions in the Philippines, and for accomplishment and dedication in the betterment of the abused, abandoned, sick, rape victims and underprivileged Filipino children of the Philippines and our less fortunate fellow Filipinos

- 2021 UST Faculty of Pharmacy Distinguished Alumni Award for Health and Community Service category for being a leader both in the practice of profession and in the society, who demonstrates commitment, compassion and competence and exhibits the importance of a UST Faculty of Pharmacy education and is loyal to the vision and mission of the Faculty through alumni involvement and/or philanthrophic support.

My mom's humanitarian efforts got my involvement in global Medical Missions and Outreach Programs. I pledge and continue to support viable and humanitarian projects both the public and private sectors across the globe. It is not enough to support everyone that I wanted to help but being able to help in a small way, goes along way for others. I am committed to helping and shaping the future amidst the COVID-19 pandemic.

Being married to another Medical Lab Scientist, Nassrollah Kamari Bidkorpeh, and a widowed mother of three boys, Roland, a graduate of Criminology at UCI, Mehran a retired HistoTech at SCPMG, and Oliver, a graduate of UCI in Chemistry and Biology and UCLA Doctor of Medicine in Dentistry and now a practicing DDS. My family is one true source of inspiration and comfort that always kept me going. I am enjoying the journey and learning more in many ways.

I know my future holds great promise with destiny unknown. I continue to be a dreamer and will dream my dreams until they become dreams, no longer. I will always be sincere, truthful, and kind in life until one day this will be experienced by the world in which we live … sharing hopes and dreams. As I travel in the direction of my dreams, I just take one step at a time each day and do the best I can.

As a testament to my honest hard work, my passion, my ceaseless dedication to the cause, I am so proud to be a co-author of this "Red Blazer" book. What a greater honor can be than to do so in the largest, most prestigious, and respected platform? My sincere appreciation to Dr. Carl Wilson for honoring me, Elma Fonacier Kamari Bidkorpeh, CLS, MLS(ASCP)CM, as one of the "Red Blazer" of Excellence and Achievement Recipients 2021-2022.

Yolanda Core Pastrana

In Love with Life
By Yolanda Core Pastrana
Communications Specialist, Filipino-American Media leader
and Cinema Arts Advocate

I was born in Manila, the capital city of the Philippines, but early on, as the daughter of a diplomat, I spent my childhood traveling the world with my parents, wherever my father was assigned as representative of the Philippine government to other countries during the 1940s through the 1950s. I have interacted with different people from diverse cultures throughout my lifetime. Schooled in the Philippines, Indonesia, Spain, and the United States, my broad education has sustained my interest and concern for humanity, the environment, arts, and culture. In Jakarta, Indonesia, our family was privileged to interact with other members of the diplomatic community and their families as well as President Sukarno, the first President of the Republic of Indonesia after it obtained its independence from Holland now known as The Netherlands. I had occasion to attend the birthday in the celebration of his daughter Megawati, who grew up to become the first and only female president in the history of Indonesia.

In 1952, I studied at the Real Colegio de La Asuncion in Madrid where I distinguished myself as the lone Filipina enrolled at the Catholic exclusive girls' convent school who graduated at the head of my class in 1953. I still have fond memories of Spain and continue to visit that European country whenever it is possible to do that.

After I graduated with a degree in Communication Arts at the Philippine Women's University in Manila in 1965, my first job was at the Embassy of the Republic of Indonesia in Manila as an assistant to the Press Attache and subsequently to the Indonesian Ambassador to the Philippines. At the same time, I started working as contributing Editor and writer for *Screenlife Magazine*. This was followed by a part-time stint during the summertime in Kalibo's DYKR radio station. In 1969-70 I was hired at the DZYK-FM radio by ABS-CBN Broadcasting Corporation, the largest broadcasting network in the Philippines. When the Philippine Constitutional Convention was established with the task to amend the Philippine Constitution from 1971-73, I became part of the historic endeavor as a technical assistant to the delegate from Iloilo province. Thereafter, I went back to working in print media editing the publications, the movie business, and miscellaneous and variety magazines. Part of my extra-curricular activities were my endeavors as a member of the National Press Club of the Philippines, Screenwriters Guild of the Philippines, and the Filipino Academy of Movie Arts Sciences (FAMAS) which I served as an officer and board member. It was an exciting life interacting with the entertainment industry's denizens.

In 1988, I decided to migrate to the United States at the suggestion of my widowed mother who was already based in California. I resigned from my position as entertainment editor of the country's oldest literary magazine Liwayway on the 22nd of December and took the flight to Los Angeles the very next day. In Southern California, I first worked as a receptionist in a Jewish publication based in Miracle Mile and then moved to be entertainment editor of the *USA Standard*, a Filipino American newspaper along the Wilshire Corridor. Other periodicals for which I subsequently edited and wrote were the *Philippine Sun*, the *L.A. Free Press, Philippine Times*, and *Star Times*. I also had a part-time radio show at KWIZ-FM in Pasadena. At this point in time, the *Philippine Press Club of America* (PPCA) was established which I co-founded along with co-publishers and editors of Filipino-American periodicals. I served as president for two terms in 1992-93 and 1993-94.

During my incumbency as the head of the press club, I established the PPCA Media Awards and the Miss Press Photography. In 2002, I founded the L.A. Cinema Indio Festival, a yearly showcase of classic and nascent critically acclaimed Philippine-themed films which recognized the achievement of Filipino filmmakers and performing artists. I also organized the Rizal Memorial Awards for Literature, highlighting the celebration of Jose Rizal, Philippines' great literati and national hero. In 2004, I convened the first Philippine Global Media Congress in Culver City. My efforts were rewarded with various awards of recognition from media, civic, and arts organizations. Among them were the 1994 PPCA leadership award of distinction; the first Golden Pen Award in 1995; the 1996 L.A. Maharlika Lions Club Hall of Fame – Media; the 2005 Chicago Hall of Fame-National Media award; the 2007 Reflections Cultural Pride Award, Los Angeles; the 2009 FAMAS Cultural Award, Philippines; the 2014 Outstanding Filipino Americans- print media, Los Angeles; and the 2017 Hall of Fame Japan-Philippines Recognition-International Media.

I was back in broadcast media from 2000 to 2006 as a TV news correspondent in Los Angeles for ABS-CBN *International's Balitang America* which aired on the Filipino Channel (TFC). I covered political as well as entertainment events. As columnist and news writer for the Weekend Balita periodical, I covered the Presidential Inauguration of President Bill Clinton in Washington, D. C., when he was re-elected in 2004 and the official visits to the United States of then-President Gloria Macapagal-Arroyo of the Philippines.

On the creative side, I have written satirical plays, including *Vote Who?* and *Sisa Revisited*, which have been staged in Los Angeles and Pasadena.

I am working at being a published author of poetry and photographic images and will be writing my memoir with the intent for it to be adapted into a screenplay in the near future.

At present, I use my communications skills as a language interpreter for legal cases in the federal, state, and county courts of the United States of America. This is a service that I have rendered to Filipinos and Filipino Americans and the U.S. legal communities for over three decades.

I still contribute feature articles to the Asian Journal and its sister publication, the *Balikbayan Travel* and *Leisure magazine* and remain an active member of the Los Angeles Press Club.

Dr. Janet Smith Warfield

THE POWER OF OUR WORDS
By Dr. Janet Smith Warfield

I had never heard of mystical/transformational experiences until I was suddenly and unexpectedly gifted with one. In a nanosecond, I had instant clarity.

My oldest son Bill began wetting the bed when his youngest brother was born. It was the last thing I needed with three young preschoolers to care for.

I ignored the conduct. Nothing changed.

I explained to Bill why a five-year-old was too old to wet the bed. Bill listened attentively, but the next morning, his bed was wet again. I was feeling frustrated.

I raised my voice. The bed was still wet.

I spanked him. The bed was still wet. Nothing the culture had taught me was working, and I was getting out of control.

Then my mother gave me a book called Summerhill by an English schoolmaster, A.S. Neill.

Neill had a strange way of dealing with "problem" students. When a child threw spitballs or talked loudly or poked other students, Neill didn't make him stand in a corner or write 100 times, "I will be good." Neill gave the child a penny. More often than not, the "bad behavior" stopped, and the child would start listening and learning.

Rewarding a child for "bad" behavior didn't make sense, but I was frustrated. Nothing that parents, teachers, or the culture had taught me was working.

The next morning, the bed was wet again. I didn't understand what I was doing or why, but I had a model to follow. I simply went to my wallet, pulled out a penny, gave it to Bill, and walked away.

Bill looked at me as if I were crazy, but ...

... he never wet the bed again.

I was amazed. It was so easy!

I was fascinated! I wanted to play with this.

One day, two of Bill's friends were in our back yard, calling each other names, and getting ready to punch each other. I walked out, drew each boy apart separately, and asked each the same question, "Do you want to fight?"

Each gave me the same answer. "No, I don't want to fight, but he's making me do it."

"Well, if you want to fight, go ahead and do it," I said to both boys together.

The boys eyed each other out of the corners of their eyes, looked at the ground, and shuffled their feet. Two minutes later, they were playing happily together again.

Absolutely fascinating!

A short time later, a man came to my door. He was angry, and he was angry with me.

Instead of becoming defensive and saying, "Oh, you shouldn't be angry over a little thing like that," I said, "I am so sorry. What can I do to make things right?"

The man's whole demeanor changed. When he walked away, we were friends.

Why do strange, unexpected words suddenly pop into your head out of nowhere? I don't know, but I know that they do.

As the man walked away, the words that popped into my head were words I had been taught as a child in Sunday School, "But I say unto you that ye resist not evil; but whosoever shall smite thee on thy right cheek, turn to him the other also" (Matt. 5:39).

As a child, I had understood Matthew 5:39 as a puzzling and unattainable moral commandment, requiring subservience of my own needs to the needs of others. Suddenly, in a different experiential context, those same words took on an entirely new meaning. They didn't require subservience of my own needs to the needs of others. Rather, they suggested extremely effective action I could take all by myself, that benefited both others and me. There was no self-denial in my actions. There was nothing but self-affirmation and life affirmation. I had never before felt so free, so strong, so powerful, so integrated, and so fully in control.

Nothing outside me changed. My living room was still there. I was still there. Our three sons were still there, playing with their toys. Only my perceptions, thoughts, actions, and emotions had changed. Suddenly, I was seeing the world through entirely new eyes, uncontaminated by all the rules I had previously been taught.

I was so excited about this new understanding and clarity that I had to tell others. As I began talking, I was met with blank stares and uncomprehending faces. I was talking, but clearly, I was not communicating. I was not being heard.

I was learning from personal experience why William James in his book Varieties of Mystical Experience wrote that mystical experiences are ineffable. I was learning why Buddhists teach, "Words are fingers pointing at the moon. They are not the moon." I was beginning to understand Alfred Korzybski's words, "The map is not the territory." I was beginning to understand why "the Tao that can be spoken is not the Eternal Tao."

The blank stares and uncomprehending faces caused me to pull back and start looking at the words I was using. How could I use analytic, divisive words to communicate a unifying holistic experience? It was like trying to hammer a nail using a screwdriver. It was like a Zen koan, a "paradox to be meditated upon that is used to train Zen Buddhist monks to abandon ultimate dependence on reason and to force them into gaining sudden intuitive enlightenment." https://www.merriam-webster.com/dictionary/koan.

I tried didactic teaching, but that clearly didn't work. All it did was throw me into self-righteousness. I was very clear that was a "space" in which I did not want to function. I began telling stories, asking questions, writing poetry, and playing with alliteration, metaphor, and allegory.

My writing was beginning to evolve into word art and away from any attempt to communicate Truth or Knowledge. That felt more in integrity, but I still couldn't answer that life purpose question: "How can I use analytic, divisive words to communicate a unifying holistic experience?"

Why do strange, unexpected thoughts suddenly pop into your head out of nowhere?" I don't know, but I know that they do.

After working and playing with words for fifteen years and struggling unsuccessfully to answer that "life purpose" question, it suddenly occurred to me to change one word in my question. What if I were to change the word "communicate" to "facilitate."

The question then became, ""How can I use analytic, divisive words to facilitate a unifying holistic experience?" That was do-able, but it required me to stand fully in my own creative and co-creative power. That was both humbling and terrifying.

Could I do it? How could I do it? Who did I think I was to take on such an overwhelming mission?

Andrew Harvey once said, "Why don't you simply model who you are?" But who was I?

The questions that kept flowing through my mind still felt like life purpose questions. I still felt driven, but now I was driven, not to talk about the change I wanted to see in the world, but to BE the change I wanted to see in the world. Part of that change was learning how to use my words consciously, intentionally, and alchemically to cocreate order out of chaos, peace out of dissonance, abundance out of lack, courage and moral strength out of fear, integrity out of rage, and POWER WITH dynamics out of "Power over," "Power under," and Power against" dynamics.

What did I need to learn and know to have the skill and discipline to be able to do this?

I began studying the power of words, taught through the first three of the Seven Liberal Arts: Grammatica, Dialectica, and Rhetorica. Developed by the ancient mystery schools of Egypt and early Greece, they remain a foundation of education.

When taught by teachers of ordinary consciousness, they become deadly school exercises learned only at a surface level by the hard work of rote and repetition. When facilitated by highly talented educators attuned to Logos—the divine principle of order and knowledge—they transform words into exciting, creative, esoteric doorways to Wisdom, inner discipline, and purification of the Soul.

Grammatica pertains to the structure of language, its history, and the underlying energy of an idea. Nouns (chair, table, apple, tree) are immobile and passive. Our minds bring together an experience that we perceive as an object. Then we give it a name. Ordinary consciousness believes the name is the object. Expanded consciousness knows that the name reflects something far more complex.

The name is simply a human-created placeholder for a continually shifting experience. It stops the moving picture at a single frame so we can name it, analyze it, understand it, and feel safe.

Verbs (run, sit, walk, fly) are changeable and active. They can create or transform our perception of time. We ran, run, or will run. Verbs pertain to human will, choice, and action.

Adjectives (beautiful, sad, dysfunctional, harmonic) and adverbs (slowly, quickly, passionately, smoothly) bring emotion into our speech. They add expansion, contraction, and rhythm.

Dialectica is logical thinking. It requires that we speak clearly and see from many different perspectives. It allows us to move quickly from the depths of hell to the heights of heaven. It enables us to build word bridges between what appear to be opposites. Like Socrates, it asks questions. Like Zen Buddhist koans, it poses mind-bending puzzles.

Rhetorica is beautiful, persuasive speech. It uses passion and tonality, questions, and pauses. It tells heart-rending stories. It speaks through poetry or drama. Rhetorica is the intention and power beneath our words.

I began noticing my words and the effects they had on those around me. Like the Director of a drama, I began playing with my words, choosing them consciously and intentionally to create the effect I wanted. If the words didn't create the effect I wanted, I would go back and reshape them to make them clearer, more succinct, more creative, more intentional, and more powerful. As my thinking became clearer, my words became more powerful, and I noticed how much more effective and persuasive I was.

I discovered that words are illusions, dancing at a masked ball. I noticed that the experiential meanings of words shifted as I connected previously meaningless words to my own experiences.

I noticed how driven I felt to get what I understood about human transformational, consciousness-shifting experiences, and the words that shape those experiences out into the world. There were so many different ways to do this.

I began to see everything as simply a process, a consciousness-shifting vehicle for transforming and evolving my own life and the lives of others.

I learned that writing about consciousness-shifting experiences cannot be objectified the way writing about how to build a bridge can be objectified. Language was part of the problem because of the way people use and understand it.

I know from long experience that each person who reads my words will understand them differently, so I simply write from the depth of my own experience, authenticity, and integrity. I also with a great deal of care, intention, attention to grammar, and attention to the energetic effect of my words.

I discovered that I was enchanted with words as art forms, not words as Truth.

I learned the distinction between judgment and discernment. Judgment was making someone else wrong. Discernment was noticing the effect another person's words and actions had on my own Soul, Spirit, and Energy Field.

I learned that when words are used, not as Truth, but as energetic vehicles to open minds and transform lives and cultures, they became fascinating toys to play with, take apart, and put together again in new ways that open doors of understanding, clarity, and evolution. Words, well used, have the power to offer those who hear or read them exciting new options for dealing with life's challenges.

I do feel driven to get what I understand about words and

transformational experiences out into the world. And yes, it feels as if this is my life purpose. How I do it is not fixed in stone. It's more like alchemy. What I say or write depends on context, environment, and the human players. The words keep shifting as context, environment, and human players shift.

The particular words are irrelevant, except in specific experiential contexts. The energy, spirit, and understanding that lie beneath the words are vital.

If you begin exploring Alfred Korzybski's famous statement, "The map is not the territory," you ultimately realize that words are nothing more than maps of experiential territory. The words are not the experience. The menu is not the food you eat. Driving North on I-75 on the West Coast of Florida is not the same as breathing in the beautiful bougainvillea, enjoying the swaying palms, or basking in a spectacular sunset.

You also realize that words almost always separate, divide, and categorize high/low; good/bad; right/wrong. Experience doesn't separate and divide. It just is. Our minds may choose to call it joyous or painful, but the experience itself just is what it is.

We humans fight over whose map is right and whose map is wrong; whose words are right and whose words are wrong. We don't need to do that. Instead, we can use our words consciously to set intentions about the kind of world in which we want to live, and together, co-create that world so that all humans feel respected and all needs are met as well as humanly possible.

Is each of us a microcosm of the macrocosm? Is your story of fear, rage, shame, or betrayal a mirror of my story of fear, rage, shame, or betrayal?

A major reason we have war is because some people set their own words up as Truth and then fight with others who have set up different words as Truth. The fact is that neither has evolved to a consciousness where they understand that words are a means to an end, not an end in themselves. This is the huge danger of religion. Religious doctrines are created to codify the spiritual experience and guide the seeker to it, yet in the process of codifying it, they frequently destroy it. Used correctly, religious doctrines guide one's own actions. They should never be used to control the actions of others.

The spiritual experience is pure awareness, beyond dualistic words, beyond my words, beyond the word "awareness." And yet it can also include dualistic words. Sometimes, it needs to include dualistic words because they can be wonderful catalysts when used in context to shift energy. They just enter the mind and they're there, to contemplate, revise, or speak.

Despite the inadequacy and imperfection of words, we have to put them out there in the best way we know how. It is through putting our words out there and engaging in dialog that we clarify, both for ourselves and others, the meaning of life---the meaning of our own life.

If words are such a challenge, why do I keep using them to write and speak? After all, gurus like Sri Maharishi taught through nothing but silence.

But I am not Sri Maharishi. I am different and unique.

Is it because I was born into a female body---impacted differently by the patriarchal culture into which both men and women have been born?

Yes, I feel driven. Yes, it feels like my life purpose to write and speak even though I am acutely aware that my words are not perfect. As a woman, it also has something to do with self-respect and standing in integrity and authenticity for what I have experienced and the way I have understood it. Then using that understanding to serve others by giving it all back.

Yes, the challenges, benefits, and energetic effects of words are something I have personally experienced, something I understand in great depth after working and playing with them for 55 years. But the drive goes much deeper than that. I cannot quit. I know what I have hold of: a semantic solution to all the human-created suffering on the planet.

I became acquainted with The Serenity Prayer through NarAnon, a support group for families and friends of addicts.

> *God, grant me the serenity to accept the things I cannot change,*
> *the courage to change the things I can,*
> *and the wisdom to know the difference.*

A copy of this prayer now hangs near the front door of my home where I can see it every day and use those "fingers pointing at the moon" to guide my steps in each and every moment.

On April 17, 2020, I filed in the State of Florida Articles of Incorporation for a new (501)(c)(3) educational foundation, Planetary Peace, Power and Prosperity Legacy Foundation, Inc. The education is free to all who want to learn and grow.

I know how to do this. The solution is semantic.

Here is our Mission Statement:

To consciously and intentionally use our co-creative power to develop ideas, present solutions, and promote action for the greater good of humanity and the planet.

Here is our Vision Statement:

To attract each human consciousness, through deep listening, clear speaking, and conscious conversation:

Away from	**Away from**
Not feeling good enough	Stepping fully into one's own, unique personal power—while not harming others or the planet that sustains us.
Abusing others or allowing oneself to be abused	Self-compassion and other compassion
Fear and terror	Inner strength and courage
Rage	Standing firmly in right action
Shame or guilt	Making amends by changing conduct
A transactional, money economy of lack planetary war and desecration	An abundance economy of giving and receiving deep inner, community, and planetary peace

ARE YOU IN?

Songwriting Shane

Singer/Songwriter/Humanitarian/Grammy Recording Artist Songwriting Shane

By Marianne Branca

Welcome to my personal life. You may know me as "Songwriting Shane" in the music and film industry here in California. Many others may know me by my Christian name Marianne Branca. But there is so much more to me that I have decided to share with you in this chapter about my life. I'm writing my story in hopes of helping someone move forward with his/her life and accomplish his/her goals and dreams through any difficult circumstance(s) that may be facing him/her along the way.

I'll start my story way back in a quaint historic town called Haddon Heights, New Jersey. My parents were born and raised with strict Italian Catholic parents as was I, and all my relatives remained very religious and are generously caring people to others. My mom and dad worked at great executive jobs at RCA "the Radio Corporation of America". My dad was a Head Engineer and one of five Communication Specialists/Sound Engineers who designed and created the very first satellite (named "Telstar") that entered outer space.

As a young child I remember it was a very energetic and trying time growing up during this era of technological competition, modernization along with a worldwide "arms race" (meaning missile warheads) being created by world leaders wanting to control the world. Although I didn't quite understand what was going on, I found a way to survive the stress in our household.

At the age of three, I suddenly began begging my parents for a piano. I remember just waking up one morning suddenly crying for a piano. My parents kept telling me "You don't even know what a piano is" and that "a piano was very expensive and called an instrument".

But I continued wanting this piano and telling my parents "I promise I will take care of it and play it. I don't want anything else for Christmas" not even the latest doll or toy advertised on TV. Thankfully, since I was the first child born on both sides of the family, my grandparents and family chipped in and helped pay for this piano for me so I could have it in time for Christmas morning. My mom made me promise to do lessons and practice on that piano.

Needless to say, from the moment I got that brand new upright Janssen piano, my parents couldn't get me to stop playing. I would wake up in the middle of the night and start playing and wake up the whole household. (I'm still laughing to myself about this as I write and reminisce those "now seemingly simple" times in my life.)

My academic studies and my music studies progressed as I began taking piano lessons with renowned Cuban concert pianist Ramondo Marquez. Mr. Marquez was the Director at the prestigious Settlement School of Music in Philadelphia (and student of the world-renowned Ignacio Jan Paderewski, a Polish pianist, composer, and statesman.)

By age fourteen, I won first place in a USA National Talent Competition sponsored by the Catholic Youth Organization. During this time, I was attending Paul VI High School in Haddonfield, New Jersey. During my sophomore year of high school, I cut a record with Capital Record, appeared on the Mike Douglas Show, had a screen test with Columbia Pictures, and was interviewed on other talk shows.

I received several awards after that, including a special monetary music scholarship from the Julliard School of Music in New York to pay for continued music studies in home because my mom would not allow me to move to New York and study at Julliard on my own or rent an apartment with anyone. That caused a great turmoil between my mom and me for a long time.

By graduation, I landed a great government job as an Executive Assistant with SEPTA (Southeastern Pennsylvania Transportation Authority) and received many promotions while gaining government and business experience. After nearly fifteen years there, I decided to take a great leap and pursued my real dream of becoming a successful songwriter and recording artist. I knew I had the talent, and I knew that it would be hard work, but I gradually made it on my own to New York City. There, I began honing my talent as a Singer/Songwriter/Actress and became an accepted member of the original AGAC American Guild of Actors and Composers of which I am very grateful to this day.

I continued writing and recording music, performed in off-Broadway theatre productions, put together a top-40 band, and sang in various clubs, casinos, etc. Soon, I began recording with top producers at Philadelphia International Records; however, the money I received in the music business was not enough to pay the mortgage, bills, and a music career in my single home in New Jersey. Just around that time, it was becoming hard for original artists and ballad writers, like myself, to compete with the new "rap" and "heavy-metal" music that was dominating the music scene.

My business sense and common sense took over, and I regretfully switched careers. I began training at Skillman Academy to become a State of New Jersey Correction Officer. Throughout my career I continued doing my music and playing the piano at church services. I, also, enjoyed visiting and entertaining the sick in hospitals and nursing homes on my days off.

What I didn't realize was that my life as a female Correction

Officer was going to be one of the most abusive business experiences I had ever lived through at that time. Nearly every day I was threatened by my peers (not the inmates). Daily, I was greeted with "Why don't you just quit; you don't belong here" or "You hoes are taking our buddies' jobs." You see, when I became an officer, I went through so much hazing by my peers and supervisors. I nearly lost my life. At one point, there were many attempted rapes and so many documented incidents of abuse and violence on my life that it was necessary for me to hire a law firm to assist in upholding my rights and opportunity to equal employment. I also wanted to be compensated for the daily violent incidents jeopardizing my safety and my life on the job.

One day I was pushed past my limit. Being a strong-willed Catholic-schooled "Jersey Girl", I remember making an announcement to the entire "line up". I looked them all dead in the face and began, "If you have a problem with me because I won't sleep with you and allow you to control me, then let's settle this fair and square in the parking lot. That's fair. And I know how to fight!"

I remember Centerkeeper Lieutenant Lutz (standing nearly 7 feet tall next to me) grabbing me as he yelled out "LINE UP! DISMISSED" and "OFFICER, SEE ME IN MY OFFICE"! Lieutenant Lutz's first words were "They all have guns! Do you realize that?"

I answered with, "Yeah, and I know how they shoot and fail at the range when we are tested. And, sir, I'm a sharp-shooter!" Needless to say, I was grounded and was ordered to work side-by-side with Lieutenant Lutz in Center for a whole week. Lieutenant Lutz and I were both angry that day.

While remaining in my good-paying job with insurance, the physical and emotional abuse continued. The slashing of my tires and busting out my windshields continued. Triple A (AAA) and local towing companies knew me on a first name basis. No one even batted an eye. They told me this was a usual practice among the good ole boys' circle of bad cops that should be in jail themselves.

I transferred to a prison which was miles closer to my home and began working at Riverfront State Prison in Camden, NJ. The harassment and discrimination continued. I was reminded daily I had two strikes against me because I "was white and also a female". Things finally came to a head one day when a lieutenant walked onto my unit to "confidentially" talk with a new inmate that was logged onto my unit during "Count". As I noticed with some hesitation, I began my regular assigned shift on A-1 Unit (comprised of the most violent offenders). I grabbed the clipboard from the Officer's Station and began walking cell to cell to count each inmate on the unit. Suddenly, as I watched this lieutenant exit our unit, my partner (LCP Officer) sitting behind the protective glass in the Locator Control Panel area yelled for me to come to the LCP STAT!! I ran to my partner who was slowly opening the palm of his hands and said, "This is what I just got from the new inmate on the second floor. The inmate said that Lieutenant Wasko just handed him these two machine-shop made shanks" (razor blades that were melted into the ends of white state-issued toothbrushes). My partner said, "He's trying to kill you like he did with Officer Baker at Bayside Prison". I realized I had had enough also, but who could I go to for help.

I remember picking up the red phone and directly dialing the chief and walked straight to his office. I recovered from the medical and emotional trauma with the help of a team of expert specialists, doctors, and psychologists. While recovering, I had to learn to trust to speak again while writing my story on pads of paper to help the professional team help me. It was hard work, but that team helped me to get back my life. When I returned home while still recovering, I worked hard to get my case heard in court. I won my case in Courthouse in the NJ State Capitol

Building in Trenton. In addition, I changed laws within the DOC in all fifty states that now require **ZERO TOLERANCE** for any workplace violence incidents to employees; all employees, officers and supervisors will face immediate dismissal for such conduct or failure to report it to the proper government authorities.

While surviving this horrendous learning experience in my life, I rehabbed while continuing my education. Colleges I attended were La Salle University in Philadelphia and Camden County College. My studies included Industrial Relations, Corporate Communications, Contract Compliance, Psychology, and Law. I earned the highest honors achieving Golden Key Phi Theta Kappa and PSI Beta.

During this time, I was also fully trained and accredited and became an experienced International CISM (Critical Incident Stress Management) member. I became more passionate about helping other police/fire/rescue professionals survive any of their critical incidents on the job. I knew how important it was to feel as if someone cared and understood what you were going through when words couldn't describe what you saw or were feeling. So many of our emergent response personnel take their jobs and training to heart while caring for others they serve. Many forget about their own needs or themselves. CISM's Director Roland Kandle was MY "rescuer". He was the only one who

came to my aid to talk sense into me when I finally ended up in a hospital completely broken and had just about given up. When I thanked him, he asked that I thank him by "paying it forward to others in need". I began training with Roland and became an official CISM member of the team doing debriefings and counseling to those professionals in "critical emergent response" situations.

The year is now 2001. I felt I could finally relax and digest life with new meaning and a new outlook. Then life happened. I received an urgent call from Director Roland on a Tuesday morning around 8:45 E.S.T., September 11, 2001. Roland's voice was urgent as he announced "Marianne, I'm calling you upon special request—repeat---your name was specifically requested to assist in the SOS search and rescue by the towers in New York. You will be a crucial part of the Urgent Response Team and the official Team Leader working side by side with me."

I responded and was driven to an exploding fiery mound of twisted steel and many imploded buildings with debris covering over a one-mile radius. My job consisted of activating, dispatching, and clearing all First Responders allowed on that site. I supervised and oversaw all movement while relaying accurate information to or from the Command Center while assuring the safety and security of our men and women in assistance. My tour of duty lasted four horrific and grueling months. As a result, I underwent my own brutal recovery and intense therapy that was needed to restore my own health due to my life-threatening assignments and intense exposure to bio-hazardous and deadly toxins. The only thing that brought me somewhat temporary relief was listening to and playing my own music again. Once again, my prayers to God with faith helped me make it through nightmares that haunt me today.

I began recording my songs with Grammy Award-winning producers on the east coast and fiercely came back to life with a new fire burning inside me. I jumped back into my songwriting and began recording with a new defiance and conviction. Man, it seemed as if I had a lot to say and a lot of love and life lessons to share. My music freed up my trapped feelings and turned them into the most beautiful orchestral rock sounds from deep within my soul. Shortly thereafter, I began winning many music awards and soon became an accepted Grammy member and Grammy Voting member which is such an honor of great achievement. So, now a new chapter of my life was beginning.

I began making arrangements to make the giant move from New Jersey to LA. My music became a mission. My experiences with violence, hatred, war, terrorism, and the effects of abuse welled up inside me, and I was ready to change the world. I titled my first album **SHANE** and **The High Command**. The collection of songs on this album showcases my various writing styles beautifully unfolding hints of the many "characters" and roles I have played throughout my life. It was recorded with the members of the legendary HOOTERS' Band in Philadelphia, PA, with Producers John O. Senior and Rob Hyman.

While emerging as an artist here in North Hollywood, I soon became politically active in the communities and worked with programs aiding the homeless and victims of violence, etc. Soon I was elected to the position of Vice President of a local Chamber of Commerce. I enjoyed being a part of the respected members of society who were hands-on educators, counselors, and corporate leaders who cared enough to use their talents to help make a difference in society and be part of the solution to so many problems facing businesses and society. Much of it revolves around plain greed and/or egos.

Around this same time, I received a "Special Invite" to attend a live recording of a special TV Show titled "90-Minute Solutions" with Host Larry King and offer "a solution for World Peace". Well, when I finally got my chance to speak, I remember speaking up "Jersey Girl" style and announced, "I can give you the solution to World Peace in less than two Minutes". (I waited for this moment from the time I first stood on that fiery mound in NY, seeing firsthand the horrific effects of terrorism and "big business" gone bad.) The words that came out of my mouth even shocked me.

It went like this: "Life imitates Art. And Art imitates Life!"

As I stopped and looked into the crowd, I saw many heads in the audience nod in agreement, I continued: "Well. all you must do is change the messages in the media, and the messages in the movies and TV, radio and in the music! We have copycat terrorists everywhere now and teenagers wanting to be sex symbols or gangsters as role models of the future. People are becoming live zombies to the facts of real life and our fateful future. Change the messages before it's too late."

I remember the shocked looks on people's faces in the audience as they listened and nodded. They had never seen me speak up like this before. Most knew of me as a Songwriting Shane, the Grammy Recording Artist who performs at many shows in LA.

I continued attending business meetings in the communities with United Chambers of Commerce, Biz Fed, etc. and began working on my new album I titled **FREEDOM** and dedicated it to all First Responders and Humanitarians out there who are helping others every day. I made sure to record an easy beautiful version of my country's National Anthem "The Star-Spangled Banner" along with songs that inspire faith, courage, and brotherly love. All you need is love.

At times, it seems hard to reach out and help others while continuing to stay the journey on the right road in life amidst a hurting society. But I have learned many times that hurt people hurt people. Many times, you may hear others say, "This is a time to Rise Up", and you may wonder "Yes, but how many times am I going to have to Rise Up?" I will tell you to "Rise Up EVERY TIME" and stick to keeping the faith. Trust me. Tomorrow is always a new day!

Lately, when I am faced with a new challenge, I try taking deep breaths while remembering all the blessings and experiences I have learned from and survived throughout the years. Then I realize once again that these miracles far outweigh the troubles in life, and I become thankful. Then I usually shout out my mantra, which usually goes like this: "Songwriting Shane is back!!!" I then return to my music and turn my love to inspirational rock that has hugged, healed, and soothed my soul, and I always thank God. Everyone has a talent or something creative he/she loves to do. Do it.

Now it's your turn to come up with a Rocking Mantra that will bring out the best in YOU!

NEVER GIVE UP! SMILE more... SING more... DANCE more... and LOVE more.

Love Always,

Songwriting Shane

Sharon Tanyag

Sharon Caring, Daring, Inspiring, Sharing
By Sharon Tanyag

Sharon T. is the CEO Of Born Famous Productions, She's a professional singer, songwriter, vocal coach & international recording artist. She released her first album "Awakening" here in the US in 2003 and reached number 7 in the Tower Record's chart. Her single "Tell Me", a dance version of the Philippines's legendary composer/producer Louie Ocampo's composition, was released in Europe in 2004 and continued her concert tours & gigs in London, Burgundy, France, and Italy. In 2007, her single "He Told Me He Loved Me" landed in Dance Billboard Hits. She is the only Filipino judge in the Annual World Championships of Performing Arts for the past several years.

She also opened an Artist Development School offering Vocal Coaching to aspiring singers and artists in 2005.

Golden Pisces has helped aspiring singers sing with power and control and develop their confidence. Sharon T's lessons include physical exercises that develop the support muscles, proper breathing techniques to control tone support, high voice techniques, blending of the voice registers and stage attitude.

Sharon T. has GROUPS produced champions and finalists in several singing competitions. Some of her students were given major roles in school plays recognizing their singing abilities. One of her students Edsel Sotiangco got signed with YOUNG MONEY (Producer to Nicki Minaj, Drake, Tyga and many famous artists). The group WTF WE THE FUTURE toured with Lil Wayne last 2013 and back-to-back tours with Austin Mahone 2014. Recently Launched a Single "Be Mah Man" in Apple Music

& Spotify & Collaborated with Jipsta for the single "New Man" which reached top 5 most played song in Apple Music.

Sharon T. Continues to expand her repertoire as a national anthem diva, singing the U.S. National Anthem multiple times in NBA games, WNBA Aces, Las Vegas Aviators including the Whitehouse.

Helping Other Artists Led her to put up Born Famous Productions.

During pandemic Born Famous Productions Launched A group band composed of seasoned and upcoming artists called W.a.V.e (We are Vegas) conducted and performed on their weekly fundraising shows/ Mini concerts for a cause to help keep musicians employed in Vegas. Also shared blessings thru feeding programs in the Philippines, handing out food and groceries to homeless and less privileged people and will continue to do Charity works to help out in any way she can.

Nancy Smith

The Voice of Your Soul
by Nancy Smith

Years ago, I went to the Grand Canyon. As I stood next to the canyon, I felt so small. The canyon is timeless. Eons of endless power of nature chiseling out this huge canyon that weaves through the land for miles. I was overwhelmed. If I were to drop my lifetime, my dreams, and hopes and all the things that I experienced in my life into this enormous canyon, my life would measure up to be less than insignificant.

Have you ever felt that way?

This experience of being less than insignificant is an illusion.

What if you could experience the depth, the width, and breadth of your Soul? What if you could see your soul from the perspective of God---the Source of all that is?

Using your imagination, stand next to the canyon again. Close your eyes and feel the canyon, the wind, the water, and the earth with your entire self. Imagine yourself as the wind carving the rocks and the dirt. Feel yourself as the water flowing against the rocks and dirt pushing against what is around you. Feel yourself as the rocks and the earth with the wind and the water pressing against you. You are the earth, holding layers of sediment filled with remnants of all life that lives on your service. Feel what it would be like to hold and nurture and provide for the life that walks on you. That life is thriving because of you.

Each element you sense in the Grand Canyon is made up of tiny pieces that come together to make the whole. You are a tiny piece, and you are that whole ginormous thing of it.

Do you still feel small? The life you live is precious and important and has meaning to more than just you. The illusion I experienced of insignificance at the Grand Canyon is rooted in the belief that I am separate from all that is around me.

Do you know if your NOW path is aligned with your Soul Path? As human beings we all go through life with big dreams and big struggles. We have the freedom of choice in how we live and what to do with our lives; however, there comes a point in time when you wonder if you are on the right path.

> *"During my biggest challenges in life, I learned that we are created from love and we will return to that love once all is said and done."* ~Divine Love Affair an Akashic Journey

When I remember and open up to what I call Divine Soul Powered Love, it's a game changer for me. This is a miracle, and it's here for you, too. I will help you remember and return to the love NOW!

How do I help you access your Divine Soul Powered Love? I use my intuition and my own spiritual gifts for that needed boost to tune into your soul's essence. Let me help you awaken your heart and build a deeper relationship with your soul. Your potential for creative and inspired choices waits for you. For over 20 years I have helped people on their journey to find and listen to the voice of their soul. I help my clients understand their own soul filled messages and meaning

I started my journey to divine soul power as an empathic child. My inner experiences guided me to learn as much as I could the Soul side of life. My intuitive awareness showed me that spirit is here, right now and ready to go. Spiritual connection doesn't have to be a "hard to reach" mystery. Connection to Soul, spirit, God Source is just a thought away!

When I was a tiny girl, I had a sense of being loved in a large way. It was as if everything and everyone around me was made of love. I returned excitement and love to everyone and everything.

My mother nicknamed me Smiley because I greeted everything with a smile.

My parents took us to church as a young family. I watched with interest as the prayers and songs glowed in colors around the sacred alter. Sometimes I saw colors around people's heads. Sometimes I heard extra voices singing with us. Later I learned I was seeing auras and energy though clairvoyance and clairaudience. I defined this joyful presence as God, the Holy Family, and my angels.

I learned that what I felt and saw inside myself was not always reflected in the world around me. The world didn't always smile back. I had trouble with my Catholic education. I was introduced to the concept of sin. I was told we were filled with sin and not deserving of God's attention until we were forgiven by God. I learned my first formal prayer:

> *"Lord, I am not worthy to receive you, but only say the word and I shall be healed." ~ A Catholic prayer to prepare for receiving communion.*

When I learned this prayer, I felt my heart squeezing shut. I felt anxious, and my stomach hurt. It never occurred to me I didn't deserve the love I was feeling. I was taught I had to earn love; it wasn't free. By the age of seven, I had a conflict with my parent's sternness, my catechism lessons, and the love I experienced from my angels. It made for one hot mess. In self-preservation, I escorted the angles to the back of my consciousness.

When I was ten, my mom gave birth to baby number eight, little Jackie. Mom threw a big christening party. The house was filled with guests, and my siblings and cousins were outside playing baseball. I was told to go upstairs and get the baby. I started down the stairs with Jackie snuggled tightly in my arms.

At the top of the landing, I heard a commanding voice say *"STOP."*

"The angels," I recognized them and thought to myself. "I had better listen." I stood on the landing at the top of the stairs. I waited for what seemed like forever. I squeezed my eyes shut and asked, *"When can I go?"* In my mind's eye I saw a traffic light. The lights changed from red to yellow and then to green. *"Okay,"* I said out loud, and continued down the stairs.

I had to walk past a bank of large windows to lay Jackie down in her bassinet. As I was just about to step in front of the first window, a ball came crashing through it, shattering and spraying broken glass everywhere. The shards just missed hitting my baby sister and me. I knew then that if I hadn't listened to the voice telling me to stop, we would have been badly hurt.

I whispered, *"Thank you."* In my heart I knew my angels were keeping me safe.

From that moment on, my journey with Spirit began to grow on purpose, by my choice. I went to the angels when I felt lost, and then I felt happy in in my heart. I believe the angels raised me.

I literally woke up to spirit while in a difficult marriage. As a young mother I found myself in a failing marriage. I lived my life day to day in despair, caring for my children, going to work, and dealing with my husband's mercurial swings.

One night I dreamt a beautiful light was shining down upon me. It warmed me. The light was brilliant colors that made a mandala in a perfect circle. I could hear voices talking to me, encouraging me, and urging me on. They told me to look at my life from a different perspective. I could feel their love for me. They gave me a sense of myself being bigger than the woman who was going through day-to-day despair.

When I woke up to attend to a crying baby, I could feel the light still shining through my iced-up bedroom window. I was pretty much "walking in my sleep", so I didn't clearly look at the window, but I knew it was there. Early the next morning I woke and remembered the dream about the circle of light. I went to the window; a perfect circle had been melted in the thick ice on the bedroom window. I was awestruck.

The message of the circle helped me look at the bigger picture of my life. I realized that my life had meaning beyond the sadness that I felt. I had heard several voices that night and realized I have many spiritual advisors and cheerleaders. I was not alone.

How to REALLY communicate through prayer. I've used many styles of prayer. I've used the ritual prayers— from the *Our Father* to the rosary. I practiced Buddhist mantras. I've prayed in tongues. I prayed *expressive ways*, like Mom's favorite prayer, "Jesus, Mary, and Joseph, God Almighty!" When up against the wall, it is best to call in the whole team. Even prayers said in emotional outbursts are still prayers.

Eventually my marriage crossed a line. My husband's temper had gone too far. I filed for a divorce. After the divorce, our young family fell into a pattern with every other weekend visitation with dad. The kids often returned home crying, sometimes they were sick, sometimes they were hurt. My anxiety was through the roof. I developed insomnia. I would try to lull myself back to sleep by praying the rosary. On one of these occasions around 4:00 a.m., a woman's presence filled my consciousness.

She was tall, hovering above me on a red-dirt hill. As I looked up at her, I also felt her by my side and in my heart. She had a loving presence. She was strong and stern. She lifted her arm towards me.

She said, *"Pray like this."*

She reached into me and blended with my thought and emotions. She expressed my pain and fear from the deepest part of my being. Every word she said was an honest and clear expression of me. As we prayed, I felt a heavy burden lift from my belly and heart. I felt a gentle light of hope. I felt I could breathe deeply again

She took me to a red dirt hill. We were in a kind of desert—the growth on the hill was scrubby small bushes mixed with patches of short, dry grass. She guided me down the side of the hill. She carved out the initials of my children's names from the dirt.

She told me, *"You came together with your husband to create these children. Now you are apart from your husband. You must still raise these children in partnership with their father. Do not run and do not doubt yourself. Do not raise your children in hate and fear. Do not lose yourself in pain and fear. Be strong and be present. Speak so you are heard. Listen with compassion."* She handed me the carved dirt initials. *"I put these children in your care. Pray to me every day as I have taught you. I will help you. Be honest and accurate. Don't pray to appease me; pray to show me your heart so that I may see you, love you, and heal you. I will be with you and you will be with me."*

As our time together ended, I felt lighter. She made it clear to me I wasn't alone. She gave me healing, nurturing love.

My uncle, a Marianist Priest, said that I had experienced an apparition. He sent me a book with pictures of the story of Our Lady of Guadalupe. I recognized the red hill and the landscape of the area we had walked together in my vision. I was stunned and grateful for this validation of her visit.

Your Soul knows what to do

When You are in a transition in your life, it's usually a redirect from your Soul. You are meant to find your true self after loss. A pandemic or economic devastation is most definitely a soul redirect. When you are not sure how to make sense of what is going on, or what your next steps are, look to your Soul.

The 5 languages of your Soul

You can learn the language of your Soul. Your Soul is creative energy and has many ways to communicate with you. Here are five ways your soul connects with you:

Self-love connects you to your Soul. As you feel your feelings, you begin to hear what your inner being (essence) is telling you. You become aware of your true and unique self. What brings you Joy? What brings you well-being? Doing this will Reconnect you to your aware self and open your heart.

Create Sacred Space. Creating sacred space simply means to take the time to listen to and accept yourself as a divine being. The "space" you are creating includes your higher mind, your Soul, and God the source. You can do this through meditation, a gratitude practice, and mindset.

Meet and connect with your Spiritual team. You are not alone. You are constantly receiving information from a higher source and helpers in spirit. This team helps with inner healing, guidance, and more! Once you create your sacred "space" you will hear your spiritual team more fully.

Fuel yourself with Divine Grace of the Creator. The "fuel" of fear, lack, anger, and pure will- power can drain you. The "fuel" from a partnership with Divine love of the Creator will elevate and sustain you.

Be aware of your unconscious inner team. You have an inner (ego based) team of protectors, children, controllers, and so much more. These are parts of yourself that have been developed through this life and past life experiences. Meeting your inner motivators helps you know what's driving your life.

Your Soul's plan and contracts are embedded in your unconscious self. You can shift your thoughts and emotions when you partner with your Soul and your ego.

The Akashic Journey to Your Soul is a program I developed to help you on your spiritual path. This program is laid out in my book *"Divine Love Affair an Akashic Journey."* The Akasha is the energy and love of the Creator. This book is a Nautilus award winner!

The Akashic program is designed to help you develop a strong relationship with the Creator and your Soul. You will learn techniques and protocols that will fill your spiritual toolbox. You will learn the different levels of conscious awareness. You will develop a strong connection to your spiritual helpers. You will learn about past lives and soul contracts. As you access your Akashic records, you will learn your Soul's dream for your life now.

My work as a medium and spirit artist has opened the door to many of my clients who have lost dear ones and need help creating meaning during their grief process. As an ordained Minister in the Spiritualist tradition, I have shown over and over again that life truly continues after the change called death and that we can communicate with our loved ones. I combine the Akashic soul work with mediumship into a practice I call Akashic Mediumship, The language of Spirit and Soul.

You can contact me through www.angelscapes.net or email me nancy@angelscapes.net.
Enroll in my free 7 steps to Soul Power at www.Angelscapes.net
I am on Facebook as Nancy of Angelscapes.
Join my Facebook groups:
Soul Power Living tools for a life you want and love.

Thank you, I am grateful.

Sonia D. Bermejo

Sonia Dionela Bermejo
A Biography by: Naiia Lajoie

SONIA DIONELA BERMEJO, publisher and executive editor of Manila Up! International

Magazine, Exquisite Magazine, and TV Producer of (MUTV) Manila Up TV Entertainment.

There is one undeniable truth about life---whatever you want to do, you can learn and teach yourself with self-determination and with God's blessing--and this is the case of Sonia Bermejo. Starting off as a model for an American promoter, a magazine commercial ad model for a Singaporean magazine, and a TV commercial model for a popular basketball team, Sonia built her career as a real insider of the industry from a very young age.

Sonia Dionela Bermejo was born in Masbate, an island province at the crossroads of Luzon and the Visayas in the Philippines. Her parents were originally from Bacon, Sorsogon, in the nation's Bicol region. After the untimely passing of her father however, she moved to Manila at the age of two. Having grown up there, Sonia considers Manila her home. Sonia attended high school at the Immaculate Concepcion Academy in Makati. She then continued onto college at Philippine Women's University in Bachelor of Science in Business Administration.

She also studied fashion designing at Cora Dolorosa and put up her own boutique, while working as a Public Relations Directress for a gourmet restaurant, planning different theme and parties every month, inviting people in the social scene. She also worked for a TV network as well.

Her true skill shines in times desperate of multitasking. She managed a co-model and singer, recording artist of Dyna Records, while producing fashion shows and working as the manager for an airline social club in Philippine Village Hotel, all at the same time.

With impossible social and work schedules, Sonia decided to leave her home and go to America for a short break. What started with no intention of staying longer than a vacation left her with true love for the city of Los Angeles, and she's been living here ever since.

After a lengthy period of shift working in an office environment under various titles, including secretary, office manager, billing manager, and production manager, Sonia utilized her adaptability and experiences in the corporate atmosphere to eventually own a surveillance company. Though Sonia had no prior background and knowledge with camera surveillance, she made her way up and above the competitors by learning and studying the industry with pure dedication. A true multitasker, Sonia was processing loans and involved in real estate at the same time. Even after the real estate crashed, her brilliance shined as she managed rental property and combined her hobby of flower arrangement and history in designing into a part time job as an event planner.

Sonia does not attribute her life's work to any specific set of skills. Rather she sees skills as something that can be learned whereas drive is what lives in you. "Create a want, and you will get it," she puts it simply.

Her time in the business has been full of twists, turns, and changes, leaving her with a variety of experiences in countless aspects of life. However, Sonia's new chapter has just begun as the publisher of an international magazine. Not even in her dreams did Sonia imagined herself in this position, but she believes that this is God's plan for her. "Only through His grace everything we do will be blessed."

This resilience and constant upward mobility are what ultimately garnered Sonia the title of magazine Publisher and Executive Editor. Her humble beginnings took place while she was the executive director of an event; "Beautiful Life" produced by Monet Lu. Having seen this souvenir program, Sonia boldly told him that she could transform it into more of a magazine-style program book "boldly" because she had no prior knowledge or experience in this world.

Despite this and fortunately having recently met a layout artist, Sonia set forth on creating a magazine. She offered her suggestions when it came to ideas and content layout to which her friend responded that he was amazed at her "natural eye" for putting together such a publication. It came as no surprise then that the souvenir program-turned-magazine was a big hit. Her artist friend inspired and motivated her to become a professional publisher---a prospect that initially scared Sonia. This would mean she would have to enter a new line of business. Yet from that first issue trial, for the next edition she managed to double the pages, invited friends from all over the world to contribute, and thus came the birth of Manila Up! Magazine in late 2015, internationally recognized and distributed.

Manila Up! Magazine is a print and digital publication catered to, promoting, and connecting Filipino- Americans, Asian-Americans across the globe. Defined by the concept of connectivity, its basic mission statement is to "establish and expand the common ties we as Filipinos and Asian-Americans share within our communities and beyond".

Sonia is grateful that the magazine is being recognized by Filipinos and Asians in the states and abroad. And yet, she doesn't believe that this is anywhere near the end of her journey. Sonia said that she'll keep on doing what she was destined to do---following God's plans.

It is with this thought process that she is so able to inspire people and why she continues to use the magazine as a platform for others to share their start-ups or for people to become known both abroad and back in the motherland. In promoting and celebrating their personal victories, they in turn can inspire the next generation.

In addition to this pivotal success and continuously welcoming new writers onto the Manila Up! team, Sonia is also particularly proud of her extracurricular endeavors. She helped to organized fundraisers for the RSG Foundation on which she served as the vice president. From 2004-2016, they would raise money for the poorer population of Bulacan so that they could celebrate Noche Buena (Christmas Eve). During the last year of her active involvement, the foundation raised money for 10 students with exceptional grades, motivating them to continue their schooling by providing them with their daily expenses throughout the school year.

Another memorable moment of success for Sonia came during Manila Up!'s 2nd anniversary. In attendance were "Project Runway" winner Kentaro Kameyama as well as celebrity Chinese designer Kiki Wang. A back-to-back fashion show was held showcasing their works; it was Kentaro's first show after winning the competition. It was also Kiki Wang's first show in Los Angeles. The show was a huge success with the help of her friend and Director, Geo Sargent. After this celebration in late 2017, in the early 2018 Sonia launched a TV show, Manila Up! TV (MUTV). It is now on its 3rd season streaming live on Facebook as well as on their YouTube channel.

In 2019, Sonia set into motion yet another expansion of her self-made Manila Up! empire. *EXQUISITE International Magazine* was introduced as the sister publication of the then 4-year-old *MUIM (Manila Up! International Magazine)*. To meet the growing expectations and cultures encompassed by *MUIM's* readership, the content of this new magazine encapsulated lifestyle and entertainment topics that would extend beyond Filipino culture – yet Filipinos could still enjoy. This included the glamour of Hollywood or stories born from the heart of Los Angeles, Sonia's current residence.

With all these accomplishments spanning a very eventful – and continuously so – life, Sonia remains humble. Perhaps it is the memory of coming from a love of producing fashion shows and owning her own modeling agency back in Manila and having to begin anew in so many different industries upon landing in the US. While she did not start as a writer, what did help her survive in the publishing industry were her passion, perseverance, and patience. The "NOs" she received only motivated her further. Above all else, she only takes on what she inherently loves doing.

Sonia is hopeful for the next generation of future publishers. While she attributes finding her place to divine intervention and God paving the way for her, she feels as though with millennials being more technologically inclined, there are a lot more tools at their disposal, thereby giving them a greater chance at success due to the accessibility of social media and the potential global outreach. While it is tough and highly competitive, Sonia encourages young entrepreneurs to remain determined and creative; with that they can achieve whatever they put their heart into. She herself has survived many trials and tribulations, so she has no doubt that others can overcome the challenges, whatever it may be.

In offering advice to newer writers, Sonia is reminded of her own mentor who showed her the know-how of the publishing world. Ernest Gonzaga passed away a couple of years ago; he was the publisher and executive editor of *IMAGES ASIA*. He guided her and taught her how to remain relevant and stay in the business. He even contributed to *MUIM* before his passing. Sonia also admires Bill and Melinda Gates, not solely for their success and riches, but for the fact that they share their wealth. In addition to giving to the poor, they promote and expand research in science and technology, aiding in making the world a safer place for the generations to come.

Sonia's creative personality is due to her husband giving her freedom. "My husband lets me do whatever I want to do." While that might sound rudimentary, he does not get in the way nor inhibits her creativity. By doing nothing, he is giving her everything. As a child, Sonia's family was not highly motivated to push their kids to be business-minded. As such, it was out of her own volition that she wanted to learn and gain more life experience---which has obviously paid off tenfold. While she laments that her younger self should have been more focused and serious earlier in life, the fact remains that she did begin working as such an early age based on a pure curiosity---something which eludes many to this day.

Sonia now helps with the "Angels for Street Kids" feeding program in Manila. She has contributed as recently as December of 2020 and hopes that the continued proceeds of Manila Up! sales will be portioned out to them. Sonia's dream is to create a program in which the parents of said kids can have a sustainable income---one that does not require or rely on monthly handouts to feed their children. Perhaps parents and kids alike can run their own business, and by doing so, are able to fend for themselves rather than resorting to relying on the mercy of others.

Another issue that touches Sonia is anything pertaining to human trafficking; an issue which is rampant throughout the world yet is particularly high in the Philippines. Women and children, being used as labor – or worse – sickens her into action. With so much going well in her life, there seems to be a correlation between the more she possesses, the more she would like to contribute. She dreams of a world where there are no forms of slavery.

Despite these occasional dark thoughts – only born from a want to make the world a better place – Sonia otherwise lives a simple life. She seeks solace in prayer. She enjoys sewing, gardening, and flower arranging – ultimately anything that involves creating something. If permitted, she wants to be with her only granddaughter, Isabel. She gives her so much joy. Isabel is a smart, sweet, and very loving 3-year-old kid. Highly praised to the early training of her parents, Lionel Dionela and Natalia Marquez-Dionela. The family is the most important thing to her now more than ever.

For Sonia, her greatest accomplishment is that despite all the failures and success that have created this rollercoaster of a life, she is still standing. Moreover, she can stand on her own. In doing so, she raised her son while also reinventing herself time and time again, creating new venture after each venture. What is more is that she continues to be excited to learn more every day. At this point, the only thing Sonia can ask for is to continue the magazine, so that it may serve as a platform for any writers, photographers, inspirational people, motivational stories, and readers to share inspiration and be inspired.

"It is not the wealth that makes a person happy; it is what you have lived through in your life."

-Sonia Dionela Bermejo

Latasha Fennell

Blazing into Success
By Latasha Fennell

Thinking back as a little girl, I knew I was destined for success! I remember all the extremely difficult moments in my life but never gave up hope and continue to believe in myself and trust in God. I started setting goals and working hard from an incredibly young age. There were a lot of setbacks and hard times where I felt stuck, confused, and broken, but I never gave up, and of course, I took a lot of risk and left wrong turns to get where I am today.

I was a curious country little kid; I grew up fast and had to do things way too early for my age. My parents divorced when I was around the age of 12. Both of my parents were hard-working, loving people and always had high expectations for my sisters, brothers, and me. It was expected that I work hard, go to college, and have a successful career, but I had no idea how and what direction to take to get there. My parents never went to college, and I didn't even know anyone in my neighborhood growing up that actually went to college. All the people I knew were hard-working. good people that worked a 9 to 5 job to take care of their family just like my parents.

One major setback that I could remember, and I could not forget was when I was younger, I was bitten by a brown recluse spider. This incident happened to me when I was in the 5th grade. I almost lost my left arm because of this poisonous spider. This incident caused me to give up every goal I could ever think of setting and actually achieving. Could you imagine being trapped inside a hospital for months and having over 10 surgeries to make your arm even usable because you refused to have it removed? God had something better waiting for me and took me through the storm to see the rainbow at such a young age. I was discharged and back in school as if it never happened. I was eager to catch up with my schoolwork and friends and do all the things the doctor told me I would never be able to do. No matter what setbacks I faced in life, I was never going to give up; I was determined to prove the doctor wrong.

I was never confident about my situation but dealt with it the best way I knew how. It was not until I was in high school where I met a young teacher that I admired and looked up to. She was a great role model for me. In her I could envision the path I needed to be successful in life and how to start a career. She pushed me to go after all dreams and made sure I didn't give up hope and was by my side the whole time. After high school I tried to join the United States Navy. It was a different path from going to college as my parents talked about, but I wanted to travel the world and see it for free; joining the military would make it possible. I knew I could be could successful if I left my hometown to be on my own. So, after trying to enlist in the United States Navy, the medical doctor placed me on a hold because of that left arm that wasn't supposed to be usable. My nightmare was back to haunt me. But I was always hopeful, and when I have my mind made up about what I want to do, I can convince anyone. So, I did just that and worked hard and passed my medical screening, and I enlisted in the United States Navy.

Funny thing is I really didn't find myself until I joined the United States Navy. I was still not comfortable with my body and still wasn't ready to tell my story about my childhood. I met many people who didn't look like me but accepted me because we were going through some of the same trials in life. The Navy was a no judgement zone. Getting to meet new people and traveling around the world gave me the tools and experience I needed in my life to better myself and blaze into success! I was finally on my way to doing what I wanted to do and had gained so much confidence along the way.

It was in my early years of the United States Navy when I fell in love and married and had a child. At this time, I had to make another tough lifelong decision. I was faced with continuing to stay and serve in the United States Navy or get out to raise my son. I decided to do both---stay and continue to serve in the Navy and raise my son although this was going to be hard and meant that there would be times, I would have to leave my son and husband behind to serve my country. I have always been incredibly determined and driven and knew I could do it all with prayer, support, and love from my husband and family. So, I did just that and continued my naval career.

During this time in my career, I learned so much about people and business with the job I was assigned in the Navy. My job title in the Navy is Logistic Specialist. This job is customer service driven, managing money, parts, equipment, and contracts. This is an important and major job in the United States Navy. Not only do I have to take care of my work center you must take care of your command and the entire Navy. The Navy provided a lot of training to do my job; I learned how to be a better me and a great leader. The Navy is big on leadership and guidance. Being a good leader is what drives me. I moved up in ranks---fast in the Navy; moving up in ranks means you will be a manager and oversee high dollar parts and equipment. But most importantly you will manage and lead sailors. This was more than a full-time job; most of the time this meant overtime because you are never off as a chief, and you will become great at solving many problems. I quickly learned to love problem-solving because it meant helping people and most of all making things better for them.

My passion will always start and end with people pushing and motivating people to be successful! After 21 years and counting of serving in the United States Navy, I have mentored and have been a mentee many times in the navy. Being a woman in the navy isn't easy; being a woman in life isn't easy either; it often makes you chose when the correct timing in life to do things. By timing I mean when to have a family and when to go to school or even start a business. As a woman you have the chance to make a positive difference in your family, community, and society. I knew doing all of this would be hard but not new. I also knew I couldn't be the only woman in life at a crossroad of deciding on making the navy a career and running an outside business and doing what I love and most of all having it all and being successful at it.

This pushed me in every direction and made me work harder but mainly pushed me into the right direction of getting my business license and starting my own business in 2018 called Boss Lady Bling Blingy. During this time Boss Lady Bling Blingy was just an online based business, and most of my items were sold to 90 % military driven customers. I wanted to share my blingy accessories with the San Diego people and eventually the world, but I was comfortable with making items for the military. There's an old saying my mentors used to tell me: if you want to be successful, you must get out of your comfort zone and do and learn things you don't normally do. I was never scared of growing or been challenge. I just didn't like the fact of starting over and facing the unknown results I might get of doing it. With all that being said, I stepped out of my comfort zone and started making and designing more blingy items for non-military customers to wear and make them feel good about themselves when wearing my items.

I was so excited that I made and created so many items that month that my spare bedroom became unrecognizable. I was ready to show San Diego who Boss Lady Bling Blingy was, and I went out and started looking for a local market or a place to do a popup shop to sale and show case my work. I signed up for my first popup shop. I will never forget my first popup shop in Imperial Beach, California. It was on a Friday in mid-February at a farmer's market. I felt I was more than ready. I was there all day and only sold one item! I didn't even make enough to pay the booth rent that was being charged to even be out there. I was crushed and heart broken and started to think maybe my business Boss Lady Bling Blingy was not ready.

My husband insured me it was ready, and I was just at the wrong place and needed to be somewhere else to shine. I must admit my husband was so right; it was all about location and marketing yourself.

So, I went back to just selling my items online, but, in the meantime, I was searching for another market to try again. I was determined to not give up; after all I wasn't a quitter. I went out and signed up for another market, but this this time it was a Home-based Artist market. This market was local in the heart of Imperial Beach not far from the first market I attend, but this market was designed for small home-based business owners. This was the right fit for my handmade items, and I cannot forget that view of the ocean. This was the place where Boss Lady Bling Blingy was known to so many locals in the area, and my name and business began to blossom and grow. The first weekend of setting up was a success! I was able to sell majority of the items I made at this market. I also met a lot of amazing artists at this market and other entrepreneur's that gave me pointers on my business and helped me get my business name out to the public and eventually into boutiques and art gallery.

My small business started getting the attention it long desired from the public with the help of IB Popup shops, The Cove Beauty Boutique, Cynthia Artistic expressions, Eye Catchin Lash, and Beauty Bar and social media. My business was even published into the local San Diego New paper from an RAW event I participated in at The House of Blues for some of the best of the best local artists in San Diego Ca. It was at this moment I knew my small business was blazing into success! This event took and introduced Boss Lady Bling Blingy Business to a new level and on the road to Los Angeles, CA, where I started working with a company named Color in Motion by Raven Wilson. I worked with some of the most Top high-end designers, models, and photographers in Los Angeles Ca.

Color In Motion (CIM) took my business on the road to success and has attended every local high fashion show in Los Angeles and every LA Kid fashion week events in Los Angeles, CA, and Hawaii fashion week. Boss Lady Bling Blingy business has been featured in over 15 magazines. I have created my very own local jewelry Look book with three series, Boss Lady Bling Blingy helps and serves the local community and my country. Boss Lady Bling Blingy represents a high level of being a role model, leader, philanthropist, mentor, mother, wife, and business leader. I am an impactor and a phenomenal example for women. Boss Lady Bling Blingy was also accepted in the All Women Rock and Red Blazer family owned by Carl D Wilson. Boss Lady Bling Blingy has dominated the streets of high-fashion style and the fashion magazines for countless seasons with no expiration date in sight. Although my small business has accomplished a lot and still has so far to go, but with prayers, support, motivation, and ambition, I will always be unstoppable and successful with the path of my business and in life because anything is possible when you don't give up and keep the faith and believe in the power and prayer of God.

My Bio

Latasha Fennell is the proud Entrepreneur of Boss Lady Bling Blingy Jewelry. She was born in Memphis, Tennessee---raised in the areas of Proctor and West Memphis, Arkansas. She grew up as a country girl with sparkles in her eyes for bigger and brighter things has always been her enthusiasm for "things that blings."

This fierce fire in her body commanded her on the path of the Bon Vivant lifestyle.

After graduating High School, she joined the United States Navy as a Logistics Specialist and made it to the rank of Senior Chief Petty Officer / E-8. Twenty-one years later, she still serves in the United States Navy, protecting and serving her country. In between serving and working in the local community of San Diego, California, Latasha purely passionately created her own business, Boss Lady Bling Blingy. It offers thoroughly detailed hand-crafted art from the heart, designed in a nearly obsessive as Latasha sits hours, pondering ideas and indulging in her favorite tunes while creating things that Bling Blingy.

Latasha strives to bring you flair if you dare to have fun. Her one - of - a - kind handmade jewelry is created by using traditional techniques, with an emphasis on simple and elegant designs. The entrepreneur and artist use a variety of precious stones to create most of her pieces, that are always ready and always available for the runway, magazine, prom, and everyday wear.

The creator of Boss Lady Bling Blingy was self-taught in making jewelry and has gained most of her work ethics from working in the Military as a Logistics Specialist. This has fed into her practice in business and financials. Latasha has a diverse background and decides to incorporate her military experiences with her first passion, fashion, and jewelry Design. For this reason, in 2018 she founded the Boss Lady Bling Blingy brand. Her Bling Blingy pieces are unique and eye-catching. Boss Lady Bling Blingy loves a Design challenge, so if there is something you'd like Latasha to make especially for you or if you have any questions, please don't hesitate to reach out to her online.

Contact Boss Lady Bling Blingy
Facebook: @ Ladie Bling
Instagram: @LadieBlingy4
Phone: 619-617-4586
www.BossLadyBlingBlingy.com
https://sqaureup.com/store/BossLadyBlingy
Email Address: Jewelry4u@BossLadyBlingBlingy.com

Di Carter

Be the Reason They Don't Quit
By Di Carter

Part 1- "Bless the world with your story; share the light God gave you" Di Carter

… Coming from a small poor village in Brazil, going to England, cleaning a lot of toilets along the way, and landing into United States with $100 dollars on my pocket. You get the picture, right?

My life wasn't easy, and I am sure yours hasn't been either. We all face many struggles and fears through our journey that we call life. I literately had to fight against the odds of success.

You might see yourself throughout my story, and the connection you will feel is real. Take a deep breath and enjoy it. This exercise will clear your mind and make you smile.

Here are a few questions you might have as you start this chapter. Who is the girl who clean toilets? What can I learn from her story? Why would our journey be similar?

Girl, what are you waiting for? Keep reading so you can be blessed today. Open your heart and enter the world of your imagination. Let me take you back to where all began!

My name is Di Carter. I am a serial entrepreneur and a network marketer professional. Today, I will share a piece of my heart with you.

I was born in Brazil, South America, raised by my 18 years old, single mom and gay babysitter who made me feel like a princess everyday even though we didn't have any money. Life from the get-go was not the perfect family picture, and I grew up without my biological father.

I came from a very poor family where having shoes and new clothes was a luxury. We all learned quickly how to make our own toys with plastic bottle of coke and had to be satisfied with what we had to eat most days were rice and beans.

My mom stopped going to school in the fourth grade so she could help her family. I am not ashamed of my mom's past. In fact, I am very proud of her for doing all she could to break the chain of poverty with no education

At 10 years old, my life changed dramatically. Why? My mom found the perfect man "a well-respected gentlemen, a senator", where my life began to change. I went to the best school from that point on in my life, and no one knew my story. I remember vividly being around the most educated, well-dressed kids with well-known names when my last name meant "poverty, broken family, no future"

Early on, I knew I wanted to impact many lives. I just didn't know how?

Between those ages of 10 to 15 years old... all I did was donate all my expensive toys and my fancy clothes to the kids in the village.

I remember saving my lunch money so I could take all the kids in the village to eat ice cream. It felt so good to be able to give to the ones that had nothing. I can't put into words their appreciation for being able to enjoy the things we take for granted.

Imagine getting your favorite toy at Christmas that was how they felt.

Those moments impacted my life, and I felt the urge to create something. I believe those were the early stages of my entrepreneur mind.

I used to wonder how I could do more for the less unfortunate. What would I do if I had the opportunity to create something bigger than myself?

The word impact never left my soul to do more for others.

At 15 years old, I had my first encounter with Jesus; from that point on, everything changed for anyone who would be around me.

At 16 years old, I landed in the USA as an exchange student. I only knew how to say, "How are you?" "I am hungry" and "Where is the bathroom?"

Wow…. How did I get here? I remember being inside an airplane for 9 hours saying, "Commit to the Lord whatever you do, and your plans will succeed." Proverbs 16:3

I learned how to speak English, I impacted many lives, and I felt so happy. I was fascinated with American culture.

It was time to go back to Brazil and this time, my stepdad was sick with diabetes and no longer had money to help with my education.

At 18, I had an opportunity to go to England to work … The goal was to clean toilets for 6 months at Home Depot and pay for my flight attendant school.

WHAT A DREAM!!! … If it all worked out, I'd be able to travel the world.

At 19 I landed in the USA with $100 in my pocket. What I know for sure: God had a plan for me all along, and he has one for you. I got married, divorced, and lost all my friends from high school. When all the 21 years old kids were celebrating having their first drink, I was feeling alone and had no hope for the future.

Is it a coincidence that you are reading this book at this point of your life?

Fast forward.... 7 years later I am a flight attendant. Who would have thought a little girl from a poor village would be traveling the world, getting a degree, and marrying a pilot?

Pinch me!!! He is a God of second chances!!!

Part 2- How big is your faith?

At 30 I became a mom of two beautiful blonde-haired and blue-eyed twin girls, and I am a true Latina. Picture this, I get asked at least once a month if I am my girls' baby-sitter; I have dark brown hair, dark skin, and dark eyes.

Once I became a mom, my life as a surgical technologist didn't make any sense anymore. I needed to find a way to stay home and find that balance that I always wanted

At this point in my life, I had my second encounter with Jesus.

I called this the point of our lives where we start seeing the blessings. Think back in your life where everything started to click and started to make sense. I finally understood the meaning for impact, the burning desire to do and be more. I knew there was something out there for me. "Where God guides, he provides." Isaiah 58:11

At 32 ... I was working full-time as a surgical technologist in the O.R on my feet, fatigued, over-weight, and unhappy with my health. I couldn't take one more day waking up at 5 a.m. feeling like a number at work. What I really didn't like was not be able to kiss their boo-boo's 24/7. I was seeing my family through my cell phone pictures more than in real life.

Just by telling you my story, it hurts to know that I wasted so many of those precious moments. If I only would have made the decision sooner to follow God's gifts, I wouldn't be in tears when I tell you, my story.

I found a way to work on my own hours and build a network marketing business. I knew it wouldn't be fast. I have twins, and with that I learned how to be patience.

I couldn't quit my job right away, so I kept working until the time was right. I was a workaholic; God had to intervene. I got fired, and I was grateful that I was building my plan B, C, and D.

"I will walk by faith even when I cannot see." 2 Corinthians 5:7

Part 3 – The shocking truth about Social Media & Entrepreneurship

We called it "The new Gig Social economy" where we don't need to leave the house to make connections to the outside world

Do you currently use any of those apps? Facebook - Instagram – Uber- Amazon – You tube - Airbnb

What Does It Mean to Be a Social Entrepreneur?

It means to be able to influence your network by using social media and create a greater impact while having fun making an income. You find the needs of society, and you are providing the solution to their problems.

So, how did I impact thousands of people spiritually, financially, and mentally? I hope today you can understand the power of social media and how much you can impact the world with your ideas and dig into your creative side. Let's start!

Spiritually - How many people are heartbroken?

We know that hurt people hurt more people, but broken crayons still color. In 2013, I went to a women's conference where the speaker was Lisa harper, a well-known Christian motivational speaker. I left that conference with a vision from God. "For I know the plans I have for you." Jeremiah 29:11

I spent a few weeks brainstorming how I would impact my community in a positive way. As I was listening to Christian radio, the idea came to my mind, aha! I had an aha moment, a whisper in my ear "You found your calling." It was clear. I heard "Child, you are going to organize a Christian concert for hundreds of heartbroken people to worship my name"

Being a new mom of twin girls, I couldn't leave my house, but I knew with social media I could reach out to thousands of people on my community.

I started by creating a name for the event, a logo, and a website. I researched online how to promote, find sponsors, sign contracts, and finally a place to hold the event. It took a lot of faith to bring your vision alive, and it took social media to plant the mustard seed.

I created a business page where I built an audience of fanatical Christian fans and non-believers.

Christfest PC was born in 2013. I started to attract more people using my profile page by posting weekly and sharing my journey along the way.

God opened the doors and brought a beautiful young lady named Rachel Jervis, who was the brain behind the scenes.

After six months of planning, working hard, and putting endless hours on this vision, I found myself lying on the floor of my bedroom praying to God "Lord please help me; I built it. Now it's your turn to show up." All I could hear was, "You did well my child".

Here are the results - Our first concert had 500 people; our second concert had 900 people.

Today over 70 people from various churches around my small town have volunteered at Christfest. We had our 4th Christian concert this last summer, and we have impacted thousands of lives, and many broken people have been saved. "Your vision matters; everything matters." Di Carter

Can I get an Amen?

I understood the power of social media, and Christian Social Entrepreneur was born.

Financially – How Can I impact more lives with all this knowledge I have learned from Christfest?

In 2016, I realized I learned how to manage a team of volunteers, how to motivate them, and what it takes to grow a non-profit organization.

I have always wanted to open a business. Once again, I turned to social media, where I found a few business friends and started asking questions. I had 30k in 401k from a previous employee that I could transfer to my husband 401k or invest in my own start-up business.

After seeing the results of my social entrepreneur adventure, I realized that I could do it again!

I went to Brazil, South America, did my research, and found a niche market that needed a distribution center to supply the small businesses with their cleaning products, equipment, and office supplies.

Let me explain---we don't have Walmart's or Sam's Clubs in every small town in Brazil. I found the solution for a problem!

I started the whole process again… name of the company, logo, business plan, hiring people, financial planning, and Inventory. I had to travel to Brazil a few times. We built a company from ground up to a 7-figure business. Pinch me!!! It was not an overnight success; this moment over here calls "My vision matters, and God is my anchor".

The decisions were made through my smartphone using WhatsApp, Facebook, and skype.

I understood The Power of social media and The CEO of Qualimax.

Mentally – How could I simplify social media for woman like me?

I wasn't done with Social Marketing. This is my 3rd business, and I chose Network Marketing.

Social Media Success Formula

1. Tell stories (Create the trust & likability factor)
2. Share the products / Opportunity (Curiosity Post)
3. Ask the question, and let them decide

My biggest question when people ask what do you do? "I use social media to create a second income." Di Carter

The truth is …it takes guts to go after your dreams when others are watching you struggling and hoping that you fail. It takes perseverance and coaching from people like Eric Worre, Ray Higdon, and Femalepreneurs. When the student shows up, so does the teacher.

Are you coachable? Can you see your future? What do you care more about---your bank account being ZERO or what others think of you? As a Social Entrepreneur, you will get a lot of No's

You will be developing your communication skills, mindset, and lastly Influence. That is when you will impact dozens, hundreds, thousands or even millions.

EVERYONE WITH ANY level of EXPERIENCE CAN DO IT.

Reality Check Question: Are you willing to put yourself out there and tell your story to attract your perfect people?

On that note, in case you say… I don't know anyone!! Think again---there are 2 billion people on Facebook alone praying that you become an example for them.

Did you know I live in a small town with 1400 people total?

There is no stop light - There is no convenience store - There is no gas station - There is no Elementary school, and guess what? - There is no food delivery.

Explain to me: why can't you build an online business?

I keep reminding myself that I came from poverty. Nothing will stop me! What is your why? Dig deep, Girl!

Don't get me wrong, I know what God has in store for his children. When will you stop the self-doubt and start going through the failures? The only way to success is falling in your knees.

When will you realized that many people go online because they are spiritually, financially, and mentally broken? Why can you be the answer to their prayers?

The shocking truth about social media is to show up knowing that Facebook is your personal billboard, YouTube is your TV show, and Instagram is the behind the scenes when you use the stories.

What I know for sure is Social Entrepreneurship has been on the rise in the past 5 years, and it's not going anywhere. What you create as a Social Entrepreneur is up to you

Once I realized that my followers needed my services to help them create content, I opened a Facebook group / page, and my website dicarter.com was born.

Following your passion will lead you where God wants you. Do you hear me, girl?

I understood the power of social media, and The Founder of Social Entrepreneur Leaders was born.

"Whatever you do, do it with all your heart." Colossians 3:23

In closing, I would like to invite you to live your dreams. Do you accept the invitation? Can you feel in your gut that this is your time?

Today, I am a 24/7 stay-at-home mom, wife, and businesswoman. I help many startup businesses creating content. Furthermore, I enjoy volunteering in my community and changing the lives of less unfortunate by going back to my country Brazil as a missionary to my people. That little girl found her calling.

What I know for sure is God doesn't stop pursuing you. I give you permission to soar like an eagle.

Di Carter

Serial Entrepreneur & Network Marketing Professional

Dolly Cortes

Living Life
By Dolly Cortes

In 2015, I became a published author for the first time. I clearly remember how I felt that evening as I celebrated with 25 other powerful and inspirational Latina women. I was happy for the first time in a long time. We were all surrounded by close to 700 people that night, and as they approached and hugged us, I realized my life would never be the same.

Just ten months prior to this event, I recognized how incredibly unhappy I was in my life, career, and 20-year marriage. I had had enough, and I made a necessary decision that changed the trajectory of my life and catapulted my desire to seek all I ever imagined and wanted.

I needed and wanted to live my best life. I decided to eliminate everything and everyone in my life that was not aligned with my values. I decided to eliminate all negativity and to focus on creating the life that I wanted in every way imaginable. I decided to surround myself with powerful and inspirational individuals that were there to lift me up not bring me down. Within months, I left my career and ended my marriage, and although the journey was difficult and challenging many times over, I refused to give up on myself. I wanted to be an example to my children, and I needed happiness and peace in my life, and I got it. It took so much effort. After many tears and struggles I can honestly say, it was not easy, but it was absolutely necessary.

Between 2017 & 2018, I wrote three more books all within a year. As I wrote, I soon realized I was healing from my past. The more I wrote, the lighter I felt, and suddenly, I was inspired to help others Write to Heal from their past traumatic experiences so their Voices Can be Heard!

In August 2018, I opened my own publishing company, Rose Gold Publishing, LLC, and since then, I have published about 30 authors. All the stories they shared are inspirational, but many have heartbreaking moments in them---moments that have affected the authors deeply but also motivated them to pursue what many never thought possible. That same year, I re-married. I refused to give up on love because I believe love is the most beautiful feeling anyone can experience and love, real love, should never hurt. Love should be exciting, not nerve-wrecking. You know you are in love when you look forward to being with your partner, your best friend, your lover, your soulmate. Pure and genuine love should bring you ultimate joy. On the other hand, when you have this feeling in your gut that makes your stomach turn as you approach your own home, that alone should tell you, something is off and doesn't belong! So honestly, get rid of it! It may not be easy, but it doesn't have to be hard.

In August 2019, just a year after I opened my company, I celebrated the first nine authors I published by introducing, The Author's Gala. I showcased each of the authors by giving them a platform to share a little about themselves, but most importantly to be celebrated as they had never been celebrated before. I wanted them all to feel complete as they walked into the venue. I wanted them all to feel the night was theirs, and we were all there to see them in their best light. It was truly amazing. You can feel the love in the room. Everywhere you looked you were surrounded by people smiling and absolute joy. The music made everyone dance, and the message was clear for each one of them. It told them they were enough, and they embraced it.

In 2020, I helped my new husband open his own company during the COVID-19 pandemic. I also launched my own magazine, became an International Publisher, and assisted in creating multiple transformations through my publishing programs. In addition, I launched my first online course, Write to Heal, for those individuals that are more concerned about healing than sharing their story publicly.

To me, life is so beautiful and yet short. It's sad to see so many people continue to live as a victim and to not strive to live a life they desire and deserve. At times, I reflect and feel as if I woke up from a 20-year sleep. Once I did, I questioned why I remained in a loveless marriage for so long, or why I continued to work in a career that completely stressed me out and did not give me joy. I knew I was better than that, but I was not giving myself the love I needed, and I was absolutely not considering my self-worth. But that was then, and this is now.

Peace was my driving force. My success came from my actions. I made deliberate decisions that have allowed me to be where I am today, and I promise you that I have never been happier. Success for me has never been about the commas in my bank account. It has been about the impact I have created for those that have crossed my path and my happiness. Some may think that is selfish, but no, it is not. Being happy, genuinely happy, is a blessing. There is nothing selfish about it. When you are happy, you share the best of you with the world, and I love that I am able to do that. I want to demonstrate to all that cross my path that genuine happiness exists.

I also found success when I fell in love again, when I laugh, when I smile, and when I interact with others genuinely. I found success when I traveled to speak in conferences and saw women react to "my story" knowing that because of me, they also "woke-up" from that sleep that has kept them where they are at that moment. I found success as a mother to my children. They respect the person I have become. I don't play games. I am real and raw and fair. I will speak my mind and not hold back, but I when I do, I do it with love. I always say that I tell people what they need to hear, not what they want to hear because otherwise, it won't serve my purpose to help improve people's lives, and I wouldn't be doing anyone any favors. Success is being comfortable with the person that I am and loving myself enough to know that I deserve my life. No apologies needed.

I do admit I am a workaholic. I work seven days a week. Sometimes, I am beyond physically exhausted. However, I have never complained because I love what I do. I am more than a publisher; I am a mother, a sister, Certified Life & Business Coach, and a friend. I continue to do my work every day because my work and the impact I create pushes me. I will never forget the lady that told me after reading one of my books, "you saved my life." I can't forget the lady that told me, "I cried the whole time. I felt you were talking to me." I have had women from all walks of life approach me and thank me for my words. Many have said, "I have tried to make my marriage work" or "you inspire me." Others have said, "I will never forget you." I feel honored when others come to me and tell me I have touched their hearts. I know my work is not about me. My work is about impacting and improving other people's lives. My work is about helping other human beings find themselves and assisting them in becoming that version of themselves that they have desired for a long time.

Unfortunately, my work has also attracted some haters. See, I believe wholeheartedly in the Law of Attraction. It is because of this Law that I consider myself fearless. I feel I am no longer afraid to try new things, to take chances. I have seen my life transform for the better ten times over! I have seen things happen in a short amount of time that only bring more blessings my way. I am happier than I have ever been, and some people don't like that. Some people want to see me fail. I know this for a fact. I just refuse to give them that satisfaction or any power. Life is too short to give those individuals energy. I rather love them from afar. I know these same individuals are unhappy with themselves; they haven't found joy in their lives, and they rather waste time hating instead of loving.

On the other hand, I love my life, and I live it based on my rules. It's actually that simple. I decide for myself. I decide what works for me, my business, and my family. No one, outside of my household has a say. They can try, but they won't succeed. I know where I stand and what my life's mission is. Like I said before, success is not about the commas in my bank account, but about living the life I so much desired, have, and deserve.

Many times, I have been asked if I have any regrets, and my answer has always been NO. I don't regret what I had to experience because it made me who I am today. Without trials in my life, how would I have known that I have the strength to go big, to go hard, to not give up? I passed that test with flying colors! But it was not easy. However, I feel the struggles I endured were well worth it because my life depended on it. I also wanted with all my heart to be the best mother for my children, that above anything, my children were the most important reason why I made the decisions I made.

I want everyone that reads my words to know that times may be difficult; however, if you really want to, you can overcome anything. Life is too precious and short to be unhappy. Life needs to be celebrated. The opportunities we all have are incredible if we are ready to receive them and if we have prepared to accept them as they show up. If we are not ready, we won't look at them as such. For example, I have come across many individuals that don't ever want to invest in themselves. They are always counting the pennies and are ignoring the dollar signs that can come their way. They are too focused on the past and are ignoring today and tomorrow. They can't see ten feet in front of them because they are too afraid to take chances on themselves. Many individuals are so afraid to make decisions about the simplest things, and I get it, but I often think how sad it must be to live this way. Why does it have to be so difficult for you to take a chance on yourself? It should not be. Leaving a job, you hate should not be difficult. Living in fear because of the "what ifs" is only holding you back! Wouldn't it be amazing instead to take a chance in starting a new business, in buying a new home, a car, in finding love again? Wouldn't it be amazing if you believed in yourself just enough to take that leap of faith that you so much deserve? I believe it would be, and you should, too!

When someone tells me it's because of my kids. I can't do this because of my kids. I want to scream! Listen to me: your kids should not be your excuse; they should be your REASON! If not for you, do it for them! Live the life you desire because when you do, your life will change, and you will be unstoppable, but you won't know this unless you take a chance on yourself!

I learned to be grateful every day. I wake up grateful for my family, my home, my career, and my friends. I appreciate that I am one of the luckiest women alive that was able to redesign the life I had. I sincerely challenge others to reflect and to consider whether or not they are indeed living the life they so deserve and to make the necessary changes if they are not.

Living life, the way God intended for us to live should not be a burden to anyone. Losing hope and choosing to live a mediocre life is simply settling. Accepting words that put us down, that don't lift us up, and that diminish and kills our soul is not why we were given the opportunity to live in today's world. We are the only ones that can make the decisions we need to make to live a life full of abundance, full of joy, full of hugs, and kisses!

In 2020 and 2021, we lost hundreds of thousands of lives during the pandemic in the United States---a very sad and tragic time of our lives and history. In essence, for those of us that are still alive, I would like to think that we were given a second chance on life. Although we are still not 100% in the clear, it should be a lesson to all of us. Living life to the fullest should not be a burden; it should be an adventure. Living life with an intention to make this world a better place should be an honor.

I won't waste time living in misery and neither should you. I won't waste time worrying or following gossip and neither should you. I won't waste time holding on to anger towards someone that did me wrong 15 years ago, unable to forgive, and neither should you.

Being a recipient of the Red Blazer Excellence and Achievement for 2021 is an honor. It is an honor to be recognized for the work I do, for the love of life that I have, and for never giving up on myself or on others. Sometimes, you don't recognize how many people can be impacted by the work you do either through action or words. I was recently told that I am the "American Dream." I did not know what my friend meant, so I asked him to clarify. He said, "You know what you want, and you go for it. You don't let anything hold you back, and you do it with love and grace."

As I mentioned before, life is beautiful and yet so short. I suggest living life with a smile on your face, with love in your heart, and with the genuine desire to make this world a better place, not just for you, but all of those that surround us. Live life with intention and celebrate each day you are granted because you can make a difference if you choose to.

Marie Lee Jenkins

Book Titles

*M.y. T.i.m.e.
(Me & You; Together Infused in a Moment of Endearment)

Before starting my work day, I had morning prayer. Still in the moment of thanksgiving, the Lord gave me the phrase, "My Time." Nothing else was revealed. Several days had passed and I was still weighing in my mind, what was the meaning of "My Time." With the same urgency, the Lord later revealed to me that the phrase was an acronym, representing our time spent together.

This revelation compelled me to write.

*M.y. S.t.o.r.y.
(My Years, Start Today on the Roads of Yesterday)

While working on the book, I had a similar, profound encounter with the Lord. A second title was added; "My Story." This time I was given revelation, including the acronym. Being redirected with clarity, it gave me a more concise narrative with a broader appeal.

("Before your development in your mother's womb, I started your story…" God)

Introduction

This is the first time in my life where my thoughts are free flowing and unhindered by its contents. I can remember childhood experiences as if they were present today. I have pondered different situations, some pleasant, some not so pleasant. Yet, my emotions are not held captive by their negative outcomes. I am present in the moment. When I measure my current being, verses yesterday's actions, I reflect on the evolution of my emotions. I have shed the weights of sadness, days of depression, as well as, being accepted.

This book is made possible by the leading of the Holy Spirit, God's grace, the encouragement of my husband (Maurice) and my children (Ron, Michele, Michael). I believe that I can do all things through Christ who strengthens me! This opportunity to share my life journey will show the abundance of blessings received throughout my life. My pilgrimage has enlarged my tent. Which has provided several opportunities to pursue my passions. I have tried to correct non favorable choices that derailed forward movement. Longevity has allowed me to a recipient of rewarding venues and witness growth, maturity and adulthood of my three grown children. My estate has expanded by God's promises, extended through my grandchildren, great-grandchildren, a daughter-n-love and son-n-love. I am humbled to share my testimony with family, friends, and an audience who will appreciate struggle, hope and victory.

The pages that follow will unfold the character of my story, stature of my struggles, purpose of my pain and the unveiling of victory. I am blessed to contribute my words in print. This book will chronicle the height and depth of my testimony. I pray that my story will encourage you to never give up or give in to the pressures of life. Don't lose hope in the fight. Hold on to your integrity, reenergize your mind with knowledge, seek God's purpose for your life. Allow daily devotions to keep your peace stable. May you be granted your best life.

My sincere prayer as *"My Story" and "My Time"* is read, that you will be saturated with appreciation of the "now" blessings bestowed to me by God. One which has become my "whole new world." I hope that my story will compel those who are faced with oppositions to hold on to faith and trust God. He will bring you through. My entire life, from a toddler to senior status, is a testimony of God's awesome power, grace, mercy, forgiveness and healing. For those who will commit to my writing, I desire that it will strengthen your determination in knowing that God is the giver and sustainer of life. He is Alpha and Omega. We have our being in Him. All that we are and will ever be is because of His grace and mercy. Hope for today and eternal life rest in His son Jesus.

At this present time of my life, I am living in the moment called "The Golden Years." The front of my hair shows a stunning classical representation of maturity thru the lens of shining silver. The glistening of the sun illuminates the richness of my senior status. I have learned to take it "slow." I can take my time and march to the beat of my own rhythm. My weekends are mine to roam the mall, take in a movie, have lunch on the strip or just sit and watch the beauty of each day. I am retired! Thank God for His promise that allows me to enjoy the fruits of my labor! I have reached a serenity of time and space that refreshes me. The setlines of a new day dawning remind me of what the Bible declares. new mercy given each morning.

Having a cup of fresh brewed coffee while sitting at the breakfast nook, evokes a conversation at length with the Lord. My morning is lost in prayer, in His presence. and His response. I allow moments of remembrances; some pleasant, some unpleasant. Together they have become the bedrock of my personality, my achievements, my failures and second chances. These adorning years have permitted me the opportunity to be at a present state, where my thoughts take me back to the roads of yesterday. The most compelling aspects of my story, is being told thru the lens of my life experiences. They unveil a life shaped by trails, tribulations, setbacks, heroic events, and God moments. I am blessed to share this journey through knowledge acquired and wisdom obtained by various venues. My desire for the reader is that the words written will not just simply entertain your curiosity, but will stimulate and extract the charm of your story.

"My Story"

"When I turned two years old, I developed an itchy skin rash marked by the medical term: Eczema. This eruption on my body stole the joy of my youthful, playful imaginations. It caused my young life to be alienated from playing with other children. No one wanted to be with the little girl with scabs, boils and running puss. As I got older, I experienced segregation, not because of race, but because of my appearance. I was teased, bullied and ostracized. I endured horrible name calling, which made me crawl inside myself for protection. Each week my mother would take me to the free clinic for treatments. I had a young, white female Doctor by the name of Dr. Farney. She always greeted me with a smile. Yet I felt as if she was like all the rest, just amusing me, hoping not to have any physical contact with my skin.

Each clinic visit was worse than my last remembrance. My clothes would stick to the puss that ran from the creases of my arms, the back creases of my legs and the circumference of my neck. Although my entire body was peppered with sores, the worse drainage was from my body creases. I would cry as I was being disrobed for treatments. They would have to peal my clothing from the infected areas. Sometimes they would apply warm compresses to the outer layers of my clothing in hopes that it would soften the removal. The doctor would examine my condition to see if there were any improvements. I recognized my hopeless physical existence through her disappointing eyes and shallow voice. I watched the sadness in the eyes of my mother when Dr. Farney gave the prognosis of my condition, prescribing stronger cortisone cream, and pills with a steroid compound for the itching. Being fully unrobed, I was instructed to step into a space just large enough to stand with my arms to my sides. I was not fully developed into womanhood, yet, I felt invaded, embarrass, ashamed, wishing that I were invisible. I would always ask God, why me? Puss oozed yellow fluid that filled pustules starting in my head all the way down to the soles of my feet. So that the ultra violet light would not affect my eyes, I was given goggles. As I watched the doctor turn on the ultra violet light, tears from my eyes would flow a stream, wishing I had never been born. I felt like a freak! Why didn't this have happened to by brother instead on me? No one could explain to me why? The procedure was designed to dry out the pustules and give me comfort. But instead, it dried my skin even the more. The side effects were tortuous. My skin became thick, scaley and drier. The outer layer of my skin resembled the appearance of a reptile.

Nights were the worse! The tribal ritual continued night after night. Before going to bed, I would take a sit bath using an oatmeal substance to calm and moisturize my skin. Afterwards, my godmother would gently apply the prescribed cortisone cream. My parents would put white gloves on my hands to prevent me from scratching in my sleep. To accomplish this task, they would tie the top of the gloves around my small wrist with ribbon to keep me from removing them. Still, I would wake in the morning to a bed of new drainage, puss and blood. Somewhere in the night I struggled to free my hands.

After the ultra violet treatment with Dr. Farney, she would give me cortisone shots in my arm to help control the itch. Hours after the shots were administered; my arm felt like it was carrying a piece of lead as a reminder of the experience. Not only was I sore and itchy, I felt like I was a burden and a curse to my family. None of my brothers were infected by this horrible, disfiguring disease. I believed that I was contaminated, an outcast. So many times, I asked God why? I wanted to know: did he not love me as much as He loved my brothers? Maybe I did something "bad" to deserve this punishment. I prayed earnestly for a healing! I could not understand why God wasn't hearing me. Most of my days were sad! I had only my dolls to comfort me. They still wanted to play with me.

I welcomed rainy days. In my thoughts, I knew all the children were like me, they had to stay inside and play make-believe. Regardless of my limited mobility, I found various activities to occupy time. The television was my closest companion. I could always depend on favorite shows to engage me

I was convinced that God did not love me as much as my brother or any other child. I hated myself! I hated that I had been born. I had begun to regress within myself. I built walls that kept me from feeling what others said about my condition. I hid the little girl who was being ostracized day in and day out. In my world I sang songs, I had imaginary friends, I was included.

I recovered from the daily battle of Eczema breakouts. They only appeared, being older, under extreme stressful situations. Young, black, gifted, energized, swollen with excitement; at the tender age of eighteen, I was married with a baby (Ronnie), and making plans to join my husband in Germany. (The details "how" are in the book.)

Germany and Home

I was so hurt, disappointed, angry, fighting tears from falling down my cheeks When I discovered we did not have a place to stay. My emotions were raging and my skin was taking a beating. I had traveled half way across the world with a baby, only to find out he wasn't the husband or father I credited him to be. Apparently, we were not top priority. I was broken. I always believed he did not want to be a responsible husband or father based upon his actions. But I still had a faith hope that maybe… Perhaps, I was holding on to hopeful desires long buried with disappointments Welcomed was the trip back home. I felt as if I had spent almost two years in a confined situation.

Once we were united back in the United States, our marriage took a turn for the worse. He informed me that he could have stayed in Texas with his woman. With that admission his answer changed the protectory of us going forward. I visioned a new future without him! With all fever, with my hands-on hips, fire in my bosom, head positioned to the side for a full throttle response. I was in complete attract mode! I informed him, upon your departure. Before you return "I will no longer be your wife!" He nodded his response in a nonchalant manner. (The details" how" are in the book.)

On my own

The call was bitter sweet. It felt like a dagger had been plunged into my heart. My son would be affected by my decision to dissolve the marriage. I felt like a failure! The church would assign the scarlet letter to my life. I would be shunned by some; ostracized by others. I feared my son may not have the joy of father son activities together. I felt I had fallen from grace, losing the two steps I had gained.

That year I experienced some of my greatest challenges. I lost my marriage and because of a lie, I lost my job, also. I recovered. (The details "how" are in the book.)

Rebuilding after the Storm

Never in my wildest imagination did I think the Detective that assisted in the Police investigations would become my husband. Several months after the case was settled, I received a phone call from Detective Lee inviting me to lunch. That afternoon encounter progressed to invited dinners dates, meeting my son, family and friends, along with his assistance, through professional connections, for me to secure employment. A year had passed when he asked me to marry him. With a yes answer, to our surprise, we started a family. After sixteen years of Ron being an only child, he now had a little sister and brother. Tragedy reared its ugly head when my husband, their father died in the early hours of a Sunday morning as we slept. Devastated, confused, in disbelief. The children and I were lost in a reality of pain. My question was: why? (The details "how" are in the book.)

The Blessing did Come

God made it possible that I would love and live again.

After thirteen years of widowhood, walking with the Lord, raising my children, taking care of my parents, and walking in the call of Ministry, I was united in Holy Matrimony to Deacon Maurice Jenkins. He is a man designed after the heart of God and lives a life pleasing to Him. Maurice is dad, grand-dad, great grand-dad, an intimate name given to him by daughter Michele, daddy-babe. We share an amazing life in ministry, friendship, family, fellowship, joy, laughter and the peace of God. (How the Lord "orchestrated" this union, is in the book.)

Conclusion

This scripture has given my life success: "In all thy ways acknowledge Him, and He shall direct thy paths. Proverbs 3:6 (KJV)

My advice for success: Pursue your passions and dreams. Never give up. If you lose direction, seek guidance. Be true to yourself. Be honest. It is never too late to do the right thing. Love, pray, have hope and above all, acknowledge God in all your ways.

Your Success can be determined by your experiences. Blessings on your journey!

Cheryl Broughton

Forget Your Age and Live Your Life
By Cheryl Broughton

Hello, I'm Cheryl Broughton, author of the book Your Epic Encore, Aerialist Performer (in my 50's with advanced arthritis), founder of Your Epic Encore Coaching, host of "Over 40 Living Epic Lives" Facebook group, and creator of Epic Encore Meditation channel on YouTube. I've also been the host and producer of a mind & body fitness TV show, founder of a 7x award-winning boot camp, and co-founder of a wellness company.

Ok, let's be honest. All of that might sound nice, but what you need to hear are the messy parts, the rough and edgy parts where I wanted to give up on everything. It's crazy, but true; sometimes we must go through breakdowns in order to have the biggest breakthroughs.

Join me on a journey through some of the not so pretty events of my life and the steps I took to rise above. I hope you will find something you can grab onto that helps ignite your fire from within. Sometimes, all it takes is one story that helps create a shift in our mindset, and we are forever changed…

What is an EPIC Encore?

To reinvent or transform yourself means letting go of emotions, past traumas, events, relationships, distractions, and maybe even friends and family that are holding you back.

It means letting go of old thought patterns and habits that no longer serve you. It means stepping away from routines, roles, and self-imposed responsibilities that have been pinning you down and keeping you from living life to its fullest.

It's time to jump in the driver's seat and grab the wheel and change the direction of your life. Give yourself permission to start over no matter how many times you've tried before!

Throughout my life, I've had many successes and many failures. At one point, I learned to stop calling them failures. Instead, I discovered that these were a series of "auto-corrections" by life trying to get me back on course, back to doing what it is in alignment with my true calling.

Science has proven the events that occur in your younger years from birth to about ten years old will dictate how you will handle just about every situation in your life for the rest of your life - good or bad.

Although our bodies will grow up and mature, the character traits and mentalities formed in response to a person or event in our childhood become our ingrained, imprinted templates for how we will interpret just about everything in the future - until we learn to adjust these reactions.

When I was about seven years old, my parents divorced, and I thought they were divorcing because of me (I didn't know any better). When they surprisingly got back together about two years later, I had already lost that bond with my dad (and did not get that bond back until my late teens). I remember my parents having financial difficulties and going through bankruptcy. Although I grew up and became an adult, these two events (divorce and bankruptcy) imprinted my subconscious mind. I interpreted them to mean money will always be tight, and the relationships in my life would be challenging. This theme continued throughout my life, and I never figured out why until I took the time to dive deep into self-reflection.

After graduating from high school, I attended an art college on a scholarship for one year. Then I switched colleges, and after a few months, I dropped out. Suddenly, I was lost, and I didn't know what I wanted to do with my life, and I felt as if I had no clear direction for my future.

Then one pivotal night changed my life forever. I was driving home from modeling in a fashion show. I fell asleep at the wheel, and my car slammed into a light pole! The impact was so strong; the pressure bent the car frame and broke the light pole in half!

The windshield cracked into thousands of tiny pieces but did not break apart or fall. However, there was a protrusion, a dome shape in the glass that stuck out about two or three inches. It was the mold of my head when I hit the windshield on impact!

It is without a doubt a divine miracle that I'm alive today and did not suffer any broken bones or head injuries. I know I had angels, the Lord above, source, or whatever you want to call it - they were there looking over me. I was given the gift of life.

I have never taken that day for granted and often think back to that moment to remind myself that I was kept here for a reason.

Epic Speedbumps

Have you ever had a gut feeling you shouldn't do something, but you do it anyway? Yep, that was me at nineteen years old. A few months after the car wreck, I moved to Atlanta, GA, with a boyfriend I had dated for a few years.

Unfortunately, he would take steroids and have fits of rage and would mentally and physically abuse me. It got to a point where I couldn't take it anymore, so I got the courage to leave and moved to Raleigh, North Carolina, where my parents had just moved.

After about three months, I moved to Myrtle Beach, South Carolina, with a friend. She and I were only twenty years old and had about $200 each to our name. We rented a room in an old, run-down, creepy beach house built up on stilts.

We did whatever we could to make our money go further - including eating peanut butter and jelly sandwiches daily and having to share the same bed.

Fast forward a couple of months - she got a job managing a retail store, and I got a job managing a party supply shop. We eventually saved up enough money to move out of the creepy house, and we rented a condo on the beach!

Unfortunately, that adventure was short-lived. The party store I managed closed after about two years. I had a staff of employees, and I felt terrible when I gave them the news we were closing. I was back to square one and in another situation where I had no idea what I was going to do or how I would make ends meet.

Prior to the party store closing, I had been helping locals with their party supplies and giving them ideas on how to decorate their events, etc. So, I decided to open up "Party Perfect" decorating services. I was the only employee, and sometimes decorating an event would take me all day, but I loved it! I didn't make that much money, but I was my own boss!

I also worked events as a promo model, and sometimes I would be the event manager. In doing so, I was presented with an opportunity to work for an event management company in Los Angeles. I got that "calling," you know, that one where if you don't follow or listen to it, you know you will regret it for the rest of your life?

So, in 1994, I moved from one coast to the other - from Myrtle Beach, SC, to Belmont Shore, CA. It was just a few months after the Northridge earthquake. But I did not let that stop me! Everyone thought I was crazy for moving alone and so far, away!

Two years later, I met this fascinating man. My alarm bells were going off, and my gut told me to walk away, but I did not listen. He reeled me in with his humor, and three months later, we had our first date. In the days that passed, he seemed fine. In fact, he seemed like Mr. Wonderful! Plus, his kids were terrific!

We lived almost two hours apart, and the drive was starting to wear on both of us. So, when he asked me to move in with him just months later, I didn't think twice.

In the beginning, he was charismatic, funny, and a blast to be around. But after a few months, I started seeing this other side of him. He was a full-blown Dr. Jekyll and Mr. Hyde, yelling, screaming, threatening, and sometimes hitting his sons and me.

Many times, in his fits of rage, he would hit me with an object. One day it might be with a video camera or one of those long steering wheel locks, and the next day, it might be with a book. Basically, it was anything nearby that he could get his hands on fast enough as he was exploding.

Well, on this one day - he used his fist. He went to punch me in the face, and I turned my head. His punch landed so hard on my ear; he ruptured my eardrum. I was in so much pain; I fell to the floor. I went to the emergency care to get it looked at, and the doctor questioned me. The next thing you know, the police show up at the house, and off to jail, he went.

My boyfriend called me from jail and pleaded with me to change my story to the investigator, and regretfully, I did. They released him the next day. Sure enough, he went right back to his old habits. I knew I should not have changed my story on what happened, but I was afraid of what he would do to me.

I wanted to run away so many times, but I couldn't leave these innocent boys who were learning all the wrong ways to be a man.

Here's what's crazy - he was in the self-help field! He helped many people overcome all kinds of issues, but he couldn't help himself! This was during the time I was a mind and body fitness speaker, a mind & body TV show host, and producer and had launched a life coaching program with my fitness boot camp!

On the outside, it looked as if I had this dream life. In reality, I was living a life of hell at home and then waking up at four a.m. to be the motivator for all these amazing people who had joined my boot camp! I could never let them know what I was going through, and I had to be strong and courageous and inspire them every day.

For years, I prayed, pleaded, and cried for an answer on how to break free from him. It was not until after eight excruciating years that I could finally get out of this abusive relationship.

Epic Lessons

In 2009 I was diagnosed with advanced arthritis and told that I needed both knees replaced. For someone who made a living in the fitness industry - this was devastating news!

After going into a depression with the pain and the stiffness, I eventually shifted my thoughts and realized the doctors' diagnosis was a gift! It ignited my drive to do something crazy and epic! It was as if I wanted to prove the doctor wrong and that I was still thriving (contrary to what she told me).

I decided to make a list of all the things that one with arthritis should not be able to do. Aerial fitness was at the top! I had wanted to do this for years, but the schools were only for advanced athletes every time I researched it.

I kept visualizing and seeing myself up in the air. I didn't know how it was going to happen. I just knew it WAS going to happen. After months of searching - I found an awesome little studio open to everyday people like me.

I was the oldest student in every class, and even the most basic moves were hard, but I did not give up. I kept coming back and training more and more, and I got stronger, more flexible, more confident, and the list goes on.

After a couple of years, I started teaching and performing in aerial alongside aerialists more than half my age! I have now performed over lakes, between mountain peaks, in front of waterfalls, over swimming pools, and much more. I can do things now in my 50s that I couldn't do in my 20s - even the splits!

I couldn't believe it! I found something that made me feel alive and helped re-invent myself... I now send out gratitude to that doctor who told me I couldn't all those years ago.

I never had knee surgery and instead changed my food intake, and I found some amazing supplements that made a profound change in my joint pain.

Knowing that I could not do the high-impact workouts anymore with my arthritis, I sold the boot camp and started a health and wellness company with a couple of business partners.

Unfortunately, after about ten years, I was let go. The company I helped build, the company that I worked so many hours on that I sacrificed getting married and having kids - all of that went out the window.

If losing my career was not bad enough, it was also around this time that my boyfriend and I broke up. I spent months in another depression trying to figure out what I was going to do.

On the outside - I looked as if everything was fine. I did not tell anyone. On the inside, I was crumbling. All I wanted to do was eat bad food, not exercise, stay in bed and watch TV all day, and feel sorry for myself.

I kept thinking, "How did this become my life? I was supposed to be married for 20 or more years by now, and I should've had kids by now, and I should be planning to retire soon and watching grandkids grow up. Why do I have to start over? How do I start over again?"

Yep, that was me just a few years ago. I was mentally stuck in my old "story." I had yet to see the "gift" in the events that had happened to me. My thoughts were muddy, and I was spinning my wheels in victim mode.

Then one day, I found a much sought-after mentor worth every dime! I learned how to diffuse the negative charge I had placed on each of the events that had happened to me. I learned how to surrender and be one hundred percent real and authentic completely. I discovered that laying all my cards out on the table and choosing to face my circumstances head-on was one of the most freeing experiences ever!

After an intensive, four-year deep dive into personal and business development, I found myself! I discovered my "why." I got my voice, my light, and my reason for living back. I became trained in the methods that transformed my life, wrote a book about starting over, opened two new businesses, and attracted the most wonderful man into my life!

This journey helped me to realize that the car wreck, dropping out of college, the abusive boyfriends, the break-ups, losing my career, and all the trials and tribulations I had been through in my life were so that I could experience life's greatest lessons. It was up to me to find the "gift" or the blessing in each event and then use these lessons to help others. I suddenly started having gratitude for everything that occurred in my life vs. resentment.

Remember this: there are no mistakes - only lessons, which will keep repeating until you have learned the lesson. The good news is - what you make of your life is up to YOU!

You already have the answers inside of you - just trust the process. If you're having one of those days, months, years, etc., where you know it's time to make a shift in your thinking - you're right! Here are five questions to get you started!

Pick one challenge (an event or person) you're having a hard time moving on from. Ask yourself:

1. How did this challenge help me grow or get stronger?
2. How were those results a benefit to me?
3. What other doors opened up after this challenge?
4. How can I use surviving this challenge to help others?
5. Why is that important at this time in my life?

That was a little snapshot into my story and some of the starting steps you can take! So, let's keep going! Join my other clients who have created their EPIC Encores! Mention this book and get a Free Discovery Call with me to take your goals to the next level!

Go To:

CherylBroughton.com (coaching services)

YourEpicEncore.com (signed copy of my book)

Facebook.com/groups/yourepicencore (free tips & training)

Remember, it's never too late for Your EPIC Encore!

Any P. Oliva

THE GLORY AMID THE STORM
By Any P. Oliva Valera

How to start writing a story???... Many times, people have always asked me that, but today I will start from the beginning. I am Any P. Oliva Valera. I was born in April in the beautiful decade of the '80s. From the day of my birth until now, the path has not been easy, but it has been highly enriching.

Since we are born, everything seems to be a storm; when we are born into this world, our cry is our first battle cry. Learning new things, developing skills, and gradually heading towards our destination are constant struggles. I remember that one day when I was seven years old while I was observing the news, I noticed that it was conducted by one of the most prominent journalists in my country - Mexico - and my mother told me, "I would like you to be as important as those people for you to appear on television one day;" that comment echoed in my head for a long time. Later, at ten years old, my mother told me, "All professionals wait until they finish their degree to start working; if they worked on what they like before finishing their degree, it would be straightforward for them," and I did so. I genuinely believe that I have the gift of listening to advice and learning from other people's experiences before their experience happens to me.

At 14 years of age, I moved with my family to Guanajuato, where my uncle invited me to work in communication and politics. Immediately, I fell in love with that profession. The passion I felt for this profession has continued to this day: communicating, transmitting, creating, and giving life to stories that had no voice to other lives that were fading without anyone telling and sharing such stories. Then, on the other hand, I found politics, one of the most beautiful professions, of course, that when exercised with absolute respect and dignity, is capable of impacting and improving progressively the lives of so many people. Again, my mother and father encouraged me to dedicate myself to what was now my passion, "journalism and communication," and of course, never to give up.

I started at an early age to work in a political youth group, and from there, I had the great opportunity to work on numerous political campaigns, including those of two former presidents of my country. I achieved many accomplishments back then and gained much experience from people who became my mentors, selfless people who taught me in the field of journalism what had taken them years and effort to learn. I also had the misfortune that many doors were closed for me, and many people said "NO" to my requests and inquiries. In addition, I suffered during these storms of life from a few betrayals, which I also appreciate. EVERYTHING---absolutely everything that happened to me was designed by God to support my growth and my becoming the person I am now. Good people showed me by example to selflessly support others, help others spread their wings, and propel them to success. Unscrupulous people taught me to be strong, not to let myself be defeated, but above all, not to be like them, not to treat people the way they treat them, and not to live my life as they live it: without love, without compassion, and without mercy.

In the middle of another storm in my life, a radical change came. I got married, which implied moving to the United States and starting from scratch a new path that I had already made in my beloved Mexico at a young age. It was a different and challenging experience, and I started from the bottom again. Things were very different for me; I worked in Mexico; the United States operates different from Mexico.

In New Jersey, the state where I came to live, I was allowed to start practicing my profession, journalism, and communication. I discovered a new world of possibilities, a new way of practicing my profession. I found that there was a lot to learn and that I am still learning. For many years, I was able to receive support and guidance from others, which helped me develop professionally. For all the experiences and the individuals who supported me, I am infinitely grateful.

For some years now, God has put me in a position to give and bless others. I am now in the position to offer my time and my profession at the service of others. I am in the position to enrich and exercise the talents that God has bestowed in me to support the growth of people, families, companies, and professionals. In this new experience, being the owner of various media outlets gave a new face to my profession.

God gave me the gift to communicate effectively, transmit, and tell stories with a stamp and a style of my own. Putting that talent at the service of others is rewarding. When you exercise your God's given talents with ethics, truth, passion, and humanism, then your work as a journalist allows you to be a transforming agent in your readers' lives.

My profession in the United States has allowed me to support many organizations. I have the privilege of giving many organizations a space for expression where other people and my readers can see their efforts. I have been able to tell extraordinary stories of entrepreneurs who are a source of inspiration and that nobody had paid attention to. I have been able to tell stories of incredible Latinos who went through challenging situations and who today are being an example and inspiration for our community.

I love my entire profession and what I can do for others. I firmly believe that the act of giving to others helps you grow emotionally and spiritually; by supporting an entrepreneur, especially an entrepreneurial woman, you are driving and propelling a whole new generation. It is a passion for me to see entrepreneurs grow, to be able to see the reality of an entrepreneur from the outside, to help them design strategies that promote their growth, and to be able to develop together with their sales channels and the development of the services of their business that they cannot see. It is even more significant when the entrepreneur I am supporting is a woman. The female entrepreneur carries a significant responsibility; their mutual support and solidarity among women in business are vital. Let us remember that each person has his/her unique essence, light, and authenticity. If you find such a woman entrepreneur, please support her, and sow in her. Let us no longer display behaviors driven by gross competition. There is no competition if each one of us exercises authenticity. Professional competence must be driven by our self-improvement day in and day out in the personal, spiritual, and career areas.

One of the best attributes of a female or male entrepreneur is congruence. Success will indisputably come to you when your heart and passion are aligned with the progressive development of your work, and congruence is part of your living and your acting. Being faithful and respectful to your ideals and values will make you enjoy the fruits of your work.

My particular vision of success is to be happy. It also means to feel complete in what I do, and the way I see my growth in every aspect is enriched with the growth of the people around me who are part of my life. Success is seeing my whole family happy and being a good role model of honesty, consistency, and support for my future generations.

I want teenage girls or young women who read this book to know that sound advice from people who love them are divine gifts, sincere love is a treasure, and deep self-respect will automatically make them respect others.

Studying will always be an indispensable tool for further progress, and that the younger years are the best time, so please do not waste your time. Goals are achieved by working and by focusing on what you want. You will never be more than you are now if you do not work on yourself, shape a mature character, and master what does not allow you to progress. I discovered the talent in me, I perfect it at every moment, and I put it at the service of others. Discover your gift, your talent, and multiply it by serving your community.

During the challenges, make an effort to ask what am I living for? And not why am I living this? Discover the experience or the teaching of the process, and you will not have endured the test in vain. Remember that in life, one of the things that most delays your progress is fear; I have experienced it. Be brave, and do not be a slave of fear in any aspect of your life. Lead your life with dignity, respect, and integrity. On the path of entrepreneurship and life, you will always find storms, trials, challenges, and betrayals. Please do not allow them to steal your essence, to take away your peace and goodness. Do not stop helping others just because you had a bad experience. Do not feel wrong about helping someone who never appreciated it. If they pay you poorly for the good you did for them, it is about them, not about you. Everyone gives what they have in their heart. The tree is known for its fruits, and people are known better for their actions than their words. Be true to your principles and your heart. Get up from each fall harder and never give up.

Being an entrepreneur is not an easy task, but it is a life full of satisfaction. Assume the full power of your potential, dare to dream big, and feel success even before owning it. Startup great ideas, and surround yourself with proactive, honest, and successful people. Always seek the advice of wise and selfless people. The entrepreneur who lives by FAITH and works hard is the one who receives the most rewarding rewards.

Respect for others is essential in your passage through this personal journey of your professional and business life. It has always caught my attention how people look down on others just because of their appearance, jobs, or simply because of their nationality. They discriminate against them to such an extent that just seeing them is extremely annoying. Unfortunately, when they realize that they can benefit and learn from the people they discriminate against, they radically change their position, call them "friends," and do everything possible to be around them. Be wise to identify these selfish/mean-spirited people who will delay your development with their toxic behavior. Please treat everyone with respect no matter what position they have, and likewise, you will be treated with sincere and loyal respect.

In this walk, I have had the opportunity to play many roles as we have all do; I am a daughter, sister, wife, friend, businesswoman, professional, and mother by God's grace and mercy. I have traveled extensively and have received multiple awards for my professional performance. Always at the end of the road, my greatest reward is to see my daughter on the right life path, knowing that she is fine and that she will not keep me in her heart for having obtained an outstanding award at the end of my journey or some great appointment. Instead, I want my children to remember me for being a good role model for them and for the love, support, values, and the love of God that my husband and I sow in them. All of that for me is invaluable. It is very easy to lose sight of our true priorities and our true goal as we go through life. Redefine your life priorities every time you feel you need to do it; that is without a doubt a priority.

See the storms of life as the best opportunity for your growth and expansion and as an intensely personal and spiritual improvement course or boot camp. For those of us who are believers, it is exciting to see that the test or challenge is the raw material coming from the Glory of God manifested in our lives in various circumstances. The raw material coming from God can manifest itself as the healing that happened from a disease that the doctors told you "There was no cure"; or as your entire family surviving from a fatal accident. It can also manifest as the poor monetary management that led you to a financial crisis, and then when the solution to such crisis appeared, or when you do not understand why things happened as they did and over the years, you understand the reason they happened that way, and you are grateful for having lived that lesson.

I always focus on seeing the glory amid the storm in my life by being grateful, congruent, authentic, and original simply because I am the head and not the tail by the grace and mercy of God.

Diane Curley

To Your Success
By Diane Curley

Some days I just don't have it.

And I feel the weight of it---the pressure to perform, to achieve, to be something more, to succeed.

Success seems elusive. Failure surrounds me again.

I feel as if everything I've already done is not enough, as if it's never going to be enough, and as if I am not enough. We have all felt this way at some time. Because as women, we face a lot of pressure to succeed in our business, on our jobs, with our relationships, for our family, and in our lives. We are judged by others for it, and we judge ourselves by it. Success.

But just what is success? How is success defined? Is there one definition of success? And who decides? Me? You? Society? Is it Wealth? Beauty? Fame? Or is it Credentials? Titles? Achievements? Power? Possessions? Some combination thereof? Or something else altogether? Is it attainable?

It is exhausting.

But what if we redefine success?
What if the definition of success included our impact?
What if the definition of success aligned with our values?
What if success was defined by all the moments and not the momentum? Or the money?
What if success was not measured by what society says about us and instead was measured by what God says about us.
Could it be that we are actually more successful than we think?

With all these questions in mind, I developed a framework for understanding what success means to me. Using the word "Success" as an acronym, I can easily share with you the concepts to discover a new way of thinking and redefine success for yourself!

S.U.C.C.E.S.S.

Simplify...when my life feels like uncontrollable chaos, I certainly don't feel successful. So, I have learned to simplify in order to reduce chaos, to create peace in my life, which I value greatly. Simplify means many things to me. It could be to pause for a moment and breathe and replace the negative narrative with the truth. It could be decluttering my surroundings. It could be silence. It could be listening to music that stirs my soul. It could be focusing on completing one small task like making the bed or cleaning up the table after breakfast. It could be drinking a cup of coffee or taking a nap. Quite simply, I simplify my life in the moment. Some days are just too much to take even one day at a time. So, I simplify and take the day one moment at a time---no pressure, just one moment. Calm over chaos.

Success!

Undo...whatever's not working, undo it! Try something else. Try something new. Try again. Walk away. Run forward. Step back. Apologize. Forgive. Give in. Stand firm. Speak up. Talk back. Change jobs. Start a business. Go back to school. Travel. Stay home. Sleep in. Go out. Reclaim your time. Set boundaries. Say no. Say yes. Mistakes will be made; lessons will be learned. Pause. Rise. Begin again.

Success!

Create and Celebrate...

Creating fuels me! I don't even need sleep or food when I am creating! After I create (writing poetry, working on my website, editing a new blog post, creating social media content, updating policy, rearranging a room, or just organizing a drawer in the kitchen!), I like to celebrate! I celebrate in different simple ways (a walk around the block with my husband, dinner out, a glass of wine with a friend, "just for me" things like a manicure, or shopping!) I also like to celebrate both small wins and big wins whether my own or others in word or in deed. Sure, we celebrate weddings, graduations, holidays, birthdays, etc., and we also celebrate passing math, getting your first pair of glasses, getting your first job or a new job, buying a new home, surviving power outages, embracing Saturday mornings, getting braces, getting braces removed, enjoying a warm summer night, setting up the backyard at the first sign of spring, playing in the first snow of the season, falling in love, attending the first dance at junior high, and on and on. My favorite way to comment on someone's accomplishment posted on social media is to reply, "Celebrating you today!"

Success!

Christ/Connection/Community…

Christ says I am beloved. He says I am His. He says I am redeemed, forgiven, and loved. With Christ at the center of my life, with my life aligned to His Word, with my worth firmly held by who Jesus says I am, then I am free. Free to live; free to love. I crave that love, that connection to God. Jesus also says we are to love others. I crave that love, that connection to others and to the global community. I love freely, I love boldly, and I love out loud. Loving others is a way to share the love of Christ without uttering a word. *By this all will know that you are My disciples, if you have love for one another. John 13:35 NKJV*

Serving others is another way to share the love of Christ.

For I was hungry, and you gave me food, I was thirsty, and you gave me drink, I was a stranger and you welcomed me, I was naked. and you clothed me, I was sick, and you visited me, I was in prison, and you came to me.' Then the righteous will answer him, saying, 'Lord, when did we see you hungry and feed you, or thirsty and give you drink? And when did we see you a stranger and welcome you, or naked and clothe you? And when did we see you sick or in prison and visit you?' Matthew 25:35-39 ESV

When I love and serve others, I am loving and serving Jesus. 'Truly I tell you, whatever you did for one of the least of these brothers and sisters of mine, you did for me.' Matthew 25:40 NIV

I am committed to meeting critical needs of victims of war, poverty, famine, disease, and natural disaster. I serve on an International Disaster Assistance Response Team and have served the people of the Bahamas; Liberia; Nigeria; refugees from Syria, Pakistan and Afghanistan in Greece; refugees at the U.S. southern border; and most recently in NYC Central Park field hospital for Covid19 response. I want nothing more than to arrive at the end of my life and hear "well done, good and faithful servant!"

Success!

Empowered…I've spoken and written on the topic of women's empowerment many times. and it bears repeating here: "We are not here for your entertainment." We need to change the messaging; we are not defined by our looks, other's definition of success, social media, our titles, the sum of our highs and lows, or our mistakes. We need to reject the double standard and the hypocrisy that continues to exist. For example: in similar situations men might be perceived as assertive; women may be perceived as aggressive. Men might be perceived as protectors; women may be perceived as overbearing. Men might be perceived as intelligent; women may be perceived as arrogant. Men might be perceived as persuasive; women may be perceived as bossy - you get the idea. We also need to transform the terminology, for instance, the word minority. Used as a descriptor, the word minority deprives us of our legitimate existence and separates us, contributing to a significant adverse effect within society. Here is the definition of minority as noted in dictionary.com: noun, plural minorities.

1. the smaller part or number; a number, part, or amount forming less than half of the whole.

2. a smaller party or group opposed to a majority, as in voting or other action.

3. a group in society distinguished from, and less dominant than, the more numerous majorities.

4. a racial, ethnic, religious, or social subdivision of a society that is subordinate to the dominant group in political, financial, or social power without regard to the size of these groups.

5. a member of such a group.

Synonyms for minority include "opposition", "the outvoted", "less than half", "the few", "the outnumbered", "splinter group". When used to describe us, these words have a negative connotation and are dehumanizing. Let us advocate for encompassing and positive terminology. We exist together in community. Let our words reflect this relationship. We need to turn away from a them vs. us mindset. We need to shift our focus to all of us. We need to speak up. We need to be heard. We need to be visible. We need to listen. We need to learn from each other. We need to create a platform of inclusiveness. We need to become champions of each other." Empowered women empower women.

Success!

Societal impact…I can think of no greater measure of success than that of our impact on society. Our impact can be either positive or negative. I advocate for a positive impact---kindness, service, and love! These are simple ways to impact the lives of others in a positive way. As a Registered Nurse by profession, my role is innately one of service, currently providing clinical education, compassionate healthcare, professional oversight, and supervision to ensure quality and safety in the healthcare and entertainment industries and for the community.

Passionately supporting the mission of Lelt Foundation, a non-profit organization based in New York, as Medical Director, I established partnerships to improve the health of the population in two communities in Ethiopia through increased access to healthcare and direct humanitarian aid. I am truly grateful for the opportunity to use my talent and time in service and care of others.

Another way to impact society is to make kindness part of everyday life: say hello, say good morning, say good night, say I love you. Smile at a stranger, hug your family, open a door, donate, volunteer, offer up opportunity, say thank you, you're welcome, great job, I appreciate you! I encourage you to use your talent and time to serve others. Maybe it's serving your family, the school, people at work or in your community. There are many ways you are making an impact!

Success!

Support…we all know how important it is to be supported and supportive, yet it is not always part of our lives and experiences. It's up to each of us to change that, to challenge that, and to use every opportunity to be of support. Allow me the opportunity to share one way I can support you: Challenging the narrative and influencing social media's message as CEO/Founder of Celebrating Women LLC, I created a global platform to amplify women's voices and visibility---hosting events, speaking internationally, writing, editing, and publishing a unifying collection of interviews about women at www.celebratingwomenusa.com. You are invited to interview and be featured on all eight of Celebrating Women's social media platforms, complimentary for all! …because EVERY woman is a role model!

Another way to be supportive is to be available to listen, to share, to comfort, and to console. It looks like this: Hi! I was just thinking about you! No, I'm not busy. I miss you! How are things? It's ok to cry. You don't have to be strong right now; I'll be strong for you. What's new? I'm so sorry. My door is always open. Let me buy you a cup of coffee. We will find a way. Can I help? Let me help. I can help. It's no trouble at all. Are you ok? Come in! I love you. Are you safe? I'm here. Do you want to talk? I'm not going anywhere. You don't have to talk; we can just sit together quietly. I have time. You're not alone. You can do this. Let's do it together. You've got this! You did great! You're the best! It's my treat. We know each other so well. I'm so happy we are friends. It's perfectly normal to feel that way. Me too. You're going to be ok. It's ok. It will be ok. I got you! We've got each other. Gods got us!

Success!

Success can be found in the joy (happiness!) that comes from the faithful mission of living out our purpose---what we are called to do. Remember we are called to love and to serve.

Simply to love and to serve.

Let's start there.

To your success!

Diane Curley MSN, RN, CNOR, CHCQM, FABQAURP

"I believe in the transformative power of relationship & connection. I know that when people unite & come together, our impact is more powerful. That's why my mission as an author & international speaker is to create exceptional experiences that spark engagement, enable change, and enrich lives."

Dr. Miyoshi Umeki Gordon

I was Broken, But I did not break
By Dr. Miyoshi Umeki Gordon

Some things are not only tough to endure but equally challenging to communicate. I was raised to be strong and confident. However, a time came in my life when my faith and strength were challenged. Faced with the choice to suffer in silence or speak my truth, I chose to 'let go and let God'. I grew up in a loving and caring environment. The values my parents instilled in me and my faith in God sustained me when life seemed bleak and hopeless, fueled by the love to parent my only son. Despite the challenges I faced, I broke my silence, beating the odds through my determination and faith in God.

The reality of life can be overwhelming. However, I now realized I am worthy of love and affection, regardless of what others have said. In the eyes of God, I am loved, capable, and strong. I am powerful and have the strength to overcome whatever comes my way. By great faith, I am fully capable of overcoming the obstacles placed in my path. With a strong will, determination, and perseverance, I can conquer all life situations one tiny step at a time.

I have survived many trials and tribulations, and I want you to know that life is worth living regardless of your circumstances. While some days are challenging, all days are not bad. What matters is what you do to get through the difficult days.

I found my joy in many things, but my most wonderful joy in life is my only child, who is a gift from God. I am so grateful because my son has helped me through some challenging times and given me hope just from his sheer presence and a smile on his face.

Looking back over my life, I ponder and wonder how in the world I remained steadfast and unmovable. I have dealt with the diagnosis of an incurable myositis disease, a drug-addicted spouse, raising my son as a single parent, remarrying a man who had no empathy for my health concerns, a diagnosis of breast cancer, and emotional abuse. At the time, I had no time to think about how I was going to make it. I was focused on making it!

Now that I'm on the other side, I want to bring awareness by communicating my story to the community. I hope that by sharing my journey, I can help those who are experiencing some of the same things that I experienced.

Life is a journey. How we live it is up to us. We have choices. I continue to live with what I call 'invisible illnesses' or illness that you may not see readily. People will ask, "How do you stay looking so good?" or "You don't look sick." Believe it or not, many who are close to me are unaware that I struggle each day to remain healthy mentally, physically, and spiritually.

When life throws you lemons, you make lemonade.

While I have learned from the times that challenged me, I still find myself questioning God and wondering why He chose to give me so many battles. But then I think about the goodness of God and all that He has brought me through, and I ask myself, "Why wouldn't He bring you out of this situation, too?"

You will never walk a straight path through life. Life is not about falling to the left or stumbling to the right but is instead about remaining steadfast in your faith.

I am grateful for my spiritual journey because it strengthens my inner core and makes me a better person.

I want others to know that with an awareness of God and self comes better health. When you know God, you love yourself, and when you love yourself, you are committed to treating yourself well. Wellness begins with the prevention of diseases, which is a byproduct of longevity and living a vibrant, peaceful, and serene life. Our wellbeing is so essential---not just for ourselves but for those who love us as well.

Living life is such a blessing. Each day I wake up, I feel so blessed and highly favored. Life is not a *given*; it is a *gift* afforded us by the grace of God.

The trials and tribulations we experience serve as life lessons. I have learned so many things about myself (and I'm still learning each day) from the times when I thought all was lost. I have more wisdom, discernment, and spirituality. I have realized that it is not the material things in life that bring me joy, but the smaller things that matter most.

Have you ever sat still and waited to hear the voice of God speak to you? I have, and nothing makes me happier!

Writing about my journey has always been a dream of mine. But the time was never right. However, now, here I sit in the middle of a global pandemic and find that I have an abundance of personal time for just God and me.

One night as I lay still, God gave me the title for my book and the cover design. That was when I knew without a doubt that it was time to tell my story.

If I keep my mind on Thee, I can do all things through Christ who strengthens me. **(Philippians 4:13 NKJV)**

No matter what challenges you face in life, with the right attitude, you can overcome them. Pray about all things and have faith that God will move in your favor. While I have become a better person, God is still molding me. With God on my side, I am determined to stay focused. Life may present obstacles, but I was not built to break. The flaws I possess serve to strengthen me. I'm so thankful that God is a forgiving God and that He hasn't taken His hands off me. I am committed to giving myself to Him in order to become the person He purposed me to be.

I am a Breast Cancer Survivor, a Myositis Survivor, and an Emotional Abuse Victim; however, I will never ever give up. I am always hopeful that all aspects of my life are in constant motion moving towards better authentic living in the now. Being my real self and feeling free to express myself in a meaningful way with no mask while embracing my vulnerabilities will allow me to encourage other persons as I share what I have gone through in life. I want people to know that they can get through similar situations holding true to themselves and who they belong to--- God.

What I keep in mind is my integrity and character in which my parents taught me. I was raised to be true to myself, "Do Unto Others As You Would Have Them Do Unto You" – The Golden Rule.

Going into a new chapter of my life, I know challenges will come up against me; however, I am better equipped by God's grace and mercy to handle the situations at hand with the use of more helpful resources the reach of my fingertip. The reality is that I am living my authentic life right now. I am at peace and am serene within myself. That was the Master plan for writing my memoir, "Broken But Still A Masterpiece". Reconnecting with my true self, I came to know that I had greater strengths and a unique gift for writing my memoir. I learned to re-engage myself with positive people who gave me encouragement and inspiration. I rebalanced my life with my passion for hobbies I loved, such as scrapbooking, reading, listening to music, going to the beach, and going on vacations. I had to learn to practice self-love, and I know that it was not a selfish act. Learning to say no without feeling guilty and with no excuses for saying no, I practice positive thinking and remove the worry away from my mind. I'm focusing on my passion for helping other people. I had to reflect upon my passion because it was at a point of giving to others without even taking care of myself. With quiet time and reflection during this Pandemic, I have learned, through knowledge and wisdom, the acceptance of being true to my authentic self and living in the moment.

At times along this journey, I was left alone to suffer and wonder how I was going to do the things I needed to do. The next thing I'm going to say is so very important: We must stop judging people. Unless you walk in another person's shoes, you can't possibly know how they are feeling. I have decided to use my story and my pain to be an advocate for those who haven't found their voices.

Finding Hope

UNITED – A DIVINE PURPOSE, INC. (UADP) is 501 (c)(3) non-profit organization dedicated to providing compassion and advocacy for patients with Myositis or Breast Cancer diseases and Mental Health. UADP provides need-based financial assistance to Myositis and Breast Cancer patients.

Through education, UADP works to increase the awareness of patients, caregivers, and the general public about Myositis, Breast Cancer diseases and Mental Health (Emotional Abuse Victims). We assist in research funding through collaboration with other charitable organizations with common goals and purposes.

Miyoshi's Hope benefits from local fundraising events across the country. UADP supports men, women, and children of all ages in all stages of Myositis and Breast Cancer as well as Mental Health Awareness (Emotional Abuse Victims). UADP also offers knowledge, encouragement, and friendship to caregivers.

Through my nonprofit organization, I'm in touch with so many people who share their stories with me about how they are coping. I realize that the first step in helping them is making sure others know that abuse of any kind is wrong, and that if you are abused, there is help for you.

At this point in my life, I am better mentally, physically, emotionally, and spiritually. I know that God is not done with me. This is just the beginning. I am so grateful and thankful for this past journey because I have learned I was "Broken But Still A Masterpiece" in the making by God. *"I was Broken, But I did not break." "For we are God's Masterpiece" Ephesians (2:10)*

Being successful in life is achieving the dreams of your life's purpose. While growing up, children dream of someone or something they wish they could be or do in limelight of not realizing they were being destined for their life's purpose.

I once thought I would like to be a flight attendant because they travelled the world in an airplane. How exciting that was to me during a younger age. Our beloved parents groomed us to become the best version of who we really are by believing we could actually do it when we reached adulthood.

As I continue to be the true person I am today, I can literally say my dreams of my future have reached beyond my expectations only by God's grace and mercy through all the trials and tribulations I overcame. I feel successful in living my authentic self---how simply stated but how extremely difficult to get there. I set goals little by little, and I accomplish them. One step at a time you will accomplish your life's mission and vision.

The younger generations are very driven by success because at their fingertip is so much new technology. Their field of studies when chosen strategically can by far be exceeded with hard work, determination, and perseverance. By believing in yourself with strong faith, you are better equipped with what life brings you during those challenging days. By using those techniques that were taught during childhood years, especially what was instilled in them as children, they are able to accomplish whatever they set their minds to become.

I would ask the younger generation as well as the other generations: Do you know your purpose for living? Do you know that you have one? Ask God, "What is my life's purpose?" Life is not just about living but is also about thriving and giving back to others. Giving does not always have to be monetary; it can be giving of your God-given talent. Once you have discovered your purpose for living you have the greatest success that resides within you – living your authentic life.

Since living my authentic life, I have achieved so much. I am a #1 International Bestselling author at the graceful age of 62; I have achieved my Master's in Christian

Counseling and Communications and a Doctorate in Humanity. All goals are accomplished by people that were ordained in my life. During this transformation period, I was beginning to live my authentic self with my God-given talent and skills. I am presently living my authentic life with divine purpose. This is the Master Plan God has destined for me: "I have finally Arrived."

Dr. Miyoshi Umeki Gordon,

"A Voice for The Voiceless"

"Touching Lives One at a Time"

Holy Bible, New Living Translation, copyright @ 1996, 2004, 2015 by Tyndale House Foundation. Used by permission of Tyndale House Publishers, Inc. Carol Stream, Illinois 60188. All rights reserved.

Dr. Miyoshi Umeki Gordon

Miyoshi Umeki Gordon, Author, Entrepreneur, Speaker, Founder and President at United - A Divine Purpose, Inc. (UADP). She is also an Advocate for Myositis, Breast Cancer, and Mental Health (Emotional Abuse Victims).

Beating the Odds

Miyoshi Gordon came out of retirement to launch a 501(c)(3) nonprofit organization to help persons with Myositis and Breast Cancer diseases. She is very passionate in helping others. She is a voice for the voiceless; her motto is: "Touching Lives One At A Time." Her 30 years career in the medical field has shown that she is truly an advocate for humanity. During those 30 years, she worked in Radiology, serving the majority of those years as a Diagnostic Radiology Supervisor. After developing and surviving Breast Cancer, she seamlessly changed her career to a Human Resources Specialist which spanned five years. Miyoshi hired both Physicians and Staff from across the United States and Internationally.

Achievements

Miyoshi has a Doctorate in Humanity, Master of Christian Counseling and Communication, Fresh Anointing Christian Bible Institute; Bachelor's Degree in Health Science, Campbell University graduated Cum Laude; Associate Degree of Applied Science Radiology, graduated with Honors Fayetteville Technical Community College; Certification of Recognition for Honorable Service by American Registry of Radiologic Technologists-Retired, Certificate of Appreciation from the Department of Veteran Affairs for her time and devotion in assisting in the Welcome Home Event of Military Personnel at the Orlando Veterans Affairs Medical Center; Member of Faith Assembly of

God in Orlando, FL; Senior Pastor Carl Stephens and Pastor Alice Stephens. She has one adult son.

Photo Credit: George Joell 3 Photography

Dr. Barbara J. Hopkinson

From Grief to Resilience
By Dr. Barbara J. Hopkinson

As I walked into my twenty-one-year-old son Brent's hospital room on that last evening of May, I remember thinking "How could I be losing another son?" I couldn't believe what I was seeing. My Arizona State University Army ROTC student lay perfectly still, hooked up to life support. Other than all the monitors and tubes, he looked fine, strong and handsome, as if he was just sleeping. I'd lost his younger brother, Robbie, a full-term stillborn son, and had a miscarriage earlier. This couldn't be happening again!

Brent's father, Bob, his younger brother Brad, and I had just gotten off a six-hour-flight in a desperate attempt to get to Arizona before it was too late. Bob had picked up a phone message that morning from Brent's commanding officer, who said that Brent had been in a motorcycle accident, that it was bad, and we should come to Arizona as quickly as we could. Brad, barely nineteen, had just walked into the house after being out all night at his senior prom. It was pure coincidence that they were both at home since neither had planned to be there then. I was on a business trip, having no idea what was happening. My cell phone had no reception in my customer's building. It took them four hours to track me down through my secretary, my boss, a local friend who knew my exact whereabouts, and the company's reception desk. It seemed odd when the customer's conference room phone rang, that I was asked to take the call.

Brent was engaged to a wonderful woman, Laura. He had already passed his aviation written test, was ready to pass the physical test, and was prepared to serve at least eight years active duty in the army. Then one May morning he borrowed a friend's motorcycle and lost control of it. Those dreams disappeared on the ASU campus in the Arizona heat on the way to breakfast with his ROTC buddies—only three weeks after we'd taken him to Las Vegas to celebrate his 21st birthday.

After Brent's funeral, I had difficulty functioning. I was in a high-pressure management role in IBM. My background was in international corporate software technology. I told my then boss that the worst thing possible had happened to me; therefore, work no longer had the same power over me; I needed to change jobs! Following that, my 30-year marriage fell apart one year after Brent's death. That 'one-two' punch nearly ended me. I attempted suicide. However, it was a failed attempt and became my turning point.

I didn't know what to do but knew I had to do something. I instinctively knew helping others would help me heal, and I was driven to find out if my son's spirit continued. I talked to several local families that had lost a child, considered options, and founded The Compassionate Friends (TCF) of Greater Newburyport, MA, one of several hundred chapters of TCF USA, the largest grief organization in the world, which supports family after the loss of a child, grandchild, or sibling – any age or cause.

We held our first TCF support meeting in May 2003 during the week of the first anniversary of my son's death. I still run those meetings, annual candle lightings, and occasional other events. I have supported hundreds of bereaved families and made many lifelong friends in the process.

During this time, I also explored my beliefs about spirituality... and I tried many forms of healing, both familiar and unfamiliar to me. I worked very hard at it, found my resilience, and realized that I wanted to do more to help others find theirs.

Meanwhile, I met my second husband, Jim, online. We dated for a year, got married, and blended our families – my son Brad and Jim's 3 adult children, Melanie, Matthew and Christopher.

Everything was great... I'd found happiness again!

But I had another major hurdle to overcome and a new kind of grief to experience. While training to swim in a triathlon with my niece, I slipped on a wet tile floor that had no sign posted and detached my retina. My other eye compensated so completely that I did not notice it. It was found months later during my annual eye checkup. I was immediately referred to specialists and had three surgical procedures within a few days at the prestigious Mass Eye & Ear Hospital in Boston. I endured extreme pain and was forced to be face down for ten days because of the gas bubble holding my reattached retina in place behind my eye. Two more surgeries followed within six months, but the results were not successful; I lost the sight in my right eye (which had been my dominant eye because I was born with a lazy muscle in my left eye). Once again, a different experience in grieving... partial loss of sight. But I learned to compensate for the challenges in depth perception, additional light and magnification needed, and the resulting dyslexia.

Like everyone, I also had other challenges, including layoffs, financial struggles... even getting shingles from another very high-pressure job. I decided it was time to retire from the corporate world and focus on what I felt my purpose in life was – to help others struggling with grief to find their hope and resilience.

Based on a refillable leather journal my son Brad had given me after his brother's death, which surprised me as tremendously healing and cathartic... I decided to write about my experience and what I'd learned that might help others. I took several writing workshops and classes, hired two editors, and published my first book: "A Butterfly's Journey... Healing Grief After the Loss of a Child." Then I hired a business coach and founded my company, also named A Butterfly's Journey™ (ABJ). Butterflies are an international symbol of transition. I think of them as representing our loved ones' transition from a physical to a spiritual life and our transition of a life-with-them to a life-without-them. This title also represented my 'journey' to heal and discover if my son's spirit continues. I now believe that it does and that all our spirits do! I have heard and witnessed several signs and proof points, which I hope to detail in another book.

As I marketed my ABJ book and started reaching out to grievers and grief support organizations, I felt that I needed a grief-related credential in addition to my experience. I also thought my company would fare better as a non-profit in the grief industry. I invested and converted A Butterfly's Journey™ to an official 501(c)(3) nonprofit while I searched for a grief recovery methodology, one that aligned with my ideals. I found a great one – the Grief Recovery Method (GRM).

The three focus areas for A Butterfly's Journey™ nonprofit are these:

1. Free Resource Center for grievers
2. Group or 1-on-1 Grief Recovery Method (GRM) classes
3. Faces of Resilience ©, mobile photo shoots

The Resource Center has hundreds of broad-based resources to help with healing grief (available 24 X 7) in ten categories.

GRM is an action-based program for moving beyond loss (of any type). It has been proven for forty years on six continents, treats each griever uniquely, is complimentary to support groups and therapy, and is the only 'evidence-based' method for grief in the world. Classes are available for many types of loss as well as pet loss and for adults helping children grieve. I am certified as an Advanced Grief Recovery Method Specialist.

'Faces of Resilience' are beautifully cathartic photos of bereaved persons to promote raising awareness of the need for open discussion of the difficult topic of grief. Participants are photographed expressing a phrase meaningful to them, which is written on their skin in washable marker. Then a professionally edited photo is emailed to them, which is a catalyst for them to talk about their grief with family and friends.

I then became a best-selling author with a collaborative book including 13 other women, called "FAITH – Finding Answers in The Heart – Volume II" published in 2015.

In 2016-2017, I reached out to national grief organizations and was showcased on Open-To-Hope Radio and TV, plus I hosted larger event photo shoots at TCF National Conferences, Bereaved Parents of the USA Annual Gatherings, ADEC (Assoc for Death & Education Consulting) Conference, Grief Cruises, a Walk on the Capital and Addiction Vigils, Walks to Remember, a Healing Day after a mass shooting, and other events related to grief. ABJ was becoming known nationally.

I'd met Lynda Cheldelin Fell, the founder of Grief Diaries, and was very impressed with her work and the anthology series. I became co-author of two of those books: "Will I Survive?" about child loss, and "Surviving Pet Loss", as well as contributing to others.

Then personal tragedy struck again... My second husband Jim died suddenly of a 'widow-maker' heart attack on his way to work in October 2017, making me a widow. I experienced a whole new kind of grief and grieving experience. I'd also lost my parents when I was age 32 and age 47, plus an older brother died before I was born. I seemed to be coming full circle with grief experiences, feeling as if it informed my life's purpose.

After getting through the initial months of grieving the loss of my husband and living alone again, I kept busy with my grief work and events supported by all the wonderful family and friends that 'got it' and who helped me heal as I worked. My new understanding enriched my work and made it easier to help widows and widowers.

Then, yet another surprise and a new type of grief. My blind eye had lost pressure and was shrinking, causing my eyelid to droop and close. I was told that it would become painful, and I would need to have the eye removed at some point. That point came six months after I lost my husband. Those challenges, along with some others related to my house and car, made it quite a struggle that winter. I grieved the loss of a body part when my eye was surgically removed and replaced with a prosthetic in the spring of 2018. But I was pleasantly surprised that although there were challenges at first with the prosthetic's care and use, it made my appearance look more normal. I was very grateful that I had such expert help to overcome that challenge. I was determined that neither the loss of sight in one eye nor the loss of the eye itself would hold me back, and it has not… at least as far as I can tell. ☺

I began to teach workshops on Resilience both online and at events. In 2019, I did photo shoots and workshops at ten national and regional events including three international events in Canada, the Caribbean, and London. I was also awarded "Top Professional in Resilience After Loss" by IAOTP (International Association of Top Professionals) at a gala in Las Vegas.

Then in 2020, the Covid pandemic hit in March, and all the planned in-person events were cancelled. I got an advanced certification in GRM so that I could teach Grief Recovery Method classes online, and I converted my TCF support meetings to use Zoom software, also meeting online. I got help from a friend and took the time to organize my nonprofit financial records and update my web site as preparation to apply for grants. These grants would fund scholarships to GRM classes for those who could not afford them and fund help to upgrade the ABJ Resource Center with information on current topics, such as losses created by the pandemic and epidemics like suicide and overdose. Fundraising is tough in the current environment, but there is a limit to what I can personally fund. I take no pay from the nonprofit, so any help is appreciated.

I used the time over the last year and the growth in online media/meetings to join some new powerful women's networks and to get interviewed on podcasts, radio, and TV…This helped to raise awareness for my work. I was honored to be given a second award by IAOTP, "Woman of the Year for 2020", which will culminate in a gala in New York City, December 2021. Then, I was further blessed to receive a Red Blazer Achievement Award from Carl D. Wilson's All Women Rock organization. I am very grateful for both of these recognitions.

I have several personal and business social media pages for A Butterfly's Journey™ and Faces of Resilience, where I post photos and helpful resources daily. I am working on better technical outreach, including new landing pages and audio plus video interactive sessions. I am honored to be invited to be a part of three new anthology series books, my sixth, seventh and eighth books overall. I am a co-author of the best-seller book "The Global Achievers – Volume I", released in February 2021 and a co-author of the books, "Red Blazers – Blazing to Success" and "Finding Joy in The

Journey" coming out this summer. I hope my story will help others.

For the future, I hope to be able to help more grievers to find their hope and resilience and to encourage open expression of grief, loss, and love through expanding the Faces of Resilience photo shoots. It is so healing to talk about our grief and our feelings. I plan to expand the photo shoots to different types of events, organizations, and international destinations, and include more languages and a series of photo books for various themes, related to types of loss and relationship types. Please reach out to me directly if you are aware of opportunities.

My advice for others finding their way as entrepreneurs serving the community is to try to achieve balance and some calm between the areas in your life. Recognize there will always be challenges; some may seem unfair. You may not understand the cause or the purpose of them when they happen. Take each hurdle individually, get quiet time, get creative, and trust your ability to navigate them or find a reasonable, if not perfect, alternative. Then move on. Hindsight may illuminate in what direction the universe was taking you later.

My balance has always been family, friends, and fun. No matter what, make sure you enjoy those in your life and be grateful for them. Don't let work or your cause totally take over your life while you are blazing to your success. You are of more value to others when you are grounded, balanced, and optimistic. My family, including my son, stepchildren, their spouses, and my four grandchildren ground me and are my priority. 'Nana' is definitely my favorite role in life and makes everything else worth it!

If you would like to know more about my work, please visit my web site: http://abutterflysjourney.org or email at info@abutterflysjourey.org

A free call can be scheduled at: http://bit.ly/GRM-call or call 617-410-6309.

Patti Rae Miliotis

Though negative, worrisome thoughts
continue to cross the minds of myself
and of those around me,
I cannot, will not let these things discourage me.
I keep fighting.
In isolation, but with people and prayer and support
and love and faith enveloping me,
I stand alone, overcome by loneliness,
but at the same time smothered
with love and support.
I cannot worry. I cannot let this win.
This soon will be over. I will have defeated it.
I will live.
I will find the courage and strength to be me again.

1*20*02
AJM
By Patti Rae Miliotis

Growing up in the mid 1950's as a Navy Junior (otherwise known as a military brat), mine was an uncommon childhood. My father was a Navy Mustang---a 17-year-old who started as a lower ranking Seamen but obtained a prestigious promotion raising him from a non-commissioned officer to a commissioned officer, based on his achievements rather than formal education.

Because of his frequent reassignments—about every three years—I was exposed to a wide variety of cultures. I lived in inner cities, in suburbs, in island villages, on a beach overlooking Diamond Head, and on a cliff with a view of Mount Fuji. I attended thirteen schools by the time I graduated from high school in Yokohama, Japan. As a result, I had no American hometown and had limited but joyful interaction with extended family through my youth. This early life's experiences generated a willingness to take risks and created a level of adaptability that informed my adult choices and allowed me to forge an independent path.

In 1968, when I graduated from high school, girls were not always encouraged to go to college. In fact, my guidance counselor advised me to find a secretarial pool. I ignored that 'advice' and proceeded to apply to universities. My parents had a resident status in California, so I attended the UC system and graduated from UCLA. I began majoring in Russian and Political Science, hoping to find my future in the US diplomatic core. At the time, most girls were expected to become teachers or nurses. I knew from babysitting at an early age that I loved children, so I recognized that I could always fall back on those options.

During my studies, I took two elective courses that changed my path. One was serving as a classroom aide in a Montessori preschool; the other was being a tutor in a young elementary special-needs classroom. Oops! I switched my major to psychology. From that point forward, I designed Independent Study courses to work with children at UCLA's experimental classrooms. I also worked with researchers studying the generational inheritance of mental disabilities. Working with autistic preschoolers at the UCLA Neuropsychiatric Institute Preschool changed my aspirations and reset my professional goals.

Following graduation, my first formal job was a caregiver at Sunland Training Institute in Gainesville, Florida, a home for the mentally handicapped. This was a temporary position on my way to New Orleans, where I was hired to design and run a day program for the youngest and most severely ill child residents of a state mental institution. It was 1973. I was 23 years old and directing both a developmental educational program for the children as well as training staff and graduate students to work alongside me. These children, who ranged in age from four to ten, had educational and social developmental needs that were unable to be met in the on-campus special needs programs. I was given a dormitory room to use as my classroom and a small amount of suitable furniture to accommodate my program.

My professional goal had been attained in my mind at that point!

Recognizing after two years in this capacity that I needed more formal education in the development of processing and functional-social use of language, I took my master's degree in Audiology and Speech Pathology at the LSU Medical Center School of Health Professions.

I put that degree to good use when I moved to Boston in the fall of 1976 as a speech pathologist at St Francis Children's Hospital. I was given the responsibility of servicing the speech and language needs of special needs children who attended the Kennedy Day School at the hospital. As part of my job, I participated in the monthly case discussions with neuropsychology and speech and language pathology researchers, who were studying the pathologies in progress of some of my students. These exercises intrigued me and set me on a path to my vocational passion.

Within a few years, I was invited to work with these scientists in the Neuropsychology Research Center at the VA Hospital in Metropolitan Boston. I became a Research Assistant to Dr Nelson Butters, who was a pioneer in both amnestic disorders and in the early stages of the field of neuropsychology; brain-behavior relationships. My job there was to oversee the administration of his team's research activity.

Meanwhile, my personal life progressed while at the Center. I got married and had my first child, a boy, Geordie. Although I continued to work part-time until I had identical twin girls three years later… Alexandra and Arianna. At that point I left work to stay home and care for my children.

As my children grew into school age, I found numerous challenges because of their above average intellect and unique learning styles vs the cookie-cutter education system in our country. After much discussion regarding options with the educators, I decided it was best for them if I home-schooled them in the early years and was able to help guide their choices to optimize later school years. Thankfully, the children were also quite athletic and socially adept, which gave them a wide range of focus areas. It was a constant challenge for me but one worth making a difference in my children's lives.

I returned to my career in neuropsychology research when my children were adolescents. Just before I turned age fifty, I was invited to train for my PhD in Behavioral Neuroscience at Boston University School of Medicine. I completed the first year of that program.

Life was busy and progressing happily until May 24, 2001. Approximately 10 P.M. that evening, we got the phone call that changed our lives. Earlier that day, I'd taken my fifteen-year-old daughter Alexandra to her pediatrician because she had slid into second base in her softball practice and injured her hip. Also, in the previous two weeks, she'd complained of headaches and bruises, but we thought that was normal because she played three sports concurrently, and it was a hot weather spring. During the visit, with the pediatrician, they had taken blood samples. The call that night was to tell us that her platelets were dangerously low and that we must immediately take her to the Emergency Room at Boston Children's Hospital!

When we got to the ER, they did another blood panel while Alexandra, and my husband Mark and I waited in the examination room. To our confusion, the ER resident told us that an oncologist would soon be in to talk to us; we were shocked and frightened..."an oncologist!" The oncologist did, indeed, arrive, and she gave us the devastating news that our precious 15-year-old daughter had leukemia! Alexandra, like most teenage girls might react…asked if she would lose her hair!

She was immediate admitted to the Hem-Onc (hematology-oncology) unit. Our nightmarish journey had begun. Ten months, three protocols—lots of radiation and chemotherapy—a bone-marrow transplant (from her identical twin sister), and innumerable sleepless nights followed. Alexandra was rarely well enough to be home during those ten months. I was with her the entire time. Our family visited daily around their high school, college, sports, work, and lives. My heart broke to see my children, husband, and family seesaw between hope and fear while Alexandra fought her illness. She was an absolute warrior; so were they. Mark and I watched the strength and bond among our children grow as they fought this horrible disease together.

Alexandra had a rare form of leukemia which required her to spend most of those months in the hospital and caused progressive paralysis, making her wheelchair bound. The extraordinarily compassionate and capable medical staff of Boston Children's Hospital cared for Alexandra and our entire family with exceptional professional skill and extraordinary compassion. In addition, this hard-working nursing staff was taking courses, attending conferences, and interacting with other hospitals' oncology staff on their own time and at their own expense… in an effort to take better care of their patients. Their dedication was mind-blowing!

As Alexandra's paralysis progressed, family and friends established a fund to redesign our home to accommodate Alexandra's wheelchair. Sadly, on March 15, 2002, at the tender age of 16, Alexandra earned her wings. We then rededicated the funds, founding Alex's Team Foundation Inc. www.alex's-team.org. Alex's Team is a tribute to the dedication of the oncology care staff and a testament to Alexandra's strength and courage throughout her battle with leukemia. This unique organization funds innovative programs in clinical care and research and creates ways to influence the cancer community by providing multiple layers of service-driven support to nursing staff, doctors, and families. With "Courage, Caring and Commitment" Alex's Team strives "to give each child a chance to follow a dream."

Over the years, our philanthropic efforts have expanded to include programs which inspire and offer opportunities to encourage Harvard University Medical students to choose pediatric oncology research as a career path. We also help support both clinical interns at Boston Children's' Hospital and research interns participating in the world-renowned Walensky Laboratory at Dana Farber Cancer Institute in Boston.

As co-founder and chair of ATF, I am proud of and grateful that the Foundation has survived and thrived nearly twenty years with the help of family and friends. I am especially grateful that the younger generation of our family has taken over Foundation leadership to carry on its mission and for the dedication Geordie and Arianna have shown, honoring their sister.

The emotional devastation of Alexandra's death and resulting grief had an unimaginable impact on our family. For some time, the Foundation was the only common thread in our lives. My marriage fell apart; my relationship with my children suffered. We all grieved very differently. As part of my trying to recenter myself, I withdrew from my PhD studies. I moved out to a coastal town approximately twenty-five miles away from our family home, and I tried to immerse myself in the arts... photography, painting, jewelry design and creation. I had some success and accolades, but I didn't believe enough in myself as a real artist to continue that path.

I realized that I needed help with my grief and reached out to a local support group for bereaved parents. There I met Barbara. J Hopkinson, founder of that group, herself a multiple bereaved mother. A close friendship grew. Barbara is high energy and a force to be reckoned with!

Fortunately, Barbara did like my photography and thought I would be perfect for the staff photographer role in her nonprofit, A Butterfly's Journey © (ABJ, http://abutterflysjourney.org) and her mobile photo shoot project "Faces of Resilience." I was delighted and excited to join her… This would become a significant part of my healing.

These photo sessions raise awareness of the need for open discussion for the difficult topic of grief while being cathartic for the participants, and the resulting photos become a catalyst for them to talk about their grief. We broadened these unique experiences from a local to a national to an international level across many types of grief-related events.

Barbara and I are "Moms on a Mission."

I worked my availability for the photoshoots around my full-time work schedule at an assisted living facility for elders with memory disorders. Because of my past neuropsychology clinical and research experience with dementia patients, I was able to offer informed input to care and programming. As part of a small program staff, my role was to provide daily activities including music, dance, arts, cooking, and gardening. I loved my job. My artistic self-surfaced again. My introverted self even learned to enjoy performing! I looked forward to this being my job until retirement.

Worldwide PANDEMIC!

By early April 2020 I needed to leave my job. I did not feel safe at age 70, working in a closed environment with vulnerable elders. Meanwhile, daycare for my beloved two grandbabies, ages two months and two years, was cancelled due to Covid, leaving my working daughter and her husband in a bind. They needed safe care for their children to be able to continue their careers. Both transitioned to working from home while I transitioned to full-time caregiver. I have left my sweet little coastal town to be closer to my daughter and grand babies. I enjoy this as much raising my own three children.

This is a win-win for our family!

As the pandemic eases, Barbara and I hope to resume our Faces of Resilience photo shoots. My plan in my new home is to re-engage in my artwork and join my new community. (I might now have to go to the Senior Center to find new friends!) And, of Course, Alex's Team Foundation now in its twentieth year will continue to be close to my heart, and a lifetime priority.

As I look at my life to this point, I feel that Robin Williams saw it very clearly; "Everyone you meet is fighting a battle you know nothing about. Be kind."

Each of us has a story. Our ability to unfold the lessons within and to move forward even just a little bit stronger each time allow us to see light and life ahead. I believe that one's capacity to withstand and forge through to the other side of life's traumas is largely a result of love and support of those who have lived parts of that journey with us. The "strength to be me" has come from others' kindnesses.

I hope you will be able not only to extend your hand in kindness but also to reach for support during rough times. We can all lift each other… "Live, Love, and Laugh!"

Dr. Tania Simmons

Leadership Is in the Being
By Dr. Tania Simmons

I am so excited to be able to write this chapter in this amazing leadership book for women obviously around the world. It has been such a pleasure to be able to participate in this book for many people to read across the globe. My name is Dr. Tania Simmons, and I am a global entrepreneur. I am a keynote speaker. I have multiple businesses, and I do multiple things humanitarian relief work around the world as well through my foundation Healing for The Nations. But that is not what I'm going to talk about within this chapter. Those are things that I do, but what I want to talk about is about who we are and what we do, and the difference between doing and being.

When I was a young girl, my mother, who is a leading force, was a force of nature and so was my father. They're great leaders---known leaders around the globe; they do multiple works in third world nations, set up schools, and do all sorts of great works. But I remember as a little girl, character always being at the forefront in our family. Some of the things that my parents would teach me and talk to me about were evident that it was noted to be within our family--principles to live by. Obviously, one of those principles would be the development of character that was always talked to me from a young age from my mother and my father as well. My father would always tell me, Tanya, you never try to do something. You always do it. That was one statement that just vibrated within me as a young child---you never try to do something; you do it. That message was very clear to me at a young age.

The other message that was very clear to me at a young age was hard work pays off. If you are diligent, then you will reap the rewards of that diligence. So, as a young girl, I saw my father as he was actually told that he would be nothing. He tried drugs when he was in high school. He was a leader of a high school band---actually a leading band, and then his best friend died. His world evolved and changed. He then became a pastor, and his whole life flipped upside down when he came into the realization of what real faith is. At that point, he met my mother, and it was true love, of course, and they fell in love and had me within that union. From that he went on to the highest levels of education throughout the U.S. and abroad, overseas, and from Harvard, accepting him, going to Yale graduating with honors, Duke, graduating with honors, and so on. Today, he lectures at Oxford University and Cambridge, and he does a lot of great work. He is an international scholar, and I'd like to give him honor where honor is due. His name is Dr. Michael B Simmons, and he is my father. He has taught me tremendous lessons about what it is to walk in faith and to walk in true character and what that really means. Let's go over some key leadership principles that have helped me through my journey of life.

Foundation:

I believe that foundation is very, very important. I didn't always have the best childhood in ways. I did overcome sexual abuse outside of the home. I overcame a lot of different adversities and challenges, but I believe that those are the things that make us. Those are the things that make you stronger. Those are the things that will build your character. When you face and when you embrace adversity with open arms, it's like being in the gym and lifting weights. With those those weights, you want to build muscle, but in order to do that, you must have more weights. It's the same way with life. It's the same way with adversity; you accept and embrace adversity; it makes you, and it will make you stronger.

So, as I was growing up, I saw what true leadership was. I saw the character of true leaders within my parents. I saw the development of what hard work and diligence will bring. Those key principles were rooted within my character at a young age. I attribute my success to those key principles, that were instilled in me at a young age. Today, I also see the value of what true faith will bring---the faith that sees when others do not, the faith that embraces the impossible and makes it possible. In our house, the words "We can't, or I can't" did not exist. We never used those words; they were very foreign to me at a young age. I was instilled with confidence. It wasn't till later in my childhood that some of those things tried to rock my confidence. Some of life situations that occurred tried to steal my confidence. But, as I have gotten older, I have found the power of my voice. I would say when those things happened at a young age, it made me feel very powerless, and it stole the power of my voice. It wasn't until I was older that I recognized that I am not powerless, that I have choices with my confidence and my purpose. There's a purpose, and there's a plan for my life, and not only for my life, but for the people around me, the people that would come into my life, the people with whom I come in contact. My voice was so important because the things that happened to me aren't just for me; they are for others. It's for me to be able to give back, speak into, and empower those around me to be, to encourage them to be at their very best to reach their highest level of potential, and to really feel empowered and discover who they are and what they can become. This to me is purpose.

Resolution and Consistency:

Another key principle is resolution or being resolute. Having a fortitude of knowing who you are and where you come from was instilled in me at a very young age although those things were definitely tried. My identity was definitely challenged throughout my adolescence. Knowing who you are is very important. Your identity doesn't come. Sometimes people can take their identity from what they do. When they lose their job or when there is no longer a successful business, or when there are challenges, or when you have to be flexible or adaptable, then their identity is challenged. But when you come into a fool knowing that your identity is not based on what you do, but on who you are, then, that is, make sure you are definitely resolute and have a solid, strong foundation within yourself to be able to overcome just about anything. Resilience is another key attribute that was established in me at a very young age. I remember us traveling all over the world because my dad was a scholar, and he would go to these high-level Ivy League schools and institutions to study and get more schooling. I would meet new people all the time, whether it be new classrooms, new teachers, new students. I was always meeting new people at a very young age. Looking back, it actually established an extrovert personality within me. Even to this day, I love meeting new people. I love connecting with new people. But there were also definitely challenges that came along with that as well---on the flip side of that, the people around me. Even now I have had long standing friendships for years and years. I can honestly say I have a few of those friends but not a lot of them. It has made me appreciate my friendships even more. So, I value connection. I value heart connection above all, and I feel that in business it is very important to make sure that you are very astute to other people's needs---that you have an ear of empathy when you are listening to people because trust is very important in building solid relationships. Consistency of character is key when you are building relationships whether that be personally or in business. People need to see what you bring to the table and who you are; we show people who we are by our actions we do every day, what they experience from us and how they, and how we make them feel.

Presence of a true leader:

People remember how we treat them and how they feel within our presence. It is one of my main goals---to make sure that people around me feel loved, secure, and cared for. I think for me that is very, very important. For me, that gives me purpose to know that I love people well, and they experience that love on a high level.

For me this is very much purpose driven. I'm very intentional in my everyday decision making. I think in your family or in your friendships or in your business relationships. It's very important to make sure people understand that they're your friend first, that they are cared for, that they are safe, and that you can be trusted. To me this is true relationship building, which helps grow your business very organically. The bottom line is to care for people very well, to make sure that you treat people, very, very well. People matter. You matter. My life has not always been easy. However, it has been very rewarding. I would not change it for anything, because it's made me who I am today. Overcoming sexual abuse at a young age, psychological abuse in different relationships, emotional trauma, and losing my first husband at the age of 22 making me a single mom of two at a very early age has, I can see catapulted me in different ways. As I have followed and allowed the process to make me from the inside out, one thing that I'd like to get across within this chapter is that you are never a victim. You are a victor; you are called to victory. Every day there is more than you know, waiting for you. You have great purpose. Don't set any limits around yourself, believe in yourself, and the sky is not the limit. Some things are taught, and some things are caught. These things were caught in my household as a young child, and I'd like to give honor to my parents for instilling these attributes in me at a year early age. These key elements of character development have carried me through my life.

I hope these things have encouraged you as you've read them. In this chapter, be true to who you are. Know who you are. Never settle for less than what you deserve, operate from the core of who you are, embrace every day with the fullness of life that you've been given, and move forward with absolute confidence in security, knowing that the best days are ahead of you. Blessings. I hope that this chapter has blessed your heart and blessed your life as you have read it. Take these words to heart knowing that there is so much more ahead of you than there is behind you.

To your success always,

Love,

Dr. Tania Simmons.

Lynda Bergh Herring

PLOT TWIST
(That Did Not Go As Planned)
By Lynda J. Bergh Herring

When I was a little girl, all I wanted to do was be a ballerina. I watched the Rodgers & Hammerstein version of Cinderella on television, and I was HOOKED! When I won the Little Miss Yorba Linda pageant in 1964, one of the prizes I received was six months of free dance lessons. I was on my way!!

For many years I focused completely on my dancing, especially ballet. Classes also included tap, jazz, Hawaiian, baton twirling, and even belly dancing, but ballet was always my favorite. I was at the dance studio every chance I got, worked as a "junior student teacher" and at the reception desk, and attended every dance conference I could. I lived, breathed, and dreamed dance. A tutu with pointe shoes was my favorite outfit. I even planned to major in dance in college and was accepted to the University of Irvine.

Shortly after graduating from high school, and in anticipation of saving some money for college, my search for gainful employment began. I had been doing some professional dancing for a few years, but it did not come close to paying my basic living expenses. I moved out of my family home at the age of eighteen and soon found myself working as a Police Records Clerk. It was supposed to be a summer job before I returned my focus on dance, but through a completely unexpected plot twist, I stayed on and ultimately worked in law enforcement in various capacities for a little over four years.

Through a few subsequent plot twists and turns, I ended up married to my first husband, a police sergeant, and starting my first business, a home-based typing and transcription business. This is where things got really interesting.

I thought I would be typing medical reports, school papers,

and other less than inspiring documents. Instead, I somehow ended up with five or six clients who were Private Investigators. That work was so much more interesting than those student papers and medical reports!! Then, one day while delivering some completed reports and transcribed interviews, my client received a phone call. It was an insurance company advising her there had been a work-related death on a construction, site and they needed an investigator at the location immediately. All her field investigators were already in the field and, since this was before pagers, email, or cell phones, she had no way to contact any of them. So, in another unexpected plot twist, she looked at me and said, "You can do this!" She handed me the required tools – a cassette recorder, cassettes, batteries, camera, film, flash cubes, a pad of paper, and a pen - and sent me out. This began my investigation career.

One of the earliest cases I worked involved a missing child. While I had worked on a few similar cases in law enforcement, this one was different. The child had been taken by a distant family member who, before we had a chance to rescue her, was sold to others for sex. It was not called Sex Trafficking at that point in time, but that is exactly what was going on. We were able to find the girl fairly quickly and get her to safety. Her family member went to prison, much too briefly, was released, and committed a similar crime. He is currently serving life without parole in another state.

That case fueled my passion for the fight against Sex and Human Trafficking, especially of children.

It was not until many years, actually decades, after I started working as an investigator that I heard Dr. Gary Zukav, who wrote "The Seat of the Soul", speak on a television show. He was discussing finding one's passion and explained that if you are not sure where your passion lies, you should think back to what you did when you play-acted as a child. Were you a Wife and Mother? A Police Officer? A Writer? A Firefighter? A Ballerina? Well, I was either a ballerina or when playing with my three older brothers, an Investigative Reporter!! What little girl pretends to be an Investigative Reporter?!? That was a huge light bulb moment for me. Huge! I had always been fascinated with mystery solving novels, television shows, and movies but had never consciously thought about becoming a P.I. until it happened. As a girl growing up in the 60's and 70's, it seemed all the investigators and police detectives portrayed on television and in movies were men; it was not a job for a petite, extremely feminine, ballerina. I'll never forget how excited I was when my father introduced me at his retirement dinner as a "female Mannix". As I look back, perhaps becoming a Private Investigator was not such a plot twist after all.

During my nearly forty years working in private investigations, I have handled cases of many types including asset locates, elder abuse, child custody, fraud, traffic collision, and more. My heart has always been with children's safety, although I have never had any children of my own. Rescuing children from traffickers is my most rewarding work even though all such work is done pro bono but also my least favorite for obvious reasons. I wish it did not exist, and maybe one day it will be eradicated.

In 2016 my dear friend Maria, who created FoRe! International, appointed me as an ambassador to raise awareness of law enforcement related PTSD and domestic violence. While, having worked in law enforcement and been married to a law enforcement officer, I possess experience related to that platform and truly believe our law enforcement needs assistance in handling such issues, I soon requested to change platforms. I will always support and gladly work with law enforcement, but a different need was calling out to me.

In 2018, I was appointed as FoRe! International's Ms. Ambassador for Children's Safety. In that position, my focus is on not only locating and rescuing children from human / sex trafficking but also the education of parents and children regarding how to avoid becoming potential targets of trafficking, especially from predators online and in the community. The manners in which children are groomed, often by friends and classmates, are unbelievable at times, and the ways in which they are used and abused are horrendous. The life expectancy of a trafficked child is five to seven years after they are recovered, which is heartbreaking. A young girl can be trafficked for months or years and then sold to a different trafficker for less than one hundred dollars---yes, less than one hundred dollars for a life. Sex and Human Trafficking is the fastest growing business in the world, second only to the drug trade when it comes to making money. This activity takes place here in your neighborhoods, not just in third world countries. Most often, a child who is taken is ultimately located only a county away, not in some far-away land. The effects of being trafficked reverberate within the family members as well, so in addition to assisting with after-care of rescued children, we also work with siblings and parents of the survivors. I have worked on more than one case where a sibling of a trafficked child felt so guilty for not reporting her little sister's contact with a perpetrator that she committed suicide---so tragic and heartbreaking and sadly not such a rare occurrence.

While working on sex and human trafficking cases, I have had the opportunity to work with multiple organizations who specialize in rescuing children including MillionKids.org, Saved in America, Shared Hope Foundation, and Operation Underground Railroad. Some of this work has been done out on the streets and some remotely. I make myself available for cases involving trafficked children 24 hours a day, seven days a week, 365 days a year. All this work is done pro bono---always has been and always will be. I would never turn the family of a missing child away because they are not able to pay my fees.

Over the years many people have asked how I handle the atrocities I see while on the job, especially dealing with crimes against children. My initial response is that I am adept compartmentalizing, but I have to admit there are nights I do not want to close my eyes because I have seen something horrific either in person or during my online research. The dark web is not a place you ever want to visit! I was blessed to have inherited my father's naturally calm demeanor, and I do not "freak out" during tense situations. I may sit in my car and cry later, but during the incident or while interacting with the victims and their families, I am able to keep it together. My faith is also a huge help, of course.

Having been asked what one needs to be successful, I believe that aside from a burning desire, the most important thing is a great Mentor. The woman who originally hired me as an investigator 100% influenced the person I am today. She was strong, incredibly intelligent, intuitive, creative, and supportive and encouraged all her employees to grow and fly. We spent many, many hours brain-storming investigation ideas, evaluating clues, and coming up with outside the box ways of solving mysteries. She was always open-minded and accepting of suggestions and creative solutions, which allowed me to be myself and to grow as an investigator and individual.

To succeed, you need to be brave. Before I began working as a private investigator, I had rarely left Orange County. Suddenly driving to Los Angeles, visiting the projects and high crime areas, became a weekly occurrence. My employer told me to just act as if I belonged wherever I was, and I would be safe.

Several years ago, an international investigation association I belong to, Intellenet, published two instructional manuals on conducting private investigations. I was asked to write two chapters for the advanced manual. I was terrified to do that, just as writing this chapter makes me nervous. But you have to step out of your comfort zone every now and then, or you will never grow. My former employer taught me that. She encouraged me every step of the way, and we even proofread each other's chapters for the manuals. When those books were published, I was so excited and proud of being a part of the project. Later, my former employer / mentor asked me to proofread a book of poetry she wrote. That was such an honor.

You need to face your fear, be it of public speaking or of putting your story on paper for all the world to see. As my former employer said, "Just act like you belong". That sure has worked for me!

Never-ending learning is also essential for success. Prior to obtaining my own Private Investigator license, I worked for many years for my original employer, much longer than necessary to meet the requirements to apply and test for my license. I did that for two reasons. One, she was the greatest boss ever. Two, I sought out training in every area of investigation I could think of. I did not want to be pigeonholed into conducting one type of investigation. Belonging to multiple organizations and associations related to my profession has helped immensely. Some of them I have been a member of for many years include Intellenet, the Texas Association of Licensed Investigators, the Association of Christian of Investigators, and the Fraternal Order of Investigators. Even after nearly forty years in the industry, I continue to seek out opportunities to expand my knowledge through training at conferences. In addition to learning opportunities, conferences are great for inspiration and networking. I have been asked to be a presenter at conferences as well but have not quite built up the courage to present to my colleagues from around the world. I'm sure that will happen someday.

Another step to success is taking chances. You do not want to find yourself 30, 40, 50 years from now regretting that you never tried that "thing" you always wanted to do. Take a trip around the world. Go skydiving. Buy those shoes. Go out to dinner and a movie alone. Get married (again)! I recently married my fourth husband, yes fourth, and I believe that is the best chance I have ever taken. Write that book (or chapter) that you've been thinking about writing. Someone out there needs to hear your story.

Finally, do not save things for a special occasion. Use the good crystal. Wear that special dress. Every day is a special occasion. Start your dream business or accept that job offer doing something you never thought you would do.

Nearly four and a half years ago I was diagnosed with a rare form of colon cancer. At the time I was in the process of a divorce, working full-time on my business, and soon found myself without insurance. This was not my first cancer fight. I had previously battled breast cancer and have had ongoing issues with skin cancer for twelve years. I wear my many scars proudly.

My cancer battle consisted of experimental treatments which took quite a bit longer than anticipated, partly due to insurance roadblocks, then the lack of insurance, and often a lack of funds. There are many organizations that assist those in the midst of cancer battles, including City of Hope, Cancer Centers of America, Chemo Buddies 4 Life, Along Comes Hope, as well as programs with drug manufacturers and clinical trials. I dealt with them all at one time or another. Many treatments were tried and did not work as hoped or planned, but finally, in May 2021, my cancer went into remission.

If you ever find yourself faced with a cancer diagnosis, my best advice is to reach out to anyone and everyone. So many people feel ashamed and are hesitant to ask for help. Do not let that be you! I've met so many incredible, inspiring people as a result of cancer battles, theirs and/or mine, and developed countless friendships that will never end. I managed to work full-time throughout my treatment, support myself, and keep my business thriving, much of the time through grim determination. I made it a point to do things for myself, which is not something I do typically. I began taking Barre3 classes, spending more time with friends, and even took an occasional day off work to just do "nothing". It was a long, difficult, extremely expensive battle, but I stayed positive the entire time. I never acted as if I was sick as I truly believe attitude is 90% of the battle. No matter how I managed, I did it. I kicked cancer's A$$!!

As the title of this chapter indicates, nothing in my life has gone as planned, and that is just fine with me. When something goes wrong, I just yell "Plot Twist" and keep on moving.

Acknowledgements

I, Dr. Carl D. Wilson, Jr. want to take time and acknowledge my mother Marjorie Wilson, who raised me to be a man that treats women with genuine integrity and respect.

I also want to acknowledge my sisters and daughter, Michelle Wilson, Carla Wilson, Marjorie Wilson, Britney Wilson, and Hibernia Kelly who are ladies that rock and support my mission to honor and celebrate women around the world.

In addition, I want to acknowledge Robbie Motter, a great mentor, the co-authors of this inspirational book, the publisher Angela Covany, the editor Dr. Randi D. Ward, and the formatter Marcy Decato for putting together a phenomenal book about women blazing to success.

www.ingramcontent.com/pod-product-compliance
Lightning Source LLC
Chambersburg PA
CBHW071948070526
44583CB00015B/1102